From Mae
to
Madonna

From Mae to Madonna

Women Entertainers in Twentieth-Century America

June Sochen

THE UNIVERSITY PRESS OF KENTUCKY

Publication of this volume was made possible in part
by a grant from the National Endowment for the Humanities.

Scholarly publisher for the Commonwealth,
serving Bellarmine College, Berea College, Centre
College of Kentucky, Eastern Kentucky University,
The Filson Club Historical Society, Georgetown College,
Kentucky Historical Society, Kentucky State University,
Morehead State University, Murray State University,
Northern Kentucky University, Transylvania University,
University of Kentucky, University of Louisville,
and Western Kentucky University.

Editorial and Sales Offices: The University Press of Kentucky
663 South Limestone Street, Lexington, Kentucky 40508-4008

03 02 01 00 99   5 4 3 2 1

Library of Congress Cataloging-in-Publication Data

Sochen, June, 1937-
    From Mae to Madonna : women entertainers in twentieth-century
America / June Sochen.
      p.   cm.
    Includes bibliographical references and index.
    ISBN 0-8131-2112-4 (cloth : alk. paper)
    1. Women entertainers—United States—Biography. 2. Women
in motion pictures. 3. Women on television. I. Title.
PN2285.S554   1999   2. Actors and actresses
791'.082 0973—dc21
  [B]   98-31976
          25+

To Emily, the future

Contents

Illustrations

Preface

Source material on women entertainers is both readily available and difficult to obtain. Current movie stars, TV personalities, and singers are known to audiences, but not all of the stars before the 1960s, for example, are known to people under fifty unless they are buffs and devotees of old movies and old TV shows. That is the reason having Fred MacDonald as a colleague and friend has been invaluable to this project. Fred has an extremely comprehensive collection of old movie magazines from the late 1920s through the 1950s and a marvellous array of old TV and radio shows. His willingness to both share much of this material and to discuss it with me is very much appreciated and was critical to the successful completion of this book. Thanks a lot, Fred.

My colleague at Northeastern Illinois University, Steve Riess, deserves thanks for his critical reading of an earlier version of this study. Undergraduate and graduate students alike who, over the years, took my course, Women in Popular Culture, must be recognized as well because teaching is inextricably tied to learning. And I have learned a great deal from my students.

Finally, this book is dedicated to my great-niece, Emily S. Dana, the future.

Grateful acknowledgment is given to the Wisconsin Center for Film and Theater Research, which supplied the following photographs: Katharine Hepburn, Mary Pickford, Pola Negri, Ethel Waters, Sophie Tucker, Eva Tanguay, Mae West, Shirley Temple, Pam Grier, Lupe Velez, Mable Normand, Marie Dressler, Gracie Allen, Dinah Shore, Meryl Streep, and Susan Sarandon.

Introduction

The subject of women and popular culture has interested me for many years. Before I became a historian of American women, I was a movie fan. In that lifelong capacity, I have been intrigued and enraptured by the portrayal of women in film. My admiration and enjoyment of the movies and of women stars in the movies have not abated. But during the last twenty-five years or more, I have also studied women's lives and experiences in this century, often emphasizing the images of women in popular culture. In 1973, my sister Joyce Schrager and I gave a slide lecture titled "Images of Women in Film" at the American Studies Association and then at the Berkshire Conference on the History of Women at Radcliffe College. At the time, the topic was considered new and audacious, a good indication of how things have changed.

Women in popular culture is a large subject. Though the movies remain my greatest interest, I have expanded my view to include women in television and, to a lesser extent, women in popular music. The following pages, albeit in a very selective manner, deal with women movie stars, TV performers, and singers whom I consider to be significant in popular culture. My personal favorites are included as well as many stars I think represent the dominant ways that our society portrays women. The general underlying premises, themes, and images that shape women's treatment in the movies or on television, I believe, pertain to all other forms of popular culture as well. This study offers a narrative of women's experiences as performers in various media at different points during the twentieth century. Though I do not treat each year or decade equally (not at all in some cases) or include every popular star, each chapter gives the reader insight into women entertainers in burlesque and vaudeville, in the movies, in clubs, and on television.

As a social type, women entertainers were the first women in this century to be visible, successful, and independent. They led lives atypical for American women as they spent their working days in the public eye instead of in the home or office. They earned fabulous sums of money; Eva Tanguay, the vaudevillian I will discuss in chapter 2, earned more money than the president of the United States. While some thought that accomplishment was appropriate, others wondered. Fan magazines, a new phenomenon that accompanied the rise of entertainment, commented on the private lives of these women stars, noting their frequent marriages and romantic break-ups. No one considered the possibility that these women, while they lived dramatically different lives, shared the culture's traditional view that all women should be wives and mothers. As the first group of women professionals, they were unwitting pioneers, forging new trails with few guideposts.

In the following discussion, I will propose a thematic framework for viewing the lives and careers of women entertainers. If you find it effective, then you can insert your favorite star and test my premises. As I will explain later in this introduction, there are helpful ways to look at women's images in the movies or on television; there are also good ways to analyze song lyrics and the personae of women singers. The following pages then will present information about women entertainers while offering an interpretive guide to the role of women in popular cultural products. By placing the women performers within their historical contexts, they will also offer understandings of American women's experiences. Hopefully, this discussion will add to and illuminate readers' knowledge of women entertainers and American women generally.

While women in their collectivity occupy my attention, I am attracted to the individual and always consider both the uniqueness and representativeness of each woman entertainer. At Northeastern Illinois University, where I have taught for more than thirty years, I offer courses on women in American history as well as women in popular culture. In both my teaching and my writing on this subject, I consider the performer, her biography and her work, as well as the ways in which her public and private lives fit within a number of larger contexts, most important, how her life is the same as or different from the lives of other American women.

Among the factors studied are the images and values evoked by the star and, as far as is knowable, the audience's reception of her performance/production. A woman star usually operates within pre-existing traditions at the same time that she brings a unique perspective and personality to her roles. She enters the field of entertainment at a particular historical moment and knowingly or unknowingly fits into a genre of film, music, or television. The woman performer also lives in her time and shares many of the values and suppositions of her society; so while movie actress Bette Davis epitomized the independent woman in her films, she declared to an interviewer that her happiest moment came when she gave birth to a child at age thirty-nine. The public and private woman did not always cohere comfortably.

The analyst of women's lives and roles in popular media must evaluate the multiple frames within which the star and her persona functions. *In my view, women entertainers become multiple texts:* biography is one text, and the star's work, be it films, television shows, or songs, is another. In addition, two *contexts* intersect with her bio and her work: the history and culture of the film, television, or musical genre in which she performs, and the society in which she lives. These four dimensions cannot be separated from each other. Knowing about a star's life is critical to understanding her personality and the screen roles she is likely to play. Because much of popular culture is bound to past conventions, how the star adapts herself to the stereotypical roles available and how she makes them her own are part of the analysis.

Many movie stars and television stars are very conscious of the work of their predecessors; they may choose to imitate or reject those who came before them, but they always operate within a well-worn tradition. The historical time during which the performer grows up and enters the world of popular culture is an equally important factor. Racism shaped the structures of entertainment available to African Americans for a good part of this century and limited the possibilities for performers to succeed. That so many black women singers did so is truly remarkable. Bessie Smith's growing up in the segregated South in the second decade of the twentieth century, played a fundamental role in her evolution. Being an extremely talented black woman singer was not enough of an asset, but singing a novel musical form increased her chances for success. Someone beginning a career as a blues singer in the 1990s, however, when that musical style was out of fashion, had fewer opportunities for stardom. Though talent is essential for a woman entertainer, she needs both method and opportunity.

The other determining context—the genre—cannot be underestimated as a force for success. Genres, conventions, formulas, whichever word is used, describe the frame within which various stories are told. The conventions exist in every medium: literature, film, television, and music. And they are amazingly constant and consistent when portraying women. When a star becomes a featured player in a melodrama or a comedy, the particular genre plays an active role in shaping her presentation. Actresses who evoke images of stoicism and grit in the face of multiple disasters can succeed in melodrama. When entering comedy, past masters of the form will influence the current conventions and treatments of the subject. A pathbreaker such as Lucille Ball takes comedy that was perfected in silent film by men such as Buster Keaton and Charlie Chaplin and transforms it in a new medium—television—and makes it appropriate for female comics as well.

The star who enters melodrama, a format that seems particularly well suited for beautiful women, enters a tried-and- true popular entertainment that began in short stories and novels before it hit the movie or television screen. An actress in this genre joins a long tradition of suffering heroines, villains, broken hearts, improbable circumstances, and romantic heroes. Some genres, such as melodrama, appear in every time period. Their appeal to basic human emotions and needs seems so strong and enduring that they exist in good and bad times. During the depression, melodramas dominated movies and became known as "weepies"; since television began, they occupy daytime television and are known as "soap operas" (after the soap company that sponsored many of them).

As you can see, sometimes the genre becomes the most important of the four dimensions, while at other times, the personal biography of the star dominates. Usually, the interaction of all four factors is critical. One must evaluate each star, each genre, and each time period in its own terms while always remaining cognizant of the interactions between the four dimensions. The fourth dimension, the times in which a star arises, is very important: Hollywood in the thirties was quite a different place than it was in the sixties or that it became in the nineties. The business of moviemaking has changed, and this change has inevitably affected opportunities for women actresses. While each of the great Hollywood studios of the thirties made more movies than the whole industry does today, more roles were available then for women. When the cost of moviemaking is exceedingly high and the risks for success even greater, producers stick to adventure formula films, a proven favorite, and make fewer movies starring women.

Considering dominant film images of women, the expression, "The more things change, the more they stay the same," applies. The larger cultural imperatives, in this case, the view of women, are major considerations in all discussions of women's images and opportunities in popular culture. Joan Crawford, for example, an enormously successful movie star, started her career during the silent-screen era. She joined a tradition of what I call Horatio Alger-type female roles: she played poor-but-honest women who make good by marrying well. This image of women predates film; it had many literary examples. But it gained particular resonance during the Depression thirties. In bad economic times, the concept of a person who makes good despite handicaps is applied to women; but the application is peculiarly sexist—the only way a woman can make good is by marrying a rich man.

Crawford's career spanned two generations, but the movie roles available to her changed as she grew older, sure testimony to the larger culture's view of older women. As a young, attractive female Horatio Alger, she struck a chord with women during the depression, and she remained an audience favorite for many years. Thanks to movie magazines and fan clubs, and Crawford had one of the largest fan clubs around, audiences knew about her personal and professional lives, and those of all their favorite stars. Fans could easily tell interested listeners who Crawford's many husbands were—in order. They kept up with the stars' activities as well as their love lives.

Beginning in the 1920s, and gaining steam in the 1930s and 1940s, the fan magazines provided the information and attention that created celebrities, a phenomenon that grew over time. While the movie studios reluctantly gave their featured players star billing (they feared demands for increased salaries and benefits), the fan magazines fed the seemingly insatiable appetites of fans for details about their favorites. The emergence of the fan-audience subculture, an essential ingredient in the making of stars and superstars, is part of the historical/ cultural context. The changing technology at the end of the twentieth century made it possible for fans to create computer chat rooms to learn and gossip about their favorite stars. The machinery and location may have changed, but the behavior has not.

From Mae to Madonna: Women Entertainers in Twentieth-Century America offers a chronological and a thematic look at selected personalities at key points in entertainment history. While the book is roughly chronological, it uses the lives and roles of some women performers to showcase not only their careers but the larger subject of women in popular entertainment forms such as the stage, movies, and television. In addition to mainstream women stars such as Lucille Ball and Mary Tyler Moore, I am drawn to minority women in the broadest sense of that term. According to my interpretation, bawdy women are also minority women. They are often on the fringes of the entertainment world, thereby offering viewers less well known and less respectable images of women. But their existence as exciting contrasts dramatizes the predictable and consistent images of women seen on the mainstream stages of America. The exceptions illustrate and confirm the general rules.

By extending the lense and including bawds, the picture of women entertainers now includes the sexy, often outrageous woman performer who reveals previously unspoken dimensions of woman's sexual nature while her popularity with men in the audience attests to male interest in hearing and seeing women behaving unconventionally. Interestingly, Bessie Smith, Sophie Tucker, and Bette Midler all appealed to both men and women while Mae West's audience at first was largely male; she consciously worked to extend her appeal to women. By discussing sex in 1910s vaudeville, burlesque, and nightclubs, Smith, Tucker, and West pioneered new images for women. American culture's stubborn unwillingness to alter its views of women, particularly on subjects such as discussing sex publicly, makes the behavior of bawdy women entertainers particularly audacious considering their success in the still straitlaced second decade of the twentieth century.

One of my main concerns, of course, is how popular cultural figures reflect, conserve, enforce, and sometimes alter the dominant views of women. If the images projected are the expected and the accepted, no change occurs. The bawdy women, particularly those who developed a popular following, challenged the traditional images thereby acting as change agents in the culture. Popular culture, after all, is an arena most people enter and from which many people acquire their general views. Advocates and detractors of popular culture have written many words defending their beliefs about the meaning of the popular cultural experience. Critics sometimes overestimate its negative power while advocates, paradoxically, downplay its meaning; while defending television, for example, advocates minimize its meaning and value. For good reason: if they acknowledge its power, they may end up supporting the negative views as well. The irony in each position is rarely explored.

Has television been helpful or harmful to children's development? Do movies that depict women only as whores keep women down or do they reflect one aspect of a minority of women's experience? There are as many answers as there are questions. Using my model of texts and contexts, the interactive and complex process that constitutes the experience makes it difficult to proclaim a simple and sure generalization that will always apply. The audience response to stereotypical and unusual portraits of women depends not only on the texts and contexts of the performers and performances but on the biography and experience of the viewer. A movie experience can be shared by people of diverse backgrounds and agreements can be reached as to its meanings; however, the commonalities can only be achieved after discussion and debate. Further, because a movie, for example, is such a rich, collaborative product, audience members from diverse backgrounds can read different meanings into it.

The era in which a 1930s movie is viewed, for example, whether it is seen in first release or thirty years later, adds another important ingredient to the analysis. Joan Crawford's grit can be seen as heroic, stoic, or masochistic behavior, depending upon the climate of opinion when it is seen and the personal experience of the viewer. Depression-era women admired Crawford and her many cohorts, such as Barbara Stanwyck, Claire Trevor, and Bette Davis, but 1990s feminists might interpret their roles as those of victims, women dominated by powerful men. The viewer and fan's ideology contributes to the understanding, thereby complicating an already complex phenomenon.

While my focus is on the woman entertainer, the performer, I cannot ignore the consumer, the movie viewer, the television watcher, and the music listener. Audience members are not robots; they make conscious choices. But the choices exist within a difficult-to-know universe; that is, the viewer may be fulfilling a fantasy by watching a particular movie, she may be looking for real-life guidance in maneuvering through unchartered romantic waters, or she may be seeking reassurance in the comfort of a predictable art form. Fans may find that the comfort they seek in a genre such as melodrama yields unexpected results. As Janice Radway has shown in her study of women who read romance novels, the readers impose multiple meanings upon the predictable fare. There is often unpredictability amidst the expected.

When Barbara Stanwyck, for example, played a whore in 1930s movies, she entered a stereotypical role, one with a long history, but she remade it and played it with bravado and stoicism. The viewer received a mixed and complex message from her portrayal, not a stereotypical one. While Stanwyck, another favorite with 1930s and 1940s audiences, often played the prostitute with a heart of gold, she also brought admirable qualities of spunk, endurance, and initiative to the role. The difficult lot that was woman's, a theme stated and restated in a variety of ways, had particular meaning during the Depression and World War Two. An unspoken subtext in most of the golddigger and heart of gold whore roles was that attractive women had only one asset to sell during difficult times.

Movie goers and television watchers could sympathize with a working woman, no matter what her profession. When Bette Davis in the 1937 movie, *Marked Woman*, walked away with her 'hostess' girlfriends rather than marry the district attorney (in a typically improbable plot), she displayed the camaraderie between working women that typified the virtues necessary to survive in difficult economic times. The stereotypical portrait of the whore had been replaced with a far more nuanced image and the film does not judge the women. Audiences gained vicarious experience and thereby increased their empathy for lives different from their own. Their sympathy and appreciation for hard working women may have been enhanced.

Influence is difficult to measure and the effect of a cultural encounter may not be known immediately. I have lectured before audiences of older women and have spoken to them about their favorite stars; many told me that they loved Bette Davis and Joan Crawford movies in the 1930s and 1940s and though the plot line usually required the stars to surrender to the hero at story's end, the women viewers remembered their favorite stars' strength and endurance throughout the movie. They had forgotten the ending. In the chapter, "Whatever Bette Davis Says: Women Movie Stars as Role Models," I discuss the interrelationship between the stars' personal lives (which were well known to the fans), their screen roles, and the presumed affect they had on their audience.

While we cannot say definitively how or whether a popular cultural product changes lives, we do know that since the 1930s, mass media, beginning with sound movies, has been very popular. Women and men went to the movies in record numbers in the thirties—half of the adult population went each week—and while that number cannot be matched in the 1990s, if you combine cable and video movie viewing, you surely score a very high number of movie fans. Further, young people with discretionary income who buy records, watch television shows, go to the movies, and attend concerts, plus older adults who watch television and attend movies (the age group 25-39 is the single largest one of moviegoers) provide billions to the entertainment industry. Both young and older women and men reward their favorite entertainers by patronizing their product.

This stunning fact alone attests to the importance of entertainers in the lives of most Americans: more hours may be spent with them than with "real" people. Fans discuss the personal lives and screen roles of their favorite stars as readily as they talk about current politics. This is no small fact. Surely historians have a difficult, if not impossible, task to document this importance; but personal, anecdotal evidence supports the contention. We all talk about the lives and performances of popular cultural figures. Some of us more than others go to the movies frequently and read about our favorite stars' personal lives. Many of us watch the innumerable television talk shows and entertainment-news shows. Whether the curiosity and satisfaction achieved from this regular activity serves as vicarious pleasure or escapist fantasy, it is an integral part of our lives.

Popularity is a phenomenon that must be respected. Understanding comes next. Since most successful practitioners of the popular arts are intriguing combinations of ordinary and extraordinary people, they both stand with, and apart, from their audience. The many African-American women entertainers I discuss in two separate essays ("Black Women Vaudevillians" and "Bawdy Women Entertainers") rise out of Northern and Southern ghettoes; they often grew up in segregated America; and they emerged as successful entertainers because of talent, opportunity, pluck, audacity, and good fortune. They shared a great deal with their audiences while they had the unique ability to express the sorrows, the heartbreaks, and the blues in inimitable ways. Bessie Smith and her many colleagues dramatically exemplify, in their lives and their work, the dynamic interaction of texts and contexts.

Sophie Tucker and Bette Midler, two Jewish women entertainers, knew first hand what it meant to be outsiders; as such, they could identify with all underdogs, all minorities, in their comic and musical presentations. Both featured humor as an essential ingredient in their shows, thereby allowing laughter to unite all peoples. Again, we cannot escape noticing the important exchanges and transactions that occur between personal biography, timely circumstance, previous histories, and talent. An entertainer's career is inextricably influenced by who she is, where she came from, when she entered show business, and what the current scene is. Further, the persistence of dominant images of women pursue them throughout time. Race and ethnicity are surely two powerful features of American culture and American audiences have a strange fascination with difference. African American women may not be treated equally or respectfully in 'real' life, but in entertainment life, they receive adulation and support from white audiences. Similarly, anti-Semitism existed in 1910s and 1920s America precisely when largely Jewish audiences flocked to nightclubs to see Sophie Tucker.

Humor interests me and I find the women entertainers who became famous because of their sharply honed wit particularly fascinating. Many of the bawdy women described, as well as the "Women Comics" in the chapter by that name, share an idiosyncratic perspective. They see the funny where others see the sober. While the bawdy women make fun of sex, mainstream women comics such as Lucille Ball and Mary Tyler Moore use humor to comment on a wide range of social behavior. In Ball's case, she appropriated male forms of humor, such as slapstick, and made it her own. Moore relied on a traditional female method of humor—the verbal—showing all around her that she could discover laughter in both her actions and those of others. Her self deprecatory style comforted fans who needed help negotiating the difficult days of women's liberation.

In the chapter called "Lupe and Pam: Representations of Minority Women in Popular Culture," I feature Lupe Velez, a little known Latina movie star whose shortlived career speaks volumes about Hollywood's and America's attitude toward Latins. In a good example of how popular culture reflects the larger society's values, stereotypes of Latinas were used repeatedly in 1930s Hollywood. In this sense, makers of popular culture are equal opportunity stereotypers. Certainly African-American women and Latinas faced, and continue to face, the most persistent stereotyping, but all women have been subject to formulaic and predictable treatment throughout movie history, and by extension, the history of all popular cultural formats. Velez' personal biography and her entry into sound movies intersected with the studios' marketing of American movies into Latin America. As testimony to the persistence of stereotypical images of Latins, Velez' screen roles did not improve. Indeed, gender boundaries, to use a currently fashionable phrase, have always existed. Both women and men have been assigned explicit and predictable roles throughout American culture. I discuss this subject in "Change Within Continuity: The Careers of Dinah Shore and Mary Tyler Moore." Writers, producers, directors, and stars all came out of American culture and they shared the same imaginative universe. Cultural continuity is a phenomenon that most everyone has an investment in. Few wish to see change, let alone radical change. All of the participants in a creative product such as a movie rely on predictability and on the preservation of the status quo. Women's traditional roles, in real and fantasy life, act as anchors to a culture.

After years of watching women in the movies and on television, I have condensed the cultural imagery of women into a trilogy—three dominant images that cross time lines. Each star has had to adapt her personality to these images. In this sense, the imagery is transhistorical; it rises above time and place, unique biography, and changing social times. The fascination and challenge for the stars is to shape these larger than life images and adapt them to their personality and talent. From popular novels to silent film to current media offerings, there have been, and are, *Eves, Marys, and Liliths.* Indeed, these images exist in nineteenth century American literature as well as in late twentieth century TV sitcoms. Using Biblical women as my prototypes, I see American popular media creating sexual temptresses (Eve), innocent young maidens (Mary), and independent women (Lilith). Sometimes creative film makers merge two of the images into one; an Eve can also be a Lilith (Mae West would be a classic example) while an Eve can never be a Mary, though movie star Doris Day played whores (Eves) first and then Marys (virginal maids).

Rarely did Marys achieve autonomy, though Mary Pickford's numerous roles in silent film often displayed more freedom of action than stereotypes would suggest. Doris Day in the late 1950s and early 1960s often combined sweetness and traditional roles with spunk and initiative. Sometimes, actresses became identified fully with one image: Katharine Hepburn as a Lilith is a good example. She never played a sweet Mary nor a seductive Eve. Frequently a career woman, sometimes married, but rarely a mother, Hepburn was in the enviable position of choosing her roles carefully (she had independent income) and never being under long term contract to one studio. The audience accepted her, indeed viewed her as an autonomous, competent woman who directed her own life in each and every film she made.

All women movie stars who became extremely successful either played their particular image to perfection or found numerous ways to transform it to be both representative of the essential type as well as the exception. Rarely did women's roles break completely with expected conventions, thereby attesting to the persistence of traditional cultural views. Movies, most often I would suggest, reflect larger cultural traits rather than challenge or change them. "Mae West: Entertainer as Reformer" playfully but seriously suggests that an iconoclastic performer, by staying on society's margins and never wavering in her message and persona, can become successful and possibly influential. Eves, socially disreputable women that they are, can also, paradoxically but truly, be extremely admired.

Success and admiration are, of course, two separate phenomena; the former is easy to prove while the latter is more difficult. As I suggest later, West's humorous treatment of the forbidden subject made her notorious, often-quoted, and possibly, secretly admired. The chapter also considers the larger question of whether entertainers as a social category may be a more powerful group of reformers in American culture than the 'reformers' so labelled. If, as I speculate, entertainers have a larger audience than social reformers, and are more generally

Even as a mature, married woman, star Mary Pickford portrayed a sweet, childlike person in her movies: the eternal Mary.

Pola Negri, a silent screen actress who failed in sound movies, always projected the image of a seductress, an Eve.

Katharine Hepburn consistently played Liliths on the screen—career women who shaped their own identities.

loved, then their "messages" may have greater effect, for good or ill, on the audience. Another paradox appears in my various discussions of women's images: while the images endure, each unique star alters it and transcends it. Audiences respond to the familiar and unfamiliar and to the ways their favorites transform known material into delightful unknowns.

A frequently discussed topic regarding popular culture is role modelling. How well, or poorly, do pop stars act as role models for their fans, particularly their young fans? Is Madonna an appropriate idol for pre-pubescent girls? Are the various male rock stars admirable characters for young adolescent males? Generally, the answers are all in the negative. Most commentators, however, note that there is an important gender dimension to the subject. Young female fans can admire the audacity of Madonna, her freedom, and her success while screaming and declaring their love for male rockers. Boys admire young men stars while lusting after Madonna. In other words, young women can buy Madonna's records while pursuing a boy with the hope of marriage. They extract from Madonna's songs and performances her audacity possibly, but do not extend the view to consider alternate life choices.

Just as I have argued that the dynamic between a woman entertainer, her work, and her audience is a complex and interactive one, I would also suggest that role modelling is a far more complicated process than generally acknowledged. This is not to say that both genders shouldn't have worthy representatives on the stage and screen; of course, they should. But identification and modelling is difficult to dissect. I grew up an avid movie fan and often placed myself in the hero's position, vicariously accomplishing great feats and defeating all enemies. It never occurred to me that, because I was female, I could not be heroic, courageous, strong, and successful. The nature of projection and identification cannot be easily unravelled. Similarly, predetermining role models for young or old audiences is a highly precarious enterprise.

I would speculate that young women identify for positive reasons with both male and female stars, that they extract from each qualities they admire, and that they adapt those features to their own lives and circumstances. Boys, given our society's higher opinion of males than females, probably would not admit a non-sexual adulation for a female star as readily, though they may secretly harbor such beliefs. Further, the traits admired, even the most outrageous and rebellious ones, may serve a constructive social purpose in that the vicarious identification with a hard rocker, male or female, may substitute for actual aggressive behavior. In this sense, role modelling cannot be taken so literally; indeed, it becomes a symbolic substitute for real-life actions.

While there are specific references provided at the end of the chapters, and a bibliography at the book's end, I would like to comment generally on writings in popular culture. Throughout this century, theoretical and empirical studies have been done on popular culture. While the Europeans, most notably the Russians, Germans, and French, have written extensively on the meaning of film, and have taken the subject seriously, Americans commentators, until recently, have focused upon the empirical and avoided the abstract. In keeping with the American spirit of pragmatism, writers of popular culture have written more biographies of stars, directors, and companies than speculative pieces on the meaning of the experience. They have emphasized the personal, the individual, often the gossipy, rather than the social or the collective.

Just as biography remains the most popular form of historical writing, so individual portraits occupy center stage in all popular cultural works. Further, scholars have, until recently, largely ignored popular culture as a category of inquiry (Fred was a pioneer) as their intellectual material was confined to elites. Worthy subjects had to have a weightiness attached to them, an intellectual heft lacking in entertainers, or so it was assumed. Similarly, if a personality was popular, or if a television show had an enormous audience, that meant, by definition, it was suspect, superficial material not worth the scholar's attention. Clearly, this view has died.

Precisely because American entertainment has also been an American business, historians and critics have always had to acknowledge the economic dimension to the product. Further, an entertainment, in American parlance, means fun and escape, rather than art, the European perspective. Imagine the surprise and astonishment among American film writers when the French discovered American film of the 1950s to be an art form, *film noir*. Generally, American film makers resisted the label 'art' and remained proudly in the business-entertainment area. When considering women's roles, audiences seemed to prefer Eve images of women followed by Mary images. The Lilith shone briefly in the 1930s and 1940s when the context, Depression and War, required strong, independent women. But the return of the GIs after 1945 ended that trend. What the market would bear remained the governing principle of American moviemakers.

Freudians and Marxists, of course, have brought their perspective to bear upon popular culture. Since they operate within a clearly defined framework, their analyses are usually predictable. Marxists always emphasized the economic dimension of American popular culture and have looked with suspicion at producers, seen as profitmongers, who imposed dominant values upon an unknowing audience. But recently, some Marxists, most notably those influenced by Antonio Gramsci, acknowledge the power of culture as both an independent force and as an interactive one. Rather than arguing, as Marx did, that all ideologies are superstructures and that commercial popular culture is simply a capitalist's tool, some recent scholars have devised a more subtle and nuanced view of American popular culture.

Some Marxists present an interactive model for popular culture in which the consumer and the provider both play active roles. Though the producer of a movie, a video, a tape, or a television show works to lure buyers and viewers to their product, the success is not preordained. Nor is it so clear that the producer operates in a different space than the consumer. Both sides are influenced by many of the same values and beliefs and both sides affect the others' decisionmaking in difficult and often unpredictable ways. Fans, then, are not seen as hapless victims but as participants in the making of their own entertainment.

This approach can easily be adapted to my contention that the interactivity is multi-layered: the texts and contexts of a popular cultural image or performance intersect in many ways. Although the producers of popular cultural material are obviously powerful, they are also tied to their audience's likes and dislikes, to the genres within which they operate, and to the times in which they produce their work. Advertising and aggressive promotion cannot guarantee success.

Nothing replaces the viewing of a movie, the watching of a television series, or the listening to a song. These source materials are the original, first-hand look into the subject. Errors can sometimes be detected in writings of movie critics about 1930s movies, for example, that they have not seen—an unforgivable sin for critics. Further, each viewer brings to the watching of a movie or television show her/his own perspective. In this sense, another text and context is brought to the table, that of the viewer. What this study, and others that attempt to analyze and explain aspects of women entertainers and popular culture do is offer readers an informed analysis that can be used as guide and comparison with her/his own experiences. By adding information and perspective of someone who has studied the subject to one's own, the viewer can place the entertainer in a larger setting and clarify her/his understanding of that performer's meaning and importance.

At the same time that I suggest that my views can help fans and interested readers make sense of women entertainers, I do not think you, the viewer, should rely solely on contemporary critics for an understanding of a film or a television show. You do so at your own peril. Though surely each of us is able to enter other critics' worlds, and benefit from the analysis, we should also experience our own intellectual and emotional reaction. Interested students can rent a 1930s video and reenter the world of Mae West; viewing old movies accomplishes at least three goals: it provides insight into earlier views on women's roles; it acquaints you with our great movie stars; and it also exposes the viewer to a very important part of our cultural history. Once the viewer has had the primary experience, she can then profitably compare her analysis to current critics' views as well as to analyses written when the movie was released.

Watching "The Mary Tyler Moore Show" *without* 1990s hindsight becomes the goal. Students of history, of all kinds of history, are required to shed, or at least contain, their preconceptions and their current attitudes and to imagine a different cultural environment. The amazing discovery, of course, is that they will find both familiar territory as well as unexpected ground to explore. It is the sameness and the difference which, paradoxically, becomes a central experience in studying the popular culture of earlier times. This is particularly true when examining the careers of women entertainers and studying the images of women. As important as each text (star and film) is and as significant as the entertainer's life is, the enduring nature of women's roles and images allows all viewers to connect with each and every time period.

By going even further back to 1950s Dinah Shore Shows, for example, the viewer-student learns to read the subtext of the show. Subtexts exist in every film, television program, or song. They are the unspoken ideas, the underlying message of the work. Is Dinah projecting contradictory messages? Is she both upholding conventional views about women while simultaneously subverting them? Similarly, when Lucy devises plot after plot to escape the home, only to fail of course, is she questioning the 1950s definition of women's proper roles? Current viewers of old television programs featuring women or 1930s movies with strong Liliths in them have the distinct advantage of living in multiple time zones. They can unpeel the layers of meaning and thereby be enriched by the experience.

All of the chapters in this book rely heavily upon original sources; when I discuss the raunchy singing of Bessie Smith or Sophie Tucker, I do so after having listened to their songs, analyzed their lyrics, and considered their musical style. Though lyrics are easier to deal with than style, music does require consideration of both aspects. The tone and pace of the singer are very important in conveying meaning to the words. Similarly, I laughed along with the fans when viewing a Bette Midler concert video and only after the laughter died down was able to analyze what I saw. In all cases, I tried to use as many original sources as possible in developing my themes and interpretations of the woman entertainer. In the essay on "Black Women Vaudevillians," this was impossible to do. The performances of these women is lost forever. We must rely on contemporary accounts. By definition, then, the conclusions are more tentative.

But after all is said and done, all my interpretations and judgments are simply that. Their worth can only be determined by you, the reader. If you find the argument persuasive, the evidence compelling, and the ideas intriguing, then my views may receive a positive evaluation. If not, at least the reader will have been presented with material and ideas that may be new and novel; even with vigorous disagreement, a different framework and perspective will offer interested readers the opportunity to measure ideas and determine their validity. *From Mae to Madonna* can be read for general amusement and/or as part of an academic course on women and popular culture. In any case, it offers readers an analysis that takes popular cultural material seriously. I hope to convince you that women entertainers are worthy additions to the narrative of American history and culture.

If I succeed, you will join me in both enjoying and understanding the phenomena that you usually accept unself- consciously. All cultural manifestations mean something. How women are treated in this culture and how they view and treat themselves is a difficult, but understandable, process. The movies, television, and popular music contribute in important ways to the formation and perpetuation of roles, values, and behaviors. Though there is no easy and simple equation that can always be applied (movies=reality or songs=fantasy), there are judgments and conclusions about women's roles in society that can be learned by watching women movie and tv stars and by listening to the singers' music. Enjoy the process.

1

Black Women Vaudevillians

By the 1880s, show business had a history, one that largely excluded women. Young boys played the female parts in many nineteenth-century theatricals, and respectable women, white and African American, avoided the stage as an unladylike place to be. But in the late nineteenth century, things changed. Popular culture joined with the new and growing cities and increasing industrialization to become big business. Commercial entertainments had already existed, but most people amused themselves in informal, free, and communally developed leisure activities. The newly discovered profit-making potential of show business transformed popular culture into for-profit entrepreneurial businesses that conveniently forgot or ignored old strictures about women on display in public places. More and more patrons paid to attend the popular theater and musical shows performed by professionals. Both venues grew beyond anyone's expectations. New immigrants and longtime city dwellers flocked to the new variety shows. People still organized their own amusements, of course, but the new popular and profit-making shows increasingly captured the attention and the money of more and more people. In an interesting reinterpretation, old cultural views of women, as old as the colonial settlements, slowly changed as women moved into the music hall. "Painted women," the term often assigned to the new women singers and dancers in the new vaudeville houses, suggested their dubious status. Respectable women in all communities did not paint their faces with cosmetics or show off their bodies in skimpy clothing in public. Women performers were eyed uneasily as closer to prostitutes than professionals, but they were looked at, occasionally admired, and slowly accepted as part of the new entertainment landscape.

Entrepreneurs quickly saw the profit potential in featuring attractive young women on the stage, but they also shared the society's racial and, in this case, gender attitudes. It is no surprise, then, to discover that those same owners of mainstream vaudeville houses were slow to include women of color. By contrast, African American men, usually in blackface (they had to use black cork to darken their faces as did white men playing African American men), sang, danced, and joked in minstrel shows, the precursors to the variety shows, sometimes before white and sometimes before black audiences. While all women had limited roles in nineteenth-century theater, black women were shunned entirely. However, show business became the first venue to break down all gender and racial barriers. Theater owners always searched for ways to increase audiences—and their wish for greater profits overcame their prejudices.

At the turn of the century, both black and white women began to appear in vaudeville shows, the variety shows that became increasingly popular in the growing cities of America. Nine or eleven acts in length (usually five or six before intermission and four or five afterwards), vaudeville shows allowed diverse audiences to see jugglers, dancers, comics, actors, and animal acts, something to please each and every taste. Immigrant members of the audience enjoyed the short acts—and if they didn't like what they saw, they shouted their disapproval. Chorus lines became an accepted feature of the show, and the need for talented and pretty young women increased. The solo dancer, the singer, and the female half of a duet became standard fare.[1] Teenage boys no longer played women.

Vaudeville producers auditioned shapely young women dancers and singers as alluring bait for the ruly and unruly men who frequented the neighborhood saloons-turned-variety-shows as well as the new downtown theaters. While a serious effort was made to bring respectability to vaudeville theaters, and thereby appeal to women and children as audience members, men remained the mainstay of audiences.

The dominant image projected by the new women vaudevillians was usually of a sweet Mary in need of male protection, or rarely, a spunky Lilith; the sexy Eve startled and intrigued the growing audiences. Attractive young girls dreamed of show business success, and New York City became the mecca of the entertainment world. Many aspiring singers and dancers broke into the business in their hometown of Memphis, St. Louis, Chicago, or San Francisco. They honed their singing, dancing, and acting skills there with the hope that it would lead to national success.

While the making of any woman entertainer requires an analysis of her biography, her work, the genre within which she performs, and the society in which she lives, sometimes one variable dominates, thereby determining the outcome. In discussing black women vaudevillians, society's attitudes on race and gender clearly played crucial roles. While all women had to overcome the whorish image associated with show business, black women had the additional burden of the color line. Besides the basic prejudice that prevailed, the actual color of the woman's skin played an active role in deciding whether or not she could be on stage: the darker the woman's complexion, the less likely that she would be booked into the show. White audiences preferred lighter-skinned black women while black audiences often shared the same view, unconsciously or consciously accepting the white standard.

The subject of color, of course, is an exceedingly sensitive one in this country. In the black press, however, some black theater critics criticized the audiences' preference for light-skinned mulattas over the deeper-colored women. White was right in terms of the styles and desired images for black women, a sad but understandable phenomenon. In 1923, critic George Schuyler wrote, "Why don't they put beautiful chocolates and handsome black girls on the stage?"[2] No one answered Schuyler's question to his satisfaction. The slavish imitation of white culture's view of feminine beauty became an embarrassing reality, particularly to African American intellectuals.

The more conventional dilemma of trapping women in rigid stereotypical roles plagued black women vaudevillians. Black women, like their white sisters, had to be pretty and slim to be in a chorus line; they had to portray the sweet young thing beside the strong, male hero; and they had to be the butt of the male comic's humor. The universality of the female cultural stereotype prevailed. Not only was beauty culturally defined in the white community and accepted in large parts of the black community, but the acceptable images for women were the same. In the movies, however, Hollywood created the Mammy type for black women, a nurturing mother who cared for white children with loving kindness, clearly, a white wish. A sexy, black woman was not allowed on the movie screen for fear of offending white tastes. Heavy-set women of both colors could succeed in non-romantic roles if they combined their song with a joke. Bessie Smith, a great black blues singer, defied the stereotype and sang about romance on the vaudeville stage but also mocked her willingness to be deceived by no-account men. Audiences laughed or smirked when they heard the hefty Bessie lament her lost loves, but they quieted down when her velvety voice sounded through the room. The combination of humor with pathos and a self-deprecatory style became the acceptable trademark for women who did not have the fashionable figure and the cultural standard of good looks. Predictable images were forgotten in the face of great talent, but in a sense, the fondness for women who went against type could be seen as strong evidence for the persistence of that very type. An occasional exception can be made because it does not deny the rule.

A slim, lithe Florence Mills, who was a singing sensation and the darling of African American and white critics alike in the mid-1920s, was more likely to be cast as the ingenue in a black musical. The lighter skin, the slimmer form, and the more delicate facial features gave her and others like her a place in the theater. This formula, of course, pertained to white women entertainers too. But black women vaudevillians had to contend with both gender and racial prejudices. They had to operate within more delicate boundaries than any other group of entertainer. Black male entertainers had to observe racial stereotypical images, and white women entertainers had to follow gender rules, but only black women vaudevillians had to observe racial and gender restrictions, making them a unique group of performers.

The vaudeville circuit was hard on all entertainers, including the stars and the chorus members. Beginning roughly in the 1890s and continuing through the 1920s (the depression years saw the death of vaudeville), performers traveled from town to town, often doing two or three shows a day. They performed in one small town for three days, traveled on the fourth, and put on their next show for another three days. They stayed in substandard hotels, and in cities where the theaters catered to white and black audiences, the black women entertainers, if they were lucky, found themselves eating in segregated restaurants; more likely, they ate in the kitchen with the cooks and waiters. The whole system was run by the Theater Owners Booking Association, commonly known as the TOBA (tough on black asses). This organization booked most of the black acts and shows throughout the country and usually had the entertainers' interests last on their list of concerns.[3] In the South, the players appeared in segregated black theaters from Indianapolis, Indiana, to Jacksonville, Florida.

Edith Wilson, a singer whose career began in the 1920s, later remembered times when she was the only black woman in a show with white entertainers; she could not stay in the same hotel with the rest of the troupe or eat dinner with her fellow performers. If she was in an all-black show, the whole group stayed together in inferior lodgings.[4] Black women vaudevillians, then, found that race, gender, and the general hardships of early show business made their career choice a difficult one. Maximum-hour laws did not apply, and the women often worked a seven-day week. There was no day of rest. Working conditions varied but were generally poor; all of the dancers shared a single dressing room, and the star had no special treatment. The constant traveling and the lack of supervision contributed to society's view that women entertainers were a shady lot and that this was not a profession for respectable young women.

When the performers played in northern cities, the show was geared to a white-majority audience with the black patrons sitting in the balcony. In the South, segregated seating also prevailed, though some theaters in both regions became predominantly black theaters with few white patrons. Robert Mott's Pekin Theater in Chicago, for example, opened in 1906, established a black repertory company, and catered to a black audience. With twenty talented artists in tow, Mott produced a new play every two weeks.[5] The Lafayette Theater in Harlem also played to Harlemites with whites occasionally visiting from downtown.[6] Many other Harlem theaters in the years 1910-19 and the 1920s also attracted white audiences.

TOBA gave the women vaudevillians some measure of job security as they booked acts for theaters throughout the region and "guaranteed" the performers so many weeks of work. Contracts, however, were never written, and entertainers could find themselves in towns where the audience was sparse and the booking abruptly canceled. There was no unemployment compensation and no assurance that the theater would be heated on a cold evening. Women often found their male traveling companions to be protectors against rowdy members of the audience; the troupe sometimes functioned as an informal family with members looking out for each other. Often, casual sexual liasons formed between members of the group and this could lead to temporary, or more rarely, permanent attachments. Many of the young women began touring as teenagers, and they welcomed the support of their male colleagues.

Black vaudeville juggled many balls in the air at once. The producers offered acts that appealed to black pride and virtuosity while not offending white audiences; similarly, if the show too consciously aped white ways, many blacks objected and demanded material that reflected black culture. When black comics performing for black audiences adopted the same characteristics that white audiences expected of them, they often encountered opposition. The women were confronted with another difficulty: they were expected to preserve the womanly images shared with white women while asserting their independence. Black women vaudevillians, then, operated within boundaries that they did not create but had to follow. Racial and gender images combined with a business that offered no protection to its workers made for hard times for black women vaudevillians.

Black blues singers sang novel and bawdy lyrics within a melodic line that emerged from the Negro spiritual and the farm song.[7] They secularized and bowdlerized a religious and rural subject matter which scandalized the religious members of the community. In addition, the singers and composers adapted a musical form that came from the black community and combined it with many themes that black women shared with white women. The musical style they created, the blues, had the sound of the African American experience, while the words described the tragic, universal womanly experience.

The blues singers sang out of the particular situation they knew, but their words resonated with all women. Ida Cox sang "Wild Women Don't Have the Blues" and reminded her listeners that, though women wished for faithful lovers. "Go home and put my man out if he don't act right. Wild women don't worry." A woman rejected by her lover became a theme with which all women could identify. The eternal rivalry for men's affections was effectively captured in the popular vaudeville tune "He May Be Your Dog, but He Is Wearing My Collar Now." Ida Cox also sang "Western Union Blues" about a rejected woman and "Tree Top Papa" about an unfaithful lover. One singer might record the song and, by so doing, popularize it for many others to sing. Romance gone sour never lost its appeal to both the women and men in the audience.

Black women entertainers, like black women intellectuals in subsequent generations, found their allegiances torn between their gender concerns, which allied them with white women, and their racial identity, which brought them closer to black men. Bawdy black and white women entertainers, who will be discussed in the next chapter, defined themselves as outside the racial and gender mainstream and were able to explore the human possibilities more fully than most others. While most bawdy white women sang and joked to a very select audience in expensive nightclubs, black bawdy women singers had a larger following in black cabarets that catered to all classes of black people.

In black vaudeville, as in white vaudeville, men dominated all aspects of the business. A white majority and a black minority of producers booked most of the acts, owned most of the theaters, and acted as agents to the entertainers. A few black women, however, became producers, unusual entrepreneurs in a male-dominated business. Mabel Whitman, for example, is an interesting case of a woman who produced a show starring her sisters. She planned the program, handled all of the arrangements, and competed for bookings with the prominent men in the business. The Whitman Sisters, as they were known, performed for more than twenty years, traveling the circuit from small town to small town. Mabel created new musicals to showcase the talent of her sisters. Her troupe, however, remained the exception; they were not joined by large numbers of women producers. As competition increased and profit declined, black male producers lost out to more and more white men.[8]

Some black performers worked for the white Pantages Circuit and the Loews Circuit, but rarely for the Keith and Albee Circuit, the aristocrat of all vaudeville circuits. Stars such as Ethel Waters and Bessie Smith got dates from white producers, but the overwhelming majority of black vaudevillians worked within the TOBA and lost their jobs during bad economic times. The period of black vaudeville extended from the 1890s to the 1930s; black musicals, a subgenre that arrived on Broadway at the turn of the century, had a long run through 1910 and then disappeared from the Broadway stage for a decade. Composer James Weldon Johnson called that decade "the term of exile" from Broadway. However, the black musical returned to Broadway in the 1920s.

Besides the musical theater, of course, was the rise of the cabaret or nightclub. This venue provided new opportunities for black women singers and dancers. Connie's Inn and the Cotton Club are the most famous of numerous Harlem nightspots that employed women entertainers. Quite elaborate musicals were staged there; sometimes, productions that originated in the clubs found a new home on Broadway, such as the successful *Hot Chocolates,* which began at Connie's Inn and ended up at the Hudson Theater in 1929. Exposure to a Broadway audience, of course, expanded the black woman star's identity and led to fame in both the black and white worlds.

The new record companies also offered employment to the singers.[9] One of the new inventions of leisure products was the phonograph or record player. Large, 78-rpm records played one song on each side and became enormously popular. In 1921, Black Swan became the first black-owned record company; owner Harry Pace sought black artists to record and gave newcomers opportunities. However, by 1924, the company was bought out by Paramount Records, which then developed its own race catalog, a testimony to the popularity and to the market for black-produced music. Blues singer Mamie Smith (1883-1946) recorded on the Okeh label while singing at Harlem cabarets. Her second record, the 1920 "Crazy Blues," sold seventy-five thousand copies in the first month of release. The demand for black blues singers combined with the phonograph's novelty and the dancing possibilities of the music made this new art form a commercial success. Mamie Smith recorded nearly one hundred songs during a seven-year period in the twenties.

Recordings, of course, brought Bessie Smith and Ethel Waters great popularity and wealth. Waters's 1922 recording of "Sweet Georgia Brown" set a new high for record sales. Bessie Smith's career and accomplishments will be discussed in the next chapter. The 1920s saw numerous blues singers become recording stars. Among the well known of the period were Sippie Wallace and Victoria Spivey. Spivey's first big success, "No. 12, Let Me Roam," appeared on the Okeh label in 1927. Before the depression and the decline of the business, black

Ethel Waters began as a singer, enjoying great success as a performer of the blues.

and white fans purchased tens of thousands of their records.[10] Black women singers crossed the color line through their recordings. In person, they still played to largely black audiences, but in the privacy of the home, their music played to white fans as well.

Just as early vaudevillians had traveled the circuit for years, so the 1920s cabaret singers sang in city after city. Rather than visit every small town with a black community, however, they sang in big city clubs where they were assured of a large audience and hoped that their records would find homes in small towns and farms, particularly in the South. Besides the multiple venues in New York's Harlem, Chicago's South Side was also the home of many clubs. State Street, in the 3400 south block, housed many popular nightspots frequented by the growing black population in the city. Many of the singers in this period traveled to St. Louis, Kansas City, and faraway California, where white and black fans enjoyed the new blues sound. A national popular culture was developing by the 1920s, thanks to records and the new silent-film industry. People in small and large towns recognized the faces and voices of entertainers; they began to share the same leisure time activities and the same fantasies.

Earlier, during the height of the minstrel/vaudeville show, black companies performed all over the country. Sissieretta Jones, known as the Black Patti (a left-handed compliment because her operatic voice invited comparisons to the white opera star, Adelina Patti), organized a black musical revue company called the Black Patti Troubadours; they traveled all over the country. Jones's repertory always included a selection of operatic arias. While black audiences enjoyed and were impressed with her virtuoso singing, white audiences considered the sight of a black opera singer a novelty act, a wildly unusual phenomenon. Needless to say, Sissieretta Jones never sang on the stage of the Metropolitan Opera House.[11]

Few musical histories acknowledge the contributions of the black women in early vaudeville and musical theater. For the many who worked for a few years and then dropped out, their performances are forgotten. The following brief survey of some of the most prominent black women entertainers of the period offer a sampling of the women who ventured into this new occupation at the turn of the last century. Their biographies, combined with the times in which they performed, offers a glimpse of who went into show business in the early years, what their circumstances were, and how well they fared.

Ada (or Aida in some accounts) Overton Walker (1870–1914) is an interesting case of a southern woman, born in Richmond, Virginia, and raised in New York, who loved to dance and sing. At the age of sixteen, she joined the Black Patti Troubadours and toured the whole country. The show followed a minstrel formula, but over time, evolved into a musical comedy show. Ada Overton danced in the chorus and eventually became a featured player.[12]

In 1898, she joined the company of Williams and Walker, the most famous and successful black comic team of the time. Bert Williams and George Walker, but particularly Williams, were considered master comics and successful producers of shows. In 1899, Ada married George Walker, helping her to gain a starring role in their next three productions, but critics agreed that she had the talent to become a star.

From 1902 to 1908, Ada Overton Walker was featured in all Williams/Walker productions. Sylvester Russell, the black theater critic for the Indianapolis *Freeman* noted her presence in Williams's *In Dahomey* and said that she was "the most important female in the cast," who "owned the stage" when she appeared.[13] Walker played Rosetta Lightfoot, described as "a troublesome young thing" in this musical comedy about two black American men who go to Dahomey to take over the country for their own financial gain. *In Dahomey* became the first all-black production to open on Broadway, the legitimate theater district. The show traveled to London in 1903 and the English critics echoed the Americans. Walker's singing and dancing "were a revelation" gushed one London critic.[14]

Ada Overton Walker continued to receive positive reviews for her roles in the company's 1906 *Abyssinia Company* and in the 1908 *Bandanna Land*. However, George Walker became ill during the Broadway run of *Bandanna Land* and Ada dressed in male attire to take his place. This ploy worked for this show but did not become the regular practice. Walker never regained his health, and the great comic duo of Williams and Walker ended; Walker died three years later. Ada left the company but decided to continue working under her own auspices. She organized a vaudeville act in 1909 called Ada Overton Walker and the Abyssinian Girls. The *Variety* critic found her exotic dance as "having a wild, weird aspect and an immense amount of action in it." [15]

Though he did not like her singing voice, the critic noted that the audience responded favorably, especially to her popular renditions of songs such as "I'm Miss Hannah from Savannah" and "That Is Why They Call Me Shine." Ada Overton Walker was one of many black women entertainers whose star shone brightly but briefly. She displayed her spunk and drive by organizing her own show after her husband became ill and by continuing to work under the extremely difficult conditions available to her. Unfortunately, sickness took her off the stage and in 1914, at forty-four, she died. Her career had lasted for more than twenty years, and because she made no recordings, she's remembered only by the written reviews of her shows, primarily in the black press.

Florence Mills (1895–1927) qualifies as one of the most spectacular black women entertainers of the early years of the century. Her sudden death after an appendectomy that went wrong ended a promising and rising career. Born in Washington, D.C., Mills began entertaining at eight years old; she was a lovely looking child with a sweet voice who grew up to become a beautiful woman with a high, fluty voice. She played in vaudeville and, with her dancer-husband, U.S. Thompson, performed on the Keith Circuit. She then turned to Broadway musicals. While starring in Lew Leslie's Revue, Mills had an offer to join the Ziegfeld Follies, the most famous white vaudeville show on Broadway. She turned Ziegfeld down because, as she explained to a reporter, "I felt that if this revue turned out successfully, a permanent institution would have been created for the colored artists and an opportunity created for the glorification of the American High-Browns."[16]

In the second act of the revue, Mills sang a song that became her trademark: "I"m a Little Blackbird Looking for a Blue Bird." Theophilus Lewis, the drama critic for the black socialist newspaper, The *Messenger,* was wild about her singing. Lewis, who usually criticized black musicals for imitating the most trivial white musicals (he called the Lew Leslie Revue "extremely shoddy, garish, and vulgar"), waxed eloquent about Mills's performance: "She is the most consummate artist I have ever seen on the musical stage."[17] Florence Mills's premature death drew more than three thousand people to her funeral. Her presence was sorely missed.

Ethel Waters was another great singer of the period who had the distinction of being not only a successful Broadway and recording star, but also a major movie star. Waters (1886?–1977) was born in Chester, Pennsylvania, and began her career in an amateur contest in Philadelphia at the age of fourteen. Within three years, she was on the pro circuit with an act called the Hill Sisters. Waters performed in small clubs and signed with Black Swan Records in 1921. She then appeared in musical comedies such as *Oh, Joy! Jump Steady,* and *Get Set.*[18]

Her first big Broadway show was *Africana* in 1927. In the middle of the second act, she sang "My Special Friend Is in Town." The *Variety* critic noted, "It's one of those ditties often found in colored shows, the lines saying just what they mean, raw, of course. The first-nighters ate that one up." Composer Irving Berlin saw Waters at the Cotton Club, and he featured her in his 1933 production *As Thousands Cheer.* It was her first white Broadway show, and Waters became the highest-paid woman on Broadway.

Ethel Waters also became a distinguished actress on the dramatic stage and screen. Her role in the 1941 production of *Cabin in the Sky* assured her a large and loyal following. She eventually gave up singing for dramatic roles in Hollywood movies of the 1940s and 1950s. Her career was exceptional in that she enjoyed success in many different venues; when the Broadway musical hit hard times during the depression, Waters found opportunities in movies. Unlike most of her contemporary black singers and dancers, she enjoyed a long career. Her maternal appearance combined with her dignified and graceful face and voice made her a reassuring image for white America.

Edith Wilson (1897–1981) is another example of a successful black woman vaudevillian and musical theater star. She too began singing in amateur shows in her hometown of Louisville, Kentucky. She was only thirteen years old but, the show business bug had infected her; she promised her mother that she would return to school after a successful run, but the lure of entertainment shortened her formal education. By the time she was twenty-five years old, she debuted at the Town Hall in New York in the musical show, *Put and Take.* Wilson's smooth, silky voice and jazzy presentation made her a popular and busy entertainer.

Throughout the twenties, she appeared in many of the most popular black musicals, such as *Plantation Review* (1922), *Dover Street to Dixie* (1926), and *Hot Chocolates* (1929). When the latter show opened at Connie's Inn, the *Variety* critic was on hand to report on the perfor-

Ethel Waters had a long career in the movies as a character actress.

mance: "Connie's floor show is certainly hot in spots and hasn't been toned down much, if any, for Broadway. There is an example in 'Pool Room Papa', as done by Edith Wilson and Billy Maxey. It is a double-meaning lyric, made distinctively suggestive." He goes on to note that later in the production, Edith Wilson sings another song "having blue, blue lines." Wilson surely qualifies as a bawdy black woman enter-tainer. She enjoyed singing songs with sexual implications while also singing straightforward jazzy rhythms. In the 1930 *Hot Rhythm,* a show not notable for consistently high quality, Wilson's performance was singled out for favorable comment and her song received the evening's only "genuine encores."[19]

Wilson also recorded many of her hit songs, eventually making twenty-six albums for Columbia Records during the 1920s. She toured with the Duke Ellington band in this country and in England in the 1940s. In 1947, Wilson went to work for the Quaker Oats Company as their Aunt Jemima spokeswoman. She traveled around the country appearing before youth and community groups. She remained in that position until 1965. In a 1973 videotaped interview, she appears as vibrant and personable as she had been in her youth. Her singing voice remained strong and sure, her pace effective, and her delivery confident. She died in 1981 at the age of eighty-four. Her voice lived on through her music. In 1994, Delmark, a record-producing com-pany, put out a compact disk featuring its great blues singers, and Edith Wilson sang a "classic" blues number. Music critic Larry Birnbaum, in reviewing the CD, noted, "Pop music tends to age quickly, but the blues, at its best, is timeless."[20]

A final example of a black woman entertainer in the musical the-ater was Adelaide Hall (1901–93). A talented singer and dancer, she began as a child dancing in the chorus as one of the Jazz Jasmines in *Shuffle Along,* the 1921 hit that returned black musicals to Broadway. The show, produced by black composers Sissle and Blake, starred Josephine Baker and Paul Robeson, two major talents. Hall, a lovely, light-skinned woman, had a starring role in the 1923 *Runnin' Wild* and possessed, according to one critic, a "luxuriant voice." In 1927, she recorded Duke Ellington's song "Creole Love Call" with him, in which she introduced what later came to be called "scat singing;" without words but with expressive sounds, she used her voice as a jazz instrument. Some years later, the great jazz singer Ella Fitzgerald would become famous using the same technique. Adelaide Hall and legendary dancer, Bill "Bojangles" Robinson, starred in the twenties' longest-running black musical, *Blackbirds of 1928*. The show's producer, Lew Leslie, saw Hall as the successor to Florence Mills, his next "sepia star." In the show, Hall sang "I Can't Give You Anything but Love," one of the most enduring songs to emerge from American musical theater.

The depression years were hard on musical theater and indeed on all entertainment forms. Yet, *Brown Buddies,* the 1930 musical featuring Hall and Robinson, ran 111 performances during the height of the 1930–31 season. In it, Hall sang "Give Me a Man like That" and "My Blue Melody." Adelaide Hall also appeared at the Cotton Club in the early 1930s, but she became disillusioned with racial prejudice and the lack of professional opportunities, so in the late 1930s, she and her husband, Bert Hicks, moved to England. During World War II, she hosted a radio show in London called "Wrapped in Velvet."[21] Hall occasionally returned to this country and made a few black musical shorts in Hollywood called *All Colored Vaudeville Show* and *Dixieland Jamboree* but these movies did not lead to new offers or opportunities. She was still a vital woman interested in performing, but there were no calls for black musical stars. In 1980, *Black Broadway,* a review of the great black musical stars of the past, came to Broadway for a limited run. Hall sang "I Can't Give You Anything but Love" in the show. Edith Wilson also performed.

Only a few of the black women entertainers of the early years of this century are remembered today. Ethel Waters and Bessie Smith are perhaps the best known. Their records and Waters's movies offer contemporary audiences an opportunity to hear and see them in performance. Though they were unique in their talent, they were also representative of a much larger group of entertainers who worked fifty-two weeks a year, if they were lucky, year after year. Black entertainment was a vibrant art and leisure form with women contributing endless hours of singing and dancing. The women also offered comic and satiric treatments of important subjects.

Ethel Waters sang "Supper Time," a song about a woman preparing dinner for a man who would never arrive because he had been lynched. The lyrics of this and other songs deserve analysis in much the same way that poetry does. Audiences listened intently to the oral poetry/song performed by the blues singers. They expected both to hear serious glosses on real issues and to laugh when Waters or Smith sang a double-entendre song. The wide range of material covered by these singers attested to their comprehensive interest and concern for their community's welfare. They played the dual role of amusing and edifying their audience.

Many black women entertainers may have shared this unusual position with them; they were social critics, stable forces, and creative innovators, all in one person. The maternal-appearing Smith and Waters defied the traditional image by singing racy lyrics, but they also dismissed the frivolous pose and sang "Supper Time." They could not be stereotyped. Their creative flexibility surely drew admiring thoughts and feelings from audience members. Their example as productive and energetic professionals acted as inspiration to many talented young women who followed in their heroines' footsteps.

The many spots for performing, from amateur shows to slick Broadway musicals, attest to the insatiable interest and need for entertainment in all communities, but for African Americans in the South and North, their own talented singers and dancers could be seen in their own theaters and nightclubs. Paralleling white cultural entertainments, commercial black entertainments grew dramatically in the first two decades of this century.[22] Though black males played key roles in developing the vaudeville circuit and the theaters, white entrepreneurs took over once it became evident that this was a profitable endeavor. Again mirroring white culture, black women found fewer opportunities to perform; but as bawdy blues singers and as mainstream singers and dancers in lavish musical productions, they distinguished themselves.

Studying the careers of black women vaudevillians offers an important example of the intersecting forces that shape an entertainer's life and performance. Edith Wilson's southernness, her blackness, and her emergence into show business during a flourishing period enabled her to have the career she did. Having been born at a different time and place would have produced different results. Adelaide Hall, however, found racism too big an obstacle to overcome and moved to England, hoping for a kinder reception. The depression surely hurt African Americans, as a group, more than it did white Americans, because they occupied the lower rungs of the job ladder. Consequently, they could not afford to attend a musical put on by Ada Overton Walker or buy a Bessie Smith record.

Vaudeville was a particularly difficult form of show business—doubly difficult for women—and triply difficult for black women. But black women vaudevillians performed, whenever and wherever they could. They displayed their individual talents within the entertainment form available to them. In this sense, their biographies and creative expressions adapted to the requirements of vaudeville. These women established the foundation for future generations of talented black women singers, dancers, and actresses while sharing many problems and dreams with white women entertainers. They maintained a delicate balance, walking a tightrope between racial and gender prejudice. Their successors may not have known of their travails, but they still owed their careers to their foremothers in the theater. The boundaries that developed for black women vaudevillians lived long after that popular cultural form died.

2

Bawdy Women Entertainers

While African American women entertainers were gaining a foothold in vaudeville and mainstream theatrical stages, a new outlet appeared for black and white entertainers in the second decade of the twentieth century: the intimate nightclub. In a living room setting, women and men comics and singers told off-color jokes and sang songs with sexual lyrics. The audience was smaller and self-selected; everyone knew what to expect in this smaller environment, and moralists could easily avoid this more risqué experience. City dwellers, who considered themselves sophisticated and forward looking, could have an evening of relaxation in the nightclub. This new setting symbolized the increasing array of new forms of entertainment for consumers; the variety show, the theater, silent film, and now, the nightclub, all competed for the attention and dollars of audiences. Equally important, however, the nightclub demonstrated the fact that sexual material could not be aired on mainstream stages.

Being the pioneer in entertainment, New York City provides us with the best examples of the new show businesses. In Harlem, the Lower East Side, and the Broadway theatrical district, women entertainers flourished, including a category generally considered less than respectable: the bawdy women entertainers. These women offered eager audiences evidences of women at their most outrageous and sexy. Though they were a minority among women performers, they interest us because of their revelations about society's values. By placing those values next to the impermissible, shocking, and outrageous styles and contents provided by bawdy women entertainers, one can look into the unspoken side of human behavior. The forbidden, always the closed door of society, really becomes a window into the respectable culture. The Eve image, most prominently displayed by these bawdy women entertainers, makes the Mary image even purer. Virtue can only be appreciated when its opposite is clearly known.

Eva Tanguay, for example, a spectacularly successful vaudevillian, was such a larger-than-life personality that she is worthy of study for that reason alone. However, her life and career is even more valuable as insight into the boundaries around entertainment and popular theater in the early years of this century. The fact that she performed her outrageousness in vaudeville makes her even more unusual. The spectrum of respectable to disreputable was broad and wide; contrary to some views of America as puritanical or Victorian in the early twentieth century, Americans, both New Yorkers and citizens of smaller cities, enjoyed a Tanguay performance and made her the most successful vaudevillian of her day. The texts that were Tanguay—her crazy personality and her anarchic songs—combined uneasily with respectable society in the years 1910–19.

Bawdy women entertainers break out of the separate spheres for men and women in content and in space: they talk and sing dirty (men's content), and they do it in burlesque houses (men's space), less frequently on the vaudeville stage, and in the new nightclubs (men and women's space). They mock the society's view of sexuality and in so doing, by their very actions, repudiate the carefully drawn boundaries between the sexes. Rarely are the women performers committed feminists, acting out of a conscious and well-developed ideology; rather, they are actors and singers, hustlers and entertainers, interested in succeeding in the precarious world of show business. In that world, they have to use whatever assets are available to them, minimize their deficits, and call attention to themselves. These very acts, of course, also distinguish them from most women and many men.

In this century, though I have not done a statistical analysis of all bawdy women entertainers, I would venture to guess that minority women are overrepresented. It is not accidental that black and Jewish women are prominent numerically on the bawdy end of show business. Eva Tanguay, the first of the three women performers offered as examples in this chapter, was a different kind of outsider: born in Marbleton, Quebec, of French-Canadian parents, she moved to Holyoke, Massachusetts as a child. As a French Canadian in WASP New England, she qualifies as a minority. Sophie Tucker, our second example, was Jewish, the daughter of immigrants, while Bessie Smith was an African American southerner.

For Bessie Smith, race shaped her life and career as it did for so many other black women singers. Ethnicity influenced Sophie Tucker's persona and work. Personality, that unique combination of traits that mark each of us as distinct from one another, also becomes particularly important in this discussion. Bawdy women entertainers, by definition, had to be hams, extremely self-confident on stage, brave, and often self-deprecating. They had to be quick to determine what would succeed with their audiences and what was beyond the pale. Bawdiness allowed a lot of room for grossness, outrageousness, and shocking behavior, all traits associated with males, decidedly not females. Women who became bawdy entertainers, then, had an innate sense of self that was not reinforced by cultural representatives or majoritarian values. They succeeded in spite of obstacles.

To discuss sexuality in public was a shocking thing, especially for women. To suggest that women had sexual natures, that they enjoyed sex, and that they had a right to initiate sexual encounters were ideas outside the pale of normal thought and discourse around 1900. The Victorian era, reinforced by medical ignorance, denied women knowledge about their own bodies and assured the moral guardians of the culture that women who had sexual longings were evil temptresses, doomed forever. Since the accepted wisdom believed that all sexuality was suspect, men, though granted sexual natures, were not better off. Their sexual needs were seen as remnants from their animal pasts, urgings that had to be satisfied (not through masturbation, however), and preferably through marriage. However, if need be, prostitutes were appropriate objects for their animal lust.

Bawdy women entertainers posssessed an angle of vision unlike the society's majority. They acknowledged their sexuality, indeed publicly proclaimed it, and often, especially in the case of the black bawdy women, did not think the whole subject was such a big deal anyway. Bessie Smith often made explicit in her blues songs what she expected from a man. While singing of man's unfaithfulness, she found immediate support from her audience who knew only too well the experience she described. Boldly, Bessie asserted woman's right to sexual satisfaction, and with both humor and a great voice, she enchanted her audiences and built a huge following, both through her personal appearances and her records.

All three stars described here were not conventionally beautiful women, but they all used their physical selves to project a style and an identity that distinguished them from all others and earned them the fame and recognition they sought. Eva Tanguay, the least talented of the three (by her own admission, she could not sing, dance, or tell a joke), had a wild mop of hair which she made even wilder-looking, an unlikely sight on the 1905 vaudeville stage. Sophie Tucker was a heavy-set woman with crude features who, though well-corseted, weighed in at two hundred pounds during her long career. Bessie Smith was built like Tucker, and both women capitalized on their appearance to offer the startling observation that they were sexy and interested.

Driven by huge egos, they flourished on publicity, the worse the better. While respectable women in the audience turned their backs on the bawdy vaudevillians, the men roared and the management shuddered. When Sophie Tucker was ordered by the Chicago police to stop singing "Angle Worm Wiggle," she protested, much to the delight of her fans and the newspaper reporters. She went to court, accompanied by publicity, lost her case, but won the publicity battle. Eva Tanguay also got into trouble with the law and ended up joking with the booking sergeant. She hired her own public relations person to ensure constant publicity for her antics. All of these women understood the advantages of modern communication; they exploited every opportunity to get their names in newspapers and magazines. Favorable or unfavorable, the content was irrelevant as long as the name was spelled correctly.

The family atmosphere of vaudeville was not conducive to most of the bawdies. Tanguay was the exception. Tucker went to the intimate nightclubs and cabarets where her brand of humor was allowed and appreciated. Bessie Smith performed in the intimate clubs of Harlem and in black vaudeville theaters. Bawdy women entertainers did not and do not appear in mainstream forums such as network television, though they may appear on cable shows where public scrutiny is not as intense. Their avant-garde style and material may appeal to both sexes, but only to small numbers of self-selected people. This is a good example of how cultural values shape cultural institutions, thereby influencing the venues in which the bawds will perform.

The biographies of Tanguay, Tucker, and Smith occupy that paradoxical position in which they share characteristics with each other and with others, yet remain separate and distinct. Many of their experiences are common to not only other entertainers but all women. In a later chapter called "Women Movie Stars as Role Models," I explore some of these connections. Star performers lived lives atypical for American women, but they connected with their fans precisely because they shared with them many basic human concerns. How to find and sustain a loving relationship and how to work while raising a family, for example, were thorny issues faced by all American women.

Eva Tanguay (1878–1947) began as a child actor in productions playing Little Lord Fauntleroy and went on to do musicals. Her family had moved from Quebec to Massachusetts when she was a child; by the age of eight, she was on the stage and had become her family's primary means of support. Her outgoing, if not flamboyant, personality was already in evidence. After playing child roles, she became the young ingenue, and by 1904, had captured the vaudeville stage. For the next ten years, Tanguay dominated the medium. While workers earned two dollars for a ten-hour work day, she received thirty-five hundred dollars a performance. Though Eva Tanguay was billed as a singing comedienne, one commentator described her this way: "It is easy to analyze her act: it was assault and battery."[1] She became known as the "I Don't Care" girl, the title of her signature song.

In 1912, Tanguay earned over one hundred thousand dollars for forty weeks of performing, while the president of the United States received seventy-five thousand dollars per year, a fact not unnoticed in the press. While some critics questioned American priorities, audiences applauded and continued to attend her shows. The sight of a high-earning woman startled and shook up many observers, though surely many people quietly applauded Tanguay's financial success. Independent women upset the traditional power distribution in the family and community. Precisely because Eva Tanguay was the exception, she could be tolerated. Heaven forbid that her high earnings should be duplicated by women in various occupations throughout society.

Tanguay's onstage performance (she also behaved audaciously

Here shown in typically outrageous headgear, Eva Tanguay thrilled vaudeville audiences for many years.

offstage) was truly something to behold. She never stopped moving. Wiggling across the stage, shaking her wild hair, and screeching out a song became her typical onstage behavior. According to one observer, she covered three and a half miles during a single performance. Sensitive to the power of the press and the value of publicity (she had four press agents), Tanguay also appreciated the fact that the more audacious she became, the more attention she received. As a self-promoter, she loved writing and singing limericks to explain her fame: "When I put on tights/My name went up in lights," the lyrics exclaimed. In 1915, audiences heard, "There's method in my madness/There is a meaning for my style/The more they raise my salary/the crazier I'll be."[2]

Many of her critics, most notably Ada Patterson, a top reporter for the Hearst newspapers, were puzzled by her enormous success. Patterson described Tanguay thusly: "Everyone is filled with breathless intensity. . . . Here she comes with quick fluttering steps and restless, outstretched hands, a dynamic personality of nerves and excitement . . . a trim, alert figure, held so tense and straight that energy exudes from it . . . a wild mop of stiff, tossled blond hair which seems charged with electric vigor. . . . Every inch of her is alive."[3] In 1918, journalist Heywood Broun criticized her performance in his column in the *New York Herald Tribune*. Tanguay had sung the "Marseillaise" in a French that Broun considered vulgar and grotesque. "The only cheerful song in her repertory yesterday," he noted, "was one in which she hinted that some day she would retire. Miss Tanguay is billed as a 'bombshell.' Would be to Heaven she were, for a bomb is something which is carried to great height and then dropped."[4] Tanguay responded by taking a full page advertisement in *Variety* in which she attacked Broun for his vicious attack on a hardworking woman: "Have you noticed when a woman succeeds how they attack her until her character bleeds? They snap at her heels like mongrels unfed, just because she has escaped being dropped into FAILURE'S biggest web. They don't give her credit for talent or art. They don't discount a very hard start. They don't give her credit for heartaches or pains; how she grimly held tight to the reins when the road ahead was rocky and dreary; how smiling she made every discouraging sneer."[5]

Tanguay's spunk and aggressive pride rose from the page. She declared frankly, "That's all there is to it. As a matter of fact, I am not beautiful, I can't sing, and I don't know how to dance. I am not even graceful."[6] But she stood her ground and continued to publicize her appearance on street corners. In one positive review of her act in the *Dramatic Mirror* of 1915, the reviewer declared, "if ever the United States becomes involved in war, we recommend Miss Tanguay as recruiting sergeant extraordinary."[7]

Tanguay's songs openly proclaimed her views. Besides "I Don't Care," she sang "I Love To Be Crazy," "I Want Some One To Go Wild with Me," "It's All Been Done Before but Not the Way I Do It," and "Go as Far as You Like." In 1908, she scandalized audiences with her Salome act in which her costume was described as "two-pearled." She later recalled how she performed the dance of the seven veils:

> I was no classical dancer, so I mixed in some Highland Fling and Sailor's Hornpipe and every thing else I knew. And I sang as I danced and dropped one veil after another. I also did something else that no one else had thought of. Instead of dancing around holding the papier mache head, I hired a Negro boy with big eyes. I sat him on the side of the stage, all covered up. As I began to dance, I uncovered his head, which, to the audience, appeared to be resting on a silver tray. As I moved about the stage his huge eyes also moved, following me. The audience was electrified. But when the Mayor of New York heard about the dance, he sent word to put some clothes on or he'd close the show.[8]

An offer from Flo Ziegfeld prevented her from accepting the mayor's challenge, but Eva Tanguay continued to pack them in whenever and wherever she played. As late as 1922, she broke Loew's New York State Theater's record with a twenty-nine-thousand-dollar gross for a performance when the top ticket price was fifty cents. Her tours around the country also resulted in headline stories. Tanguay had the reputation of being a brawler; she carried around hundred-dollar bills to give stagehands after she hit them for an alleged insult. In Evansville, Indiana, in 1905, she slept through the matinee performance and received a one-hundred dollar fine from the manager. She retaliated during the evening show by threading the stage curtain with a dagger. In 1915, in Sharon, Pennsylvania, at Morgan's Grand Theater, she berated the audience for being "hicks" and cursed the management because her dressing room mirror was not large enough. Her craziness did not deter her fans. It was only when vaudeville died in the 1920s, replaced by silent movies, that her career ended.

Tanguay was famous and notorious. Indeed, the two qualities interacted: every time she did something outrageous, it increased her fame. The independent Eve image she so effectively projected has always attracted more viewers than the sweet but predictable, Mary. Tanguay combined Lilith with Eve. A host of imitators—the highest form of flattery in show business—dogged her trail. Burlesque queen Millie DeLeon, a Tanguay contemporary, created a routine called "I Don't Chair," in which she did a suggestive dance around a chair, a clear parody of Tanguay's "I Don't Care" song. DeLeon also mimicked Tanguay's rendition of Salome's dance of the seven veils. Both stars boasted that their version was the best and most spectacular. Each time DeLeon performed one of the numbers closely identified with Tanguay, she drew the comparison and extended Tanguay's and her own fame.

Sophie Tucker (1887–1966) came from an immigrant Jewish family that settled in Hartford, Connecticut. Her parents had emigrated from Russia, and her father opened a restaurant in his new hometown.[9] The clientele was often composed of traveling entertainers, and Sophie helped out both as a waitress and as a singer. The Yiddish actors who frequented the place encouraged her to go into show business; while they had the Yiddish stage in mind, she thought about burlesque and vaudeville, the American venues. At nineteen years old, Tucker, already a mother, decided that show business was to be her future. In the fall of 1906, she left her baby with her parents (her husband had already left after a brief marriage) and moved to New York City.

Tucker began a career that easily fit into the working-herself-up-the-hard-way tradition, a truly American story of rags to riches. However, because her story was that of a woman entertainer, it brought new features to the old myth. Young, ambitious, hardworking women rarely had their autobiographies become evidence of the American Dream. As a Jewish woman who believed in the Protestant ethic of hard work, Sophie Tucker sang in a New York City club for fifteen dollars a week, mixing audience requests with prepared numbers. She later estimated that she performed between fifty and one hundred songs every night. After singing at an amateur-night event in one theater, she was hired to perform on the Park circuit, which serviced New England towns.

One of the bawdy women entertainers, Sophie Tucker poses for her fans.

An agent advised Sophie to appear in blackface, because her large size and hoarsy voice were deemed unattractive. By putting cork on her face, making herself invisible, she could become acceptable to her audience. Tucker hated this practice but followed it for a few years. She was billed as the "Manipulator of Coon Melodies," another reference to African American-inspired songs. In 1909, after briefly playing in the Ziegfeld Follies, she abandoned blackface forever. By that time, she had developed her trademark style: a three-part series of songs made of Yiddish or Yiddish-inspired ballads, a comic interlude, and risqué songs.

Tucker's rendition in both English and Yiddish of "My Yiddishe Mamma" remained a staple of her repertory for more than fifty years and reminded the Jewish members of her audience of their families' immigrant roots. Beginning in the years 1910–19, composers Fred Fisher and Jack Yellen wrote her songs, many of which featured double entendres, the essence of much bawdy humor, songs that could be sung in nightclubs. Sophie Tucker became known as the "red hot mamma," a term taken from black singers suggesting a sexy woman who is not afraid to talk about the subject. The maternal and the sensual are blended in this image. "When They Start to Ration My Passion, It's Gonna Be Tough on Me," "You Can't Serve Love in Dishes," and "You Can't Sew a Button on a Heart" were songs written by Yellen for Sophie during this period.

Tucker's theme song, "Some of These Days," was written by African American songwriter Shelton Brooks and became a featured part of her act. It was in the intimate atmosphere of a club that she could wink, grin, and sneer about sex, passion, faithless lovers, and the general dangers of romance. Historian Lewis Erenburg credits Sophie Tucker with making Reisenweber's, a New York cabaret, a hit; eventually, Reisenweber named the room "The Sophie Tucker Room" after their most popular star. The bawdy singer did in nightclubs what Eva Tanguay had done on the stage. She spoke directly about sex, made fun of prudishness, and proclaimed her sexual independence. "Make Him Say Please," "You've Got to See Your Mama Ev'ry Night," and songs such as "No One Can Satisfy Any One Man All the Time," "I'm Living Alone and I Like It," and "It's Never Too Late" typified her offerings.

Tucker sang of faithless men and women who did not lament their fate. "Never Let the Same Dog Bite You Twice," "No One Man Is Ever

Going to Worry Me," and "Mamma Goes Where Poppa Goes" are good examples of this theme. As Sophie Tucker got older, and kept performing, she sang of the joys of being sixty and sexually active. "How Am I Ever Going to Grow Old?" "I Am Starting All Over Again," and "I Am Having More Fun Since I Am Sixty" all exemplifed this attitude. The heavy, well-corseted Tucker presented a mock serious/serious persona. She was both kidding and expressing her true feelings. In "I Am Having More Fun Since I Am Sixty," she sang, "The more candles on my birthday cake/the hotter I become." Audiences laughed, assuming she was joking, yet Tucker's personal history suggests otherwise. "You Can't Deep Freeze a Red Hot Mamma" and "Vitamins, Hormones, and Pills" illustrate her continued interest in the same theme. Twice married and twice divorced, Tucker sang/talked her way through a song, suggesting personal experience at the base of all her lyrics.

Sophie Tucker had a faithful following, most of whom aged simultaneously with her. She told the men in her audience not to take themselves so seriously, and she assured the women that they got better as they got older. Tucker kept a large card file of her fans' addresses and sent out hundreds of postcards regularly informing them of her next appearance in their city. In Chicago, she appeared at the Chez Paree until the end of her life. Tucker appealed to middle-aged audiences in the 1940s and 1950s and comforted women whose shapes were not as slender and fashionable as the women's magazines promoted. Coincidentally, her long career and the intimate nightclub ended around the same time to be replaced by the huge concert hall or the outdoor forum for pop and rock entertainers.

Bessie Smith (1894–1937) is our third star who thrived in the bawdy world of small theaters and nightclubs. Unlike the French-Canadian Tanguay and the immigrant daughter Tucker, Smith was born in a one-room wooden shack in a poor and segregated part of Chattanooga, Tennessee. The section, known as Blue Goose Hollow, looked like many other places in the South where the legacy of slavery persisted in the form of severe discrimination. Bessie was one of seven children; her father William was a part-time Baptist preacher who barely earned a living. Her mother Laura tried valiantly to feed and clothe her large family. William died when Bessie was still an infant, and Laura died when she was eight years old. As a child, Bessie lost two brothers and was raised by an older sister, Viola, who, according to acquaintances, looked like an old woman before she reached her thirtieth birthday. The blues, Bessie's singing material, described her hard life.[10]

Despite these terrible hardships, Bessie attended the Main Street School until the eighth grade, exceeding the experience of most of her peers in the community. While attending school, she began singing on street corners, particularly on Ninth Street, a lively gathering place where passersby rewarded talented singers with coins. While brother Andrew played the guitar, Bessie Smith displayed her silky natural voice, her expressive style, and her true emotions. Even as a child, she was large and appeared older than her years. Earning a living as a singer surely seemed a more desirable path than that of a domestic—the fate in store for most of her female friends. From street corners, she graduated to amateur nights at the Ivory Theater where one night's earnings (from the tips given by a grateful audience) exceeded the weekly earnings of a housemaid.

In 1912, Smith's brother Clarence returned to Chattanooga after years on the minstrel circuit to appear with the Moses Stokes Troupe at the Ninth Street Theater. Bessie auditioned for the troupe and left town with them. Ma Rainey, an established blues singer and member of the troupe, offered Bessie some tips on singing the blues. But Bessie, an eager eighteen-year-old, left the group after a few months to strike out on her own. She went to Atlanta where she performed at the "81" Theater and began her life as a traveling singer, touring with a number of different companies throughout the South and up and down the Atlantic seaboard.

In 1918, she and Hazel Green formed a specialty act that was booked in various theaters through the TOBA. They did one-or two-night stands at many theaters in the South: the Liberty in Chattanooga, the Bijou in Nashville, the Palace in Memphis, the Ella Moore in Dallas, the Lyric in New Orleans, the Douglass in Macon, and the Booker T. Washington in St. Louis. The circuit began its schedule after Labor Day and continued, if they were lucky, throughout the year, seven days a week, two shows a night. This routine went on for five years. In early 1923, a recording producer, Frank Walker of Columbia Records, auditioned her. He later recalled: "she looked about 17, tall and fat and scared to death and just awful!"[11]

Once she began singing, Walker forgot his objections. He signed her to a Columbia contract, and she recorded "Down Hearted Blues" and "Gulf Coast Blues." The record was a smash hit, selling 780 thousand copies in the first six months. Smith earned $125 for her efforts with no royalty arrangement, a practice that was common in those days for both new black and new white singers. During the height of her popularity, when she was a proven winner, Smith still received only two hundred dollars a record. The blues became popular with both black and white audiences and Bessie Smith became a well-known entertainer in both worlds.

In sharp contrast to the pattern of male managers and female singers, Smith took her group to Atlanta in the spring, leased a railroad car, and zigzagged across the South with her tent show until Labor Day, when she resumed her schedule under the auspices of the TOBA circuit, playing one-to two-week dates in cities from New Orleans to Detroit. By 1924, she was receiving more than two thousand dollars a week for her theater appearances and was one of the highest-paid black entertainers in America. As one old-timer recalled, "Bessie traveled with her own group of musicians. That gave her a leg up because all theaters where colored performers played were dumps, and they had what was jokingly referred to as a three-piece orchestra: a piano, stool, and drums. But with her, she had a coronet, trumpets, and a saxophone player, and she had a very popular musician leadin' the organization called Johnny Dunn, which of course helped her popularity."[12]

Bessie Smith's blues contained emotional, bawdy, and humorous lyrics. Her audiences knew that Bessie's words and style reflected her personal experience. When she sang of faithless lovers, fans both nodded in agreement and sympathized with her, knowing that her 1923 marriage to Jack Gee was rocky. In the song, "Dirty No-Gooder's Blues," she asks,"Did you ever fall in love with a man that was no good?... The meanest things he could say would thrill you through and through/And there wasn't nothing too dirty for that man to do." She concludes by singing, "That dirty no-good man treat me just like I am a dog." But Bessie might have sung these sad and victim-like words with a smile on her lips, thereby acknowledging that her love of love kept her coming back for more, despite the poor record of men.

"Poor Man's Blues" asks "Mister rich man" to "open up your heart and mind/Give the poor man a chance, help stop these hard, hard times." Recognizing the hard times experienced by many in her audience, she always connected with them by singing of their troubles. In the bawdy "Copulating Blues," she explicitly reminds her lover what she needs: "I need a little sugar in my bowl/I need a little hot dawg between my roll."[13] Audiences laughed, shouted, and generally identified with the words, the style, and the audacity of this blues singer. One of Smith's trademark songs, "T'aint Nobody's Business if I Do," always reminded audiences that she was her own woman: "If I go to church on Sunday/Then just shimmy down on Monday,/T'aint". Pleasure and respectability coexisted in her soul and behavior. Consistency was not a sought-after principle.

The blues, a very appropriate musical form for Bessie Smith, captured and expressed her sorrows, her joys, and her life experiences. She chronicled various stages of her life in her songs. When she was in a sad mood, "Wasted Life Blues," in which she sang, "No father to guide me, no mother to care,/must bear my troubles all alone," could be followed by "Down Hearted Blues" with the famous words, "Got the world in a jug/the stopper in my hand." Moods alternated and the blues singer knew good and bad days, just like her fans. A Bessie Smith performance, then, contained a wide spectrum of blues singing, from funny to sad, from passive to aggressive. She was a victim of bad circumstances and a determiner of her own fate. Bessie evoked the Eve image as the naughty woman acting as a sexual creature while also displaying Lilith, independent-woman qualities. "T'aint Nobody's Business if I Do" effectively combines both images.

By 1925, Smith had made one hundred recordings for Columbia, but her popularity waned toward the end of the decade. A theatrical appearance in mid-May 1929 in a musical called "Pansy" failed to attract an audience and a talkie movie she made the following month, *St. Louis Blues*, may have displayed her great voice, but her limited acting ability prevented a successful Hollywood career. In recent years, film critic Pauline Kael viewed the movie and proclaimed, "Here she is, the greatest of our jazz singers, all five foot nine inches and two-hundred pounds of her.... and when she lets out her huge, thick voice, full of gin and love and humor, she is one of the most beautiful images that ever filled the screen."[14]

The 1930s offered few opportunities for a revitalized career; in 1933, she made four recordings for the Okeh label, a small recording studio, and she performed for twelve weeks at the popular Connie's Inn in Harlem. There was talk of a Carnegie Hall appearance as well. Fans looked forward to her return to fame, but in the early morning hours of September 26, 1937, the car in which she was riding struck the rear of a National Biscuit Company truck outside of Clarksdale, Mississippi. Bessie suffered fatal injuries and died later that morning at the age of forty-three.

The personalities, the lyrics, and the presentation styles of all three bawdy women entertainers contributed to the public discussion about women's roles in society. Knowingly or unknowingly, they made fans and critics alike wonder about the proper and improper dreams of women. Tanguay flourished, paradoxically, in a family medium— vaudeville—where her eccentric and decidedly unladylike behavior made her a curiosity in a form of entertainment that prided itself on its wholesomeness. She did burlesque in vaudeville and got away with it. Sophie Tucker, in contrast, found vaudeville too inhibiting and flourished in the new medium of the cabaret, where a heavy-set woman as well as an older woman could sing and joke about sexual need. Bessie Smith became the "Empress of the Blues," the undisputed queen of that art form. She was both a unique talent and a worthy representative of many, many blues singers who expressed woman's romantic needs and dilemmas.

Feminists who have written about women's humor, including bawdy material, have suggested theories that can be applied to bawdy women entertainers. Folklorist Rayna Green and literature specialist Nancy Walker, for example, offer contemporary analyses that apply to 1910–19 entertainers.[15] Green argued in her 1977 essay that all women discuss sex but only within women-only settings. It is their way of initiating young women into the mysteries of life; it demystifies sex for girls and creates solidarity among women. Walker has suggested in her writings that women humorists use humor to poke fun at themselves and at their perceived male oppressors; sexual humor, then, becomes a weapon for feminist consciousness. By sharing their own weaknesses as well as male frailties in a humorous way, they gain perspective on themselves and a sense of unity among women.

The bawdy women entertainers I have discussed perform in men-women settings and, in contrast to Green's discussion, have the express purpose of amusing their mixed audiences, for which they are well rewarded financially. Further, the entertainers made gentle fun of both sexes, but especially men. Thus, while some feminist comedians in recent years have performed for women-only audiences and sought to create a common ground with them, the bawdy women entertainers of the vaudeville and nightclub circuits appealed to the humanity in everyone. Many contemporary stand-up comics such as Joan Rivers, Ellen DeGeneres, and Brett Butler directed their humor at anyone who would listen. In recent times, explicitly feminist and lesbian bawdy humor has appeared alongside the more traditional bawdy women entertainers.

Eva Tanguay's career ended when she was in her forties, Sophie Tucker performed until her death, and Bessie Smith's life was cut short by a tragic early death. Tucker insisted that her red-hot-mamma needs only increased with age. Each woman left an indelible mark in her time and place. All of them behaved as atypical women, as public Eves, women willing to be shocking, to receive public attention (to seek attention, in fact, a very unladylike action) in a most disreputable way. They revealed America's inhibited attitude toward natural human functions. They made fun of the prevailing views of feminine beauty. None were conventionally attractive, but all acted aggressively self-confident about their interest in the opposite sex and their ability to attract more than their share of partners.

They were not afraid to talk dirty and to use explicit body language to convey their meanings. Tanguay became very popular, achieving a following beyond the limited confines of the vaudeville theater, and in so doing, moved from the periphery to the center. Bawdy women entertainers have existed at least for the past one hundred years in this culture; the subject matter rarely changed, though the sexually liberated present generation combines its tolerance of bawdiness with a heightened feminist consciousness. Today, lesbian, feminist, and show business bawdiness coexist, though only the show biz type reaches a large, mixed audience. As long as polite and rude remain as social categories, however, and as long as forbidden and permitted topics of conversation exist, bawdy women entertainers will amuse us, shock us, and delight us. They will always have an audience.

Although conservative critics, then and now, argued that bawdy women entertainers were akin to prostitutes, examples of the moral decay of our culture, their argument lacked (lacks) conviction and raised more questions than it answered. After all, many entertainers were married women from respectable, working-class families; some came from middle-class families. How could these women demonstrate sexual interest and knowledge without raising the pertinent (and impertinent) question, "Do my daughters, sisters, and wives think such bold thoughts?" Though "respectable" women did not display their bodies and their rude tongues in public, did they harbor secret thoughts along the same lines as the bawds?

It would take many years, two generations, but women's sexuality did become a public subject. The bawdy women entertainers of bygone years anticipated this discussion and did it with humor, directed at themselves and against social prudery. The women entertainers enjoyed making fun of the moralists who called them threats to civilization while attending their performances; they found the audience in agreement every time they demystified sex and joked about natural urges. They shocked and amused their audiences simultaneously by their audacious dances, scanty costumes, and suggestive gestures. Twice a day, six days a week (in Eva Tanguay's case, from 1905 to 1915, and in Sophie Tucker's, for more than fifty years), they attracted enormous audiences, concrete testimony to their success. They met a perceived, though possibly unspoken, need.

Their professional success as humorists set them apart from mainstream women. Surely most women joked and laughed among themselves and within the confines of their families, but bawdy women stretched and sometimes broke the boundaries between acceptable and unacceptable humor for women's ears. By performing in public places, they displayed characteristics not taught to most women: self-confidence, an enormous ego, and personal ambition. Never mind the open discussion of sex. Imagine the shock and secret pleasure experienced by a 1910–19 woman in seeing the aggressive, in-your-face Eva Tanguay on stage. Laughing at serious and private subject matter was truly an audacious and mind-expanding experience.

Before social change occurs, imaginative change happens. Bawdy women entertainers gave large numbers of women in multiple generations in this century the opportunity to envision other traits, other pathways, and other thoughts. They viewed women as whole human beings with the full range of characteristics. Men and women may be different in central and essential ways, but they are the same in possessing sexual desires, needs, hopes, and dreams. Bawds broke down the barriers between the sacred and the profane. They blurred the lines between acceptable and unacceptable and by so doing allowed other forbidden subjects to be broached, such as: Why should women stay at home? Why can't women train for a career in engineering? and where is it written that motherhood is woman's primary adult role? Because bawdy women entertainers did all of this with a laugh, and often unselfconsciously, they were all the more successful.

Bawdy women entertainers were double texts—their personae and their material enforced and reinforced each other. They superseded the cultural context within which they lived. The traditional culture enabled them to be the stark contrast, the dashing alternative to all others. An audacious culture with a history of respecting outrageous women would have doomed their careers. All of the bawds had powerful personalities that exclaimed their message. While race helped to shape black, bawdy women and ethnicity played a role in the development of Sophie Tucker, it was the anarchic personalities of all bawdy entertainers that gave them their identity and their mission.

The text that was the bawdy woman entertainer flourished in a context of repression. Every time Eva Tanguay shocked a society woman, and every time Sophie Tucker went to jail, their celebrity increased and their next show sold out. Bessie Smith, by contrast, found a congenial and supportive culture within the confines of black America. By the 1970s, however, when Bette Midler came on the scene (she will be discussed in the chapter called "Women Comics"), the vibrant culture of women's liberation and rock 'n' roll concerts gave her and other bawdy women entertainers a venue. The large youth culture, which had the financial resources to attend concerts and buy records, identified itself as rebellious while creating a new mainstream.

So while the more staid years 1910–19 helped an Eva Tanguay and a Sophie Tucker present themselves as audacious rebels against the status quo, the 1970s allowed Bette Midler's career to feed on the new air of nonconformity. In both cases, however, the times acted as a backdrop to these irrepressible women, who preserved the long tradition of Eves as the most popular image for women entertainers. The audience for bawdiness might be small and confined to a nightclub, or it might be large and fill an auditorium to see Eva Tanguay and Bette Midler, but it has existed in every decade of this century. The odds are it will continue to attract performers and audiences.

3

Entertainer as Reformer

So far we have looked at the lives and careers of women performers in the first third of this century whose material and style challenged dominant cultural values in either of two ways: As black or white Eves, they were sexual women who were bold enough to discuss the forbidden subject in public, and as black women vaudevillians, they were outside the mainstream. Mae West epitomized the outrageous Eve, and she did it in vaudeville, on Broadway, and in the movies. Her fame has endured throughout the century and therefore kept the converstion on the subject of sex alive longer than her predecessors. Her name became a shorthand reference to the forbidden subject. In that sense, she had a transforming effect on her audiences.

Neither upholders of cultural values nor audience members anticipated, expected, or wished for the entertainer to advocate, however subtly or indirectly, changes in cultural behavior. The words entertainer and reformer rarely appear beside each other; they seem incongruous, unlikely, and unsuitable. The worlds of popular and elite culture seem miles away from the world of reform. Temperance advocate Carrie Nation and Sophie Tucker had nothing in common. Cultural historians rarely place the world of show business with the world of social causes. Yet, upon reflection, a case can be made for the compatibility of these realms. Performers in both groups wish to inform, enlighten, and influence their listeners; both aspire to change their audiences' behavior and possibly their minds and values.

Even when entertainers are not trying, they influence their viewers. They may unconsciously be change agents, though not always for the "good." But their styles, their words, and their actions affect their audiences in obvious and not so obvious ways: People talk about the performers in casual conversations, they buy fan magazines, they dream about them, and, in this sense, the stars become an essential part of their lives. Entertainers are pragmatists; they wish to convince their listeners that they are worthy of attention, that their product is worthy of repeated purchase (whether it be records, books, or the next performance), and that their persona is one to be endlessly admired and patronized. No one appreciated this perspective more than did Mae West. After all, her career depended upon her popularity and success.

Therefore, West and her cohorts' wish to engage their audience, and to convince them of their worthiness is essential to their financial well-being. Because entertainers often represent avant-garde ideas, values, and styles, their very being influences their fans. Jean Harlow's peroxided hair and Joan Crawford's arched eyebrows are only the most superficial examples of entertainers influencing audience members. Manufacturers of myriad varieties of goods have always appreciated the connections between stars and fans and have exploited the stars' personae to sell products and services. This close relationship, born early in the century, has grown continually.

Reformers also seek to educate people to a new point of view, a new idea, a new value, and a new behavior. They too wish to effect change, whether it be in politics, economics, morality, or culture. They yearn for approval and hope that their message will win them votes, the desired legislation, and elections. The entertainer has a distinct advantage over reformers; she presents her message in an engaging, sometimes amusing style. Presumably, she has the talent to enchant and engross her audience in a way that only the most charismatic reformers can match. Most reformers have sincerity, intensity, and commitment to their respective causes, but not necessarily the talent to convince all listeners of the worthiness of the issue presented.

An entertainer with a sense of humor has a further advantage: she creates laughter, relief from dreariness, and a refreshingly new perspective on the world. A comic performer like Mae West, who challenged social norms, enthralled audiences in an inimitable manner. As a funny commentator on society's values and its innumerable absurdities, she was in the rare position to make Americans think about their long-held values and beliefs in the midst of a laugh. The entertainer has another powerful tool in her repertory: she doesn't have a social agenda to advocate. Rather, she is selling herself and her iconoclastic view of the world. Inadvertently, however, she may change more minds than a self-conscious reformer. Social critic Susan Sontag wrote in a recent essay that cinema's power to draw the audience into its world and to teach many, many things is only half its power. The greater power was "to lose yourself in other people's lives"[1]

The successful movie star, alongside the effective comic performer, achieves this awesome goal and, in so doing, places herself above the reformer in effectively changing lives. Mae West, a unique entertainer whose career spanned fifty years of this century, qualifies as a candidate for entertainer-reformer status. During her long career, West represented herself as a bold proclaimer of women's sexual rights. She used humor as her valuable weapon in the battle between the sexes and in the struggle to gain a large following. In a period when women's roles on the theatrical stage were clearly defined (with comic not being one of them), Mae West winked, smirked, wiggled, and joked about sex, the forbidden subject. By the end of the 1920s, she had surpassed her many rivals for title of supreme bawdy humorist on the stage. West learned from Eva Tanguay and then surpassed her. She became the symbol of the daring, sexy woman who made fun of sex. As a woman and a comic talking about the forbidden subject, she broke three sacred conventions at once.

In prudish America, Mae West kidded with her audience, the censors, and all others who believed in the double sexual standard, in woman's passivity, and in moral seriousness as an absolute value. West exposed hypocrisy and male arrogance, all with a smile. She never alienated her core audience—men of all ages. She got men to laugh at their own foibles, not an insignificant accomplishment. By doing the audacious in public view, and particularly in the movies where she reached a national audience, West brought to everyone's attention the forbidden subject of sex. First in vaudeville, then on Broadway, and finally in the movies, she crossed the boundary from polite to rude and got applause and large salaries for doing so. Women may not have attended her vaudeville show, but they did go to see her Broad-

Striking a characteristic pose in her 1933 movie, *I'm No Angel,* Mae West epitomized the bawdy woman entertainer.

way plays and later, her movies, nightclub act, and Las Vegas shows. To many people's amusement, her appeal grew over time, and more women became fans.

The reasons that she endured so long and that women came to admire her presentation were debated by writers and critics. Each generation of commentators noted her enduring image as Diamond Lil, the 1890s good-time gal. Whether she appeared on the stage or in the movies, the persona remained the same. Perhaps, one critic argued, the sameness of her presentation was her strength. Another writer pointed to that very feature as his reason for finding her unworthy: too predictable. Mae West provided her own analysis. She argued that her gentle mocking of male egos appealed to women, and she had the fan letters to prove it. Further, each generation of viewers in this century has found West's performances fertile ground in which to explore the battle of the sexes. The war has not yet ended, nor has it been resolved to both genders' satisfaction.

Though most women did not consciously imitate Mae West's style, nor did most men change their domineering ways, everyone's "consciousness" had to have been raised. The Diamond Lil personality, dressed in 1890s gowns with a bustle in back and a corset that pushed up her ample bosom for display, amused 1920s women who wore loose-fitting chemises. The women did not imitate her fashion, but they, along with the men in the audience, enjoyed watching a Mae West performance in which a bold woman initiated sexual encounters, called men "suckers," and always left them laughing. Audiences compared her audacious remarks and actions with the respectable ones advocated by the majority. They may not have changed their behavior, but they must have had new and novel thoughts, thanks to Mae West.

It is, of course, difficult to measure the effectiveness of a performer-reformer. Popularity is one indication, and Mae West was very popular. While the passage of a reform bill ended the activists' work, Mae West's work never ended and her message was told, enforced, and reinforced with every performance and to multiple generations of fans. In the democratic environment of entertainment, audiences were the measuring stick of success: if they came, an entertainer and her message remained fresh and desirable; if they didn't, she changed her act or sunk into oblivion.

During the course of her long life and career (1893–1980), Mae

West's preoccupation with sex, a woman's right to it, the double standard, and the silly rules governing sexual behavior became her abiding concern, a concern she discussed in public venues from the latter part of the second decade of the twentieth century to the late 1950s. She began exploring the topic in vaudeville. A *Variety* review in 1916 noted, "She'll have to clean up her style—she has a way of putting dirty meanings in innocent lyrics."[2] But it was on the Broadway stage beginning in 1925 that she gained a lot of publicity for her singular focus. Under the pen name Jane Mast, she wrote a play called *Sex*, a title that ensured notoriety. No New York newspaper would advertise a play with such a bold title, yet word of mouth assured good attendance, particularly among her loyal constituency—working-class New Yorkers and college boys from the city and surrounding communities. (Yale University was one of her most popular venues when she toured in vaudeville.)

The story line of *Sex* effectively illustrates the Westian perspective. Though it sounds like the plot for a B or C movie, it stayed on Broadway for eleven months. West starred as Margie LaMont, a Montreal prostitute who followed the British fleet from port to port. The story involved blackmail, the kidnapping of an innocent society woman (not world-weary Margie), Margie's seduction of a society youth, and finally, Margie's departure to follow the fleet again. The story took more turns than a roller coaster. But Margie always remained good-natured, cynical but not sour, and a good sport who understood human nature better than most. When she helped the society woman escape from the evil clutches of a blackmailer, she was accused by the woman of being part of the plot. In revenge, Margie seduced the rich woman's son. She lured him to the altar but she did not go through with the marriage ceremony. She was, after all, a "bad" girl with a heart of gold.

Further, because she was a shady lady by profession, she could not win the rich guy; but being philosophical, another characteristic of a good-hearted whore, she accepted her fate and returns to her occupation. West's frequent portrayal of a prostitute underlined her interest in sex and her view that a woman's sexuality was her chief asset. If sex was also a commodity of exchange, the woman should be in charge of it. Though West never suggested that sex was a woman's only asset in the struggle for existence, she did believe that a woman should throw away her naïveté and capitalize on all of her strengths.

West's prostitutes became self-conscious feminists in the sense that they controlled their bodies, their business, and their futures.

Sex, like West's subsequent plays, defied the convention, in terms of both subject matter and form. While a melodrama about the seedy underworld was hardly a new subject, rarely did the prostitute emerge whole at the end of the story. In the biblical story of Adam and Eve, Eve is blamed for the loss of innocence and the exile from Eden. West challenged religious morality. Margie's misdeeds went unpunished, a wholly unusual phenomenon in traditional melodrama of the period, because religious conventions carried over to popular theater. West as Margie was always in charge; she was never a victim and never victimized. West took credit for the writing and producing of *Sex,* as she did for all subsequent creations. Mae West's total control of the theatrical production, a fact not lost on New Yorkers, offers additional evidence of her autonomy, her power, and her forthrightness.

West's melodrama had music, an unexpected and unlikely addition to the genre. But Mae West liked to sing, albeit in a low growl. She delivered songs whose lyrics were unrelated to the plot. This mixing of genres became a regular feature of her plays and movies. One of the many reasons why some critics did not respond positively to her plays, perhaps, is that they were not sure whether the play was fish or fowl; melodrama, comedy, or musical. If asked, West might have replied that it was a little bit of all three. Where was it written that a playwright had to stay within one dramatic form all of the time? West did not believe in discarding assets. Her singing and her sashaying were just that, and they had to be incorporated into all of her work.

The fact that West did not have a conventionally pleasing voice, with her Brooklyn accent ever present, did not deter her. As she aged, she "talked" a song more than sang it (as did Sophie Tucker). But her supreme self-confidence assured her that audiences loved to hear her sing, walk, talk, whatever. In an age when respectable women were to be seen, not heard, much like children, Mae West's front and center personality broke the mold. Self-confidence, an essential quality for male entrepreneurs and all energetic men, was never taught to mainstream girls. No etiquette book told women to state their opinions loud and clear. But Mae West did.

The stereotype of the Eve, the seductress, outnumbered all other images of women in popular culture. It was common in Broadway plays, novels, and silent film. The contrast was amazing: writers, alongside preachers, teachers, and mothers warned American girls to beware of sexually aggressive men, to be good girls until they married, and never, never to be like the town prostitute. Yet, these words of caution were replaced by portraits of sexually active and exciting women in literary and theatrical productions. Mae West's major contribution to the image was in making her Eve an initiator of actions, not a victim of circumstances. In contrast to novelist Theodore Dreiser's portrayal of Sister Carrie, a woman doomed by sexual missteps, Mae West's Margie LaMont, and later Diamond Lil, were take-charge women.

Lil was not a vulnerable weakling; she was not dominated by men. Nor was she seduced and abandoned, a fate commonly experienced by innocent girls; rather Lil did the seducing and abandoning, a neat example of sex role reversal. Audiences watching *Sex* saw unexpected views about women displayed and in this sense, their conventional attitudes were challenged if not changed—surely the goal of a reformer. Because West's plays were set in the past, they offered a space between contemporary values and fantasy times. Thus, audiences could admire the audacity of Margie and Lil, 1890s women, while being removed from them. They could be titillated, even required to consider the relevance of these attitudes and behaviors for their lives, while reminding themselves that, after all, this play was set in the bad old days.

Both men and women in the audience laughed at West's wisecracks, watched her uncomplaining behavior, and applauded her at the end. While most prostitutes died at the end of melodramas, West's women always remained very much alive. They may not have won the rich guy—rather, they often explicitly claimed they had no desire to settle down—but they always won their independence. Being on the go, being women who moved around a lot, and liking it also put them in a unique position. In her 1933 movie, *I'm No Angel,* West as Tira, a circus performer (barely a step above whore) told all who would listen that she considered marriage a last resort. She threw out lines such as "Take all you can get and give as little as you can," and when a fortune teller said that he saw a man in her life, she responded, "Only one?"

Mae West went on to write *The Drag,* a play about homosexuality; this play was considered even more over the edge than *Sex.* In fact, the police closed down *Sex* and prevented *The Drag* from opening in

New York. In April 1927, she and her lawyer were arrested and charged with corrupting the morals of youth. The trial became a publicity opportunity for Mae West, one of many in which she could communicate to her growing public about her belief in free expression and the naturalness of sex. She insisted that the play was not offensive, and that people, not the law, should judge. The newspapers reported her every word and willingly framed the subject according to her point of view: free expression versus censorship, a worthy reform cause.

By always insisting that she was the most glamorous woman alive and that she shared with all women and men an interest in sex, she found a hoard of reporters clamoring for her every word. Mae West never missed an opportunity to speak to the press. As she later said, the arrest, trial, and eight-day jail term were worth a million dollars in publicity. If one of the goals of a cultural reformer was to communicate her message to a large audience, Mae West succeeded. The humorous way in which she presented her ideas muted the shock some people experienced. Was she serious? Did she take herself seriously? No one ever knew.

By the end of the 1920s, she had written four plays, the fourth being *Diamond Lil*, set in the 1890s, and first performed in April 1928. Lil embraced all of the characteristics West had been cultivating since her early days in vaudeville. Wearing the elaborate costumes she so loved, Lil, the whore with a heart of gold, with a string of one-liners and a leering smile to match any Lothario's, became the public personality that merged with the private West. After Broadway, she went to Hollywood where every character she played was Lil. Between 1932 and 1943, her moviemaking years, the names and locales were different in each of her movies, but the essential personality stayed the same.

Diamond Lil was set in a dance hall saloon in the bowery. It was a hangout for the underworld with gangsters mixing with the regular drinking crowd. Dance hall girls sold their services, both on the dance floor and in the rooms above. The first and third acts took place in the back room of this establishment. Diamond Lil earned her way to the top of this shady world by being the best saleswoman around. She now sported diamonds up and down both arms and she slept in a huge wooden bed, shaped like a swan. At the opening of the second act, she lounged in the swan bed reading a copy of the *Police Gazette*, the 1890s version of a tabloid. She later sang the highly suggestive ballad "Frankie and Johnny," drawing out its sexy meanings for all to hear.

West had perfected her presentation of this song while still performing on the vaudeville circuit. Harry Richman, who had been her piano player, recalled how Mae was called upon to sing the song for E.F. Albee, the boss of the Keith-Albee circuit and a stickler for propriety. Albee had heard that West sang "Frankie and Johnny" in a naughty manner. Richman remembered that "She had a line in her "Frankie and Johnny" number that went, 'If you don't like my peaches, don't you shake my tree.' She did this line as only Mae West could do it, and the men in the audience would scream and yell and go half-crazy. . . . When she did it for Albee, she clasped her hands close to one cheek and said it very clearly, almost childishly, and at the same time cast her eyes upward, the most mournful creature in the entire world. I nearly fell off my piano stool."[3] Needless to say, Albee resumed her booking and wondered what all of the commotion was about.

In *Diamond Lil* and in all of her Hollywood movies and stage shows, Mae West was surrounded by admiring men. They all oohed and aahed over her looks, her clothes, and her style. They all sought her attention, whether they were would-be lovers or fans surrounding her after a circus performance. In one scene, when an admirer said, "your hands, your lips, your hair, your magnificent shoulder," Lil interrupted him and asked, "What're you doin' honey? Making love or takin' inventory?" The one man in the play whom Lil is interested in was not interested in her—he was a Salvation Army officer (a very young Cary Grant in the movie version). His only interest was in converting her to the righteous path. It was in an early scene with him that Lil uttered what became one of her most famous lines: "Why don't you come up sometime and see me?"

She followed up this remark with a less well known one: "You can be had." Lil believed that all men were suckers and that she had the ability to lure any and all of them down her path. This line was viewed unfavorably by the censors. The play, however, became a hit, established Mae West as a star and became one of her most popular movies, renamed *She Done Him Wrong*. The *New York Times* critic loved the movie. For the first time, that august newspaper's writer found West's acting to be superb, though the writing of the play was considered "to be a bit thick." Her overall performance, particularly her attitude toward sex, was described as "almost Elizabethan."[4] West's supporting cast helped her deliver an amusing movie, and West's singing was also positively reviewed.

Mae West had learned a lot about singing suggestive lyrics from black blues singers she had observed during her vaudeville days. She knew how to "shimmy shwabble" from watching black women dancers in Chicago's South Side clubs, and she delivered double entendre lines with the proper emphasis, pause, and smirk, combining black blues style with her own unique personality. West sang "Frankie and Johnny" mockingly; she satirized women's reliance on romance and always assured her listeners that she, not the man in her life, was in charge. Whether she sang the song onstage or in the movie, she brought her humorous and assertive style to bear on her rendition. The more she sang the song, the more her fans became assured that Mae/Lil was an autonomous woman. Years later, West said of her character, Diamond Lil, "I'm her and she's me and we're each other."

The tightly corseted, floor-length dresses of the 1890s lent humor to West's Diamond Lil personality. She was the sexiest woman around, she asserted, as she slowly sashayed around the stage in a dress that revealed nothing more than a generous bosom. Because she was tightly corseted and in three yards of undergarments that touched the floor, walking slowly was probably a necessity. To the 1920s and 1930s women in their short flapper dresses that emphasized their slimness, the thought that 1890s dresses were sexy was laughable. Further, West, not a conventional beauty (she had a wide nose, her eyes were smallish, and she only achieved some height by wearing six inch-heels), reminded everyone that she was the most desirable, attractive woman in and of the world. She was a campy, exaggerated personality, a self-parodist, who made fun of herself alongside mocking others.

In a souvenir program available to theatergoers who saw *Diamond Lil*, Mae West described the character of Lil and the general plotline of the play. She asked rhetorically: "Could Diamond Lil love anyone more than herself . . . Love anything better than the white flame of her diamonds or the red flame of men's passions?" The answer was clear to all who knew the Lil/Mae character. And the answer demonstrated her audacity, her willingness to challenge the image of women as demure, passive, and obedient. Her audacity and self-centeredness

Showing off her svelte figure, Mae West displayed her appreciation of her own assets.

also flew in the face of female modesty. Granted, Lil was not a respectable woman, thereby giving her license to behave outrageously. But might not audience members, particularly the women, begin to wonder whether loving oneself more than others might not be a bad philosophy?

In West's interpretation of Diamond Lil, she acknowledged that she was a harlot but added, "Men had to pay heavy, if they wanted her—and it is true that she did want to be paid. Still, she was not an ordinary trollop. She had brains where they belong . . . ordinary bawds had their brains where" She did not have to finish the sentence. In 1928 and in 1933 (when the movie came out) these were shocking words. The twenties may have been roaring and bootleggers may have enjoyed their profits, but rarely did the underworld appear on Broadway having so much fun. Further, defending prostitutes represented controversial behavior. The governing moral principle remained: the good succeed and the bad are punished. Mainstream entertainment did not question this viewpoint. But Mae West did, and her sold-out audiences every night shared in her conspiratorial joke.

Mae West's message in *Diamond Lil* was subversive. She departed from the usual stereotypical treatment of prostitutes by making Lil independent, successful, and dominant; she was not a victim, used and misused by men, determined by circumstances beyond her control. West's Lil used men and was always in control. Both men and women could view Lil as an atypical, humorous rendition of an old stereotype. And because Mae West did consider herself an original, everyone was happy. Women may not have literally imitated Mae West, but their inner lives were enriched by her movie and real behavior. Moreover, the inner conversations each moviegoer might have had about sex, women's needs, and men's will to control after seeing a Mae West movie must have enlarged their personal vision and sense of self.

Though audiences laughed at Diamond Lil, and all later-day renditions of the persona, Mae West had made and remade her point. Women were sexual creatures who had brains, willpower, and energy to shape their destinies. Women need not be self-effacing, self-sacrificing, tearful, or pathetic. They did not have to rely on a man for their identity, their income, or their reason for being. Mae West was not recommending prostitution to all women, but she did admire entrepreneurship. She was living proof of that view. Of course, West would have been the first to tell you that she was an exceptional person, not a representative of the masses. As an entertainer, she had great visibility and earned unheard of sums of money, and her astute real estate investments in 1930s Los Angeles made her a rich woman. But her attitude was inimitable.

Most women and men did not attend a Mae West performance to reform themselves, to change their lives, or to change their behavior in significant ways. But they exposed their minds to ideas, attitudes, and styles of living that offered interesting contrasts to their lives. Further, even in the more open era of the twenties, Mae West appeared as sui generis. As she repeatedly told reporters, she did not believe in modesty (a traditional female trait), and she was the first to proclaim her greatness. Mae West reversed sex roles or perhaps expanded the female sex role in such a way as to blur the lines between the sexes. That is, she assumed characteristics normally labeled male and acted as if it was the normal means of behaving. In this sense, her very being and her public and aggressive insistence upon her right to be bold, assertive, and sexual became a reform symbol to all of her fans and critics.

Commentators, even in intellectual magazines such as the *Nation* and the *New Republic,* tried to analyze the basis for her power and popularity but were unsuccessful. Every time she fought the censors, and she did it both on Broadway and in Hollywood, she gained headlines and broadened her audience. She kept the public conversation focused on her and on woman's sexuality for decades. True, she became other things to subsequent generations of audiences, sometimes a caricature of herself, a campy parody for the youth of the 1960s, for example, but for the generation or two that saw her in the 1920s and 1930s, she represented a challenge to the social status quo. In so doing, she qualifies as an American reformer, someone who questioned dominant values in sex relations and became a one-woman campaign for free expression and an uninhibited view of woman's nature.

Expanding the definition of reformer to include entertainers involves audacity and risk. It recognizes that the primary aim of an entertainer is not to educate but to amuse; it acknowledges that the entertainer is the quintessential individualist, while the reformer is most often a member of a group. Though the entertainer appeals to each individual in the audience, one person at a time, the ultimate effect is collective. Fans join together to form a large and impressive following. A more expansive view of culture and of how it changes requires including entertainers in the category of reformers, thereby acknowledging the significant role that entertainment plays in American culture. More people watched and listened to Mae West in this century than they did to most reformers, and her witty take on life's most important topics brought smiles and nods to her numerous fans.

4

Women Movie Stars
as Role Models

By the 1930s, the dominant medium of popular entertainment was sound movies. No one anticipated the spectacular success of moving pictures. During the depression years, fully half the
population went to the movies every week; sixty million people found
escape, relief, pleasure, and interest in the darkened theater of their
neighborhood or in the more ornate theater in the downtown district
of their city. Audiences gathered to watch their favorite star perform,
and in the 1930s, there were as many women stars as men stars. In
sharp contrast to the movies since the 1960s, when action adventures
have dominated and few movies have featured women, the 1930s and
1940s were the golden years for women movie stars.

The many women stars of the period built a major body of work
as they worked continuously. Bette Davis, for example, often made
two movies simultaneously, putting in sixteen-hour workdays. The
most popular stars such as Davis and Joan Crawford made more than
a dozen movies during the decade, a feat never duplicated. The plots
of many of the movies, of course, were predictable and the images
repeated again and again. But two important images of women appeared regularly on the screen: Eves and Liliths. The independent
woman, in fact, became a major genre for women's films during the
depression. Workingclass and professional women could be seen sur-

viving under difficult personal and professional circumstances. Katharine Hepburn, Bette Davis, Rosalind Russell and many others made careers out of Lilith roles (see table 1).

During the heyday of women movie stars, fans wanted to know everything about their favorites, so the performers' personal and professional lives blurred. The messages gleaned from both worlds came together and often revealed unexpected thoughts. The receivers of these new messages, fans (a new category of being), followed the personal and professional lives of their favorite stars in magazines designed to not only satisfy but also preserve interest in movies and movie stars. *Photoplay* and its innumerable imitators since the early 1920s regaled their readers with tantalizing details about the lives of Mary Pickford, Greta Garbo, the Gish sisters, Katharine Hepburn, Joan Crawford, and countless others.

Neither the writers nor the readers, however, ever evaluated the lifestyles of their favorite movie stars as object lessons in how to be or how not to be successful women, careerists, wives, amd/or mothers. Fans were eager to learn of Carole Lombard's romance with Clark Gable and to discover the color of Joan Crawford's bedroom, but they hardly considered the important question of how a talented woman could be a traditional wife-mother and a fourteen-hour-a-day professional simultaneously. Further, the movie magazines' depictions of each star's rise to fame and fortune after suffering became so formulized and predictable as to lose whatever authenticity or uniqueness each star possessed. The star's mother was always helpful and encouraging, each studio chief cooperative, and each opportunity recognized for the break it was.

In almost every case, these claims were false. Yet, many women movie stars believed their own press releases. In the 1930s, particularly, many actresses wanted to believe that they had inimitable talent, unusual looks, and the dynamic personality necessary to achieve the heights of the movie world, if only to contradict the naysayers who believed that only whores succeeded in Hollywood and that all nice girls stayed home and married their high school sweethearts. Further, these women accepted the mainstream cultural view that women should be wives and mothers first and last. Many tried to achieve these personal goals while ambitiously pursuing professional success.

Ever since the Zukors, Warners, and Mayers began film production in the wilds of New York and then in the tropical setting of Hol-

Table 1. A Sample of Lilith and Eve Images of Women in Films, 1930-1950

KATHARINE HEPBURN (always Lilith)
as careerist	1932	*A Bill of Divorcement*
	1933	*Christopher Strong*
	1936	*A Woman Rebels*
	1942	*Woman of the Year*
	1949	*Adam?s Rib*
as aristocrat	1938	*Holiday*
	1938	*Bringing Up Baby*
	1940	*The Philadelphia Story*
	1942	*Keeper of the Flame*

BARBARA STANWYCK
as independent Eve	1939	*Golden Boy*
	1940	*Remember the Night*
	1941	*The Lady Eve*
	1946	*California*
	1949	*No Man of Her Own*

JOAN CRAWFORD
as careerist	1933	*Dancing Lady*
	1945	*Mildred Pierce*
	1947	*Daisy Kenyon*
as independent Eve	1932	*Rain*
	1934	*Sadie McKee*
	1937	*Mannequin*
	1938	*The Shining Hour*

ROSALIND RUSSELL
as careerist	1938	*The Citadel*
	1940	*His Girl Friday*
	1940	*Hired Wife*
	1942	*Take a Letter, Darling*
	1943	*Flight for Freedom*
	1943	*What a Woman*
	1945	*She Wouldn?t Say Yes*

BETTE DAVIS
as careerist	1933	*Ex-Lady*
	1935	*Front Page Woman*
	1935	*Dangerous*
	1945	*The Corn Is Green*
	1950	*All about Eve*
as independent Eve	1934	*Of Human Bondage*
	1934	*Bordertown*
	1937	*Marked Woman*
	1938	*Jezebel*

lywood, many young women have defied cultural expectations and tried to become movie stars. Few made it; most did not. The few who did, however, were regularly featured in the movie magazines and thereby became inspirations to countless readers who had the same ambitions, albeit not always the same talent and opportunity. The spunk, perseverance, and courage described in the fan magazines convinced attractive young women that they too could become female Horatio Algers, a variation of the Lilith image. Frequently featured stars such as Joan Crawford, Katharine Hepburn, and Greta Garbo became familiar figures to their readers. Each fan could recite the personal biography of her favorite star. The vicarious pleasure garnered from reading the rags-to-riches story that was Joan Crawford's life endeared her to her large audience of admirers.

While popular culture promoters often highlight the victims of Hollywood's highly competitive system, the women stars I will discuss in these pages were not only survivors, but often triumphant winners in the Hollywood wars. Judy Garland and Marilyn Monroe are frequently cited examples of the movie industry's exploitation of women, but there were numerous stars who adapted quite successfully to their environments. Stars such as Katharine Hepburn, Joan Crawford, Bette Davis, and Barbara Stanwyck not only survived moviemaking, they endured and prevailed to have long and substantial careers.

The survivors and succeeders existed in impressive numbers particularly in the 1930s and 1940s. For every Monroe and Garland, innumerable actresses survived; in the 1930s, when women's movies were a well-developed genre, women stars flourished. Myrna Loy, Claudette Colbert, Joan and Constance Bennett, Carole Lombard, and many others, including those already mentioned, enjoyed lucrative careers. Many stars such as Barbara Stanwyck and Jean Arthur appreciated the ephemeral quality of glitter and carved out lives for themselves after the flash dimmed. The women stars offer all women useful insights into developing survival skills; they also, by example, offer instruction in developing independence. On the screen and in their personal lives, these women embodied the Lilith image. The subtext discernible in the numerous fan magazine articles is that these women, though atypical, provide some lessons for all American women. Their uniqueness could help representative or mainstream women survive as well.

Women movie stars were the first visible group of professional women in this country and the first conspicuously successful group of women in the public sphere. After all, most American women who have been written about in the history books until well into the twentieth century received notice because they were either some great man's wife, a witch, or a gun moll. Women's sphere, as clearly discussed by women historians in the last thirty years, had been the private, domestic sphere, and though many women accomplished their wifely and motherly roles superbly, such accomplishments were not deemed worthy to be recorded in the usually male-dominated record books.[1] Thus, women movie stars emerged as a new phenomenon: a well-known group of women whose screen performances gave them astronomical incomes and lifestyles unlike their sisters and brothers.

Women movie stars lived like public men. They appeared and spoke before large, mixed audiences. They dedicated buildings, invested in businesses, sometimes managed their own careers, and became public personalities. They had a distinct identity separate from their lover/husband. They existed separate from their children and from their parents. In short, they became a pioneering new social type: a successful career woman. Few understood the meaning and the implications of this new type, including the movie stars themselves. They often lived in two worlds simultaneously: the new uncharted one of careerdom, and the old, traditional one of private wife and mother. That the latter rarely succeeded dismayed many of the stars; few understood the reasons for their often multiple domestic failures.

Becoming a movie star, entering this magical and difficult world, required a strong personality, and most women stars had it before disembarking at the Los Angeles train station. The women who made it in Hollywood, with few exceptions, were self-confident, decisive women who were not afraid of hard work or temporary frustration. Contrary to popular myth, most women stars understood the difficulties of being a beautiful woman in a setting where physical beauty was a marketable commodity. They knew that they were their own best friend and that they should read their contracts carefully. These strong women displayed their strength and knowledge both on and off the screen. They showed themselves to be unusual women whose identity and worth were either self-or studio-determined, but never dependent on their husband's fortune or social position. Even when their studio shaped their career image, they imposed their own imprint upon it. Bette Davis is the best example of this.

Hollywood press releases, of course, did not explore or focus upon the star's strength; neither did they encourage the development of women's psychic and economic independence. Rather, when Bette Davis rebelled against Warner Brothers' inflexible and slavish contract, she was portrayed as temperamental and difficult. But she insisted upon her right to decide whether a role was good or bad for her. When Warner Brothers sued her in the English courts for breaking a contract, she lost the battle but won the war. From then on, the studio gave her the right of script approval, a fact that was well publicized. Obedience, passivity, and towing the line were female virtues in Hollywood as well in greater America, but both male and female actors often broke that stricture. While cowboy stars and male stars in general might be allowed some leeway, women stars were expected to be good and agreeable. Bette Davis's suspension in 1936 was seen as an object lesson, but the outcome produced the opposite result. Warner Brothers began paying her more attention and, as a peace offering, gave her a very juicy part in *Marked Woman*, a role that richly depicted an independent woman.

Hollywood's goal, then, was not to recruit strong-minded women. On the contrary. But they discovered, much to their disgust and anger, that many of their most attractive screen personalities were individualistic women. Rosalind Russell greased her hair with vaseline, dressed poorly, and grimaced through her interview with Carl Laemmele in the early thirties in order to get out of a contract she hated. He had been told that she was the next glamour girl. Laemmele quickly acceded to her wishes. Russell's reputation as a shrewd businesswoman, on and off the screen, became well known and prompted one Hollywood reporter to write, "In Hollywood, Rosalind Russell is regarded as the one star who has done more to make women with brains popular."[2] Carole Lombard staged innumerable comic antics, swore like a sailor (which even surprised some veteran Hollywood types), and lived her own iconoclastic life. Katharine Hepburn told reporters whatever outrageous story entered her head and shut up one particularly nosy reporter in 1934 by telling him that yes, she had two children, and they were both black.

Of course, we know more about the successful women stars than about the many who had bit parts or no parts at all. One of the striking features of the stars' backgrounds is the makeup of their families. Many stars came from middle-or working-class families, and an as-

A 1944 picture shows movie star Bette Davis, one of the great actresses during Hollywood's Golden Years.

tonishing number for the period came from single-parent homes. The few outstanding examples of upper-class women who became stars, Katharine Hepburn and Rosalind Russell most notably, came from two-parent families with strong models for self-development. The various family types may produce average people or desperately unhealthy people as well. They may develop independent doctors, independent wives, and independent women secretaries. But the most conspicuous group of publicly successful women are the movie stars, and many stars emerge from one of these family types. Unique personality, of course, is an extremely important determinant of success and one nearly impossible to isolate and define. But home environment and parental models play critical roles in the development of strong, independent women.

Katharine Hepburn and Rosalind Russell, two stars who came of age in the 1930s, can be joined by Elizabeth Taylor, Shirley MacLaine, and Ava Gardner, stars who began their careers in the 1950s, as good examples of women who came from stable families. All of these women, but especially Hepburn and Russell, who represent the first generation of movie stars of the sound era, were raised to believe in their own worth. Hepburn has spoken admiringly of her suffragist and birth-control-advocate mother and of her doctor-father. Both parents contributed to her sense of self-assurance. "Good Lord," she once said, "one of my earliest recollections is my mother making speeches, and raising hell—a real suffragette, and in those days, that wasn't an easy thing to be—about 90 percent of the people in America—men and women—were against you if you were a suffragette—made fun of you—she didn't give a damn—it was something she believed in. Now with Dad trying to make a living as a doctor, of course it could've got in his way professionally—but they talked it over—decided people have to do what they feel—it wasn't only the vote that was the issue."[3] Hepburn's consistent image presented in all interviews with her is that of an idiosyncratic, self-confident person, someone who would succeed in whatever profession she chose. In 1950, she told an interviewer, "I have to be a person, not a piece in a pattern."[4]

Rosalind Russell's father was a lawyer and her mother was an editor at *Vogue* magazine. She has recalled how her loud voice annoyed her mother at the dinner table, while her father assured her that because she wanted to be heard, it was a useful instrument. She always projected her voice beyond the third row of the theater. "It's okay to

In *Woman of the Year,* Katharine Hepburn epitomized the independent woman as journalist Tess Harding.

have talent," she has noted, "but talent is the least of it. In a performance or a career, you've got to have vitality. I've worked with actors and actresses far better that I'll ever be—as far as raw talent goes. But what they have just doesn't register because they don't have the drive underneath to project. . . . Sometimes what you have to do is almost claw your work onto film."[5]

American magazine complimented Russell in 1941 by saying that her distinctive quality was that "she dared to be herself."[6] Russell played career women in many of her films, thereby joining her personal and professional selves. Even when she allowed romance in the form of Fred MacMurray to distract her in the movies, the real-life image of a competent woman was projected onto the screen.

A member of the second generation of Hollywood stars, Elizabeth Taylor arrived in California from England at the tender age of seven and went from a child star to an adult star successfully. She has observed how schooling at Metro-Goldwyn-Mayer (MGM), a traumatic experience for many child stars, amused her; even Mr. Mayer failed to intimidate her. Taylor's family provided her with emotional encouragement and support. Dick Sheppard, in his biography *Elizabeth,* defines her strength and endurance as based on four things: "a sound family foundation and a consequent inner assurance which has never failed her; the mutual love and devotion of those closest to her; a bond with the public which transitory crisis could never sever; and a professional knowledge of the crafts of film acting second to none."[7]

Though her mother had some of the characteristics of a pushy stage mother, she also acted as a refuge for Elizabeth. In 1950, at seventeen years of age, Elizabeth Taylor told interviewers that she was a traditional girl and very concerned with her mother's opinion of her. "I'm being painted as a good-time girl," she told Louella Parsons, "who stays out all hours of the night. That is hard to take. If you could see how my mother cries, you'd know what I mean."[8]

In December 1974, when Taylor was already forty-two years old, the movie magazines still referred to Mother Taylor's influence upon her daughter. Sara Taylor disapproved of Richard Burton, Elizabeth's current love, while Mother Taylor admired Henry Wynberg, "a wonderful, considerate gentleman."[9] Observers of Elizabeth Taylor as a child star noted how unambitious and undemanding she was, in contrast to an all-consuming careerist like Margaret O'Brien. "No one," wrote a Hollywood reporter in 1955 "can accuse Elizabeth of storm-

The quintessential Eve, Elizabeth Taylor is at her most glamorous in this publicity photo from the 1950s.

ing front offices, demanding, fretting or weeping over lost roles."[10] She was a cool professional who projected an image of a purposeful actor.

During her long tenure in Hollywood, Elizabeth Taylor had her face on more magazine covers than anyone else. Her every move has been recorded, and she once complained that her life was comparable to a young woman schoolteacher's in a small town. But despite the public adulation, she grew in self-awareness. In two separate interviews in the mid-1950s, when she was twenty-two and twenty-three years old respectively, she observed how all of the people around her protected and approved all of her actions. "Instead of pointing out my faults, people always told me how good I was. I never learned responsibility."[11] She continued by saying, "All my life I've been riding on a pink cloud. Because I'm a movie star, no one has the courage to tell me that I'm wrong. I have been told I was great when I was awful. . . . I am the little princess for whom everything is done."[12]

The interview is the perfect vehicle for creating intimacy, albeit false intimacy, between a star and her fans. Taylor's voice emerges from the print interview, and later, from the video interview. In both cases, audiences can connect with their star and believe that they have learned about the star's personal life. Since Elizabeth Taylor's private life has been more exciting, dramatic, tense, and life-threatening than her screen life, fans have probably blurred the lines between her filmic image and her "real" image. Her admirers have watched her survive serious illness, the trauma of widowhood, and the loss of lovers; they have also seen her emerge from each trial intact. No Hollywood script writer could imagine a fuller life story than Elizabeth Taylor's.

Shirley MacLaine, another second-generation movie star, exemplifies a kind of strength and independence that has been more generally associated with the 1960s stars. While Taylor's strength as a survivor was admired in the 1950s, MacLaine anticipated the sexually emancipated behavior of subsequent stars. Movie magazines noted in the still unliberated year of 1963 that MacLaine's marriage to producer Steve Parker was unconventional; he lived in Japan and she made movies in California. As she explained to one interviewer, "When you marry and have a child, you become a unit. But each individual in the unit should be allowed to express himself, not always perform in concert. We give each other freedom."[13] MacLaine picked her screen roles and generally shaped her own public identity. As one columnist wrote, "The surprise is not that Shirley has moved to the top, but that she has done it on her own terms without cheesecake, without studio-supervised romances, even without a swimming pool."[14]

Ava Gardner, an actress who usually portrayed the worldly-wise whore, arrived in Hollywood at the age of eighteen, fresh from a North Carolina farm. She learned quickly about the dangers and the lures of Hollywood. "I didn't know *anything*. I had barely finished high school—at a rural school three miles' walk from my home. . . . And here I was, plumped down in Hollywood. . . . I spent hours in beauty shops having my hair glued into fancy hairdos—I didn't have enough sense to know I looked terrible with fancy hairdos."[15] By 1950, at the age of twenty-seven, Gardner realized that fame and fortune, love and romance, were illusory qualities. Her marriage to Mickey Rooney at eighteen had ended in divorce, and she discovered that, "there isn't a chance for happiness in marriage or anything else unless you accept people—*and especially yourself*—for what they really are."[16]

Ava Gardner continued searching for personal happiness for many years, but early in her tenure in Hollywood, personal experience taught her to be wary. She had many more marriages, all ending in divorce. Her financial success as an actress enabled her to exile herself from moviemaking and live abroad. Though Gardner was unable to combine a successful career with a happy home life, she was not destroyed by Hollywood culture.

Many actresses have come from one-parent families where the mother was a positive model of independence for the daughter. Bette Davis's parents, for example, divorced when she was eight years old, an unusual phenomenon in 1916. Her mother Ruthie had to earn a living to support Bette and her younger sister, Bobbie. An attorney, Mr. Davis, seemed disinclined to participate in the financial or emotional rearing of his children. Thus, Bette Davis saw her mother work at various jobs until Mrs. Davis learned photography and became moderately successful at it. In high school, Bette decided to become an actress and, after graduating, spent some time at the Robert Milton-John Murray Anderson School of the Theater in New York. By 1930, at the age of twenty-two, she was on her way to Hollywood under contract to Universal Studios. Once in Hollywood, the path was stormy, but Davis's determination kept her going.

Her 1932 marriage to high school sweetheart Harmon Nelson

ended in 1938, a classic example of career clashing. He wanted her to ease up on her work and devote more time to him. "Only one thing could save our marriage," she told an interviewer. "My giving up my career. I thought about it. Seriously! And I decided it was no use. For if I should quit now before I finished all the things I set out to do, it is altogether too likely I would turn resentful, even bitter."[17] Early in that marriage, Davis had become pregnant and aborted rather than interrupt her career, a decision agreed to at the time by her husband and mother.

Silent stars Mary Pickford, Blanche Sweet, Mae Marsh, and the Gish sisters are all examples of women raised by mothers alone. Marsh's father died when she was four. The Gish sisters' father deserted the family when they were very young. Sweet's father deserted her mother when she was one, her mother died a year later, and she was raised by a grandmother. Pickford's father was killed in an accident when she was five. Her mother always played an active role in furthering Pickford's career. When Mary Pickford formed her own corporation and became its president, her mother Charlotte became all of the vice-presidents. From the age of seven, the young Mary became the bread-winner of the family. Director D.W. Griffith enjoyed the role of father/ protector to these fatherless women. He cultivated their image of vul-nerable girls. Blanche Sweet said it: "He became the father figure. Anything he told me to do, I did. *Anything* to win his praises."[18]

Though the Griffith screen image for these women was that of dependency, sweet weakness, and vulnerability, all of these women also displayed a realistic ability to handle their careers and exploit their advantage. When it suited Mary Pickford to go to Hollywood and earn a great deal more money from Adolph Zukor, she took the first train, leaving Griffith, art, and New York. Her private personality was entirely separate and different from her screen image of Mary. Being women alone, raised by women alone, made these actresses wary but decisive, traits quite the opposite of those projected on the screen. Marys would have a hard time surviving in Hollywood. Pickford retired on her untaxed millions after discovering that sound movies were not her métier.

Carole Lombard, Joan Crawford, Judy Holliday, and Doris Day are more examples of movie stars raised by single parents. Carole Lombard's parents divorced in Fort Wayne, Indiana, in 1915, when she was seven years old. Mrs. Elizabeth K. Peters moved her two sons and daughter (Jane Alice) to Los Angeles. As an eleven-year-old, soon-to-be Carole caught the attention of a silent movie recruiter while boxing with her brother in the front yard. She did her first bit part in a silent movie called *The Perfect Crime*. After junior high school, Lombard decided to become a movie star and hung out around the Pickford and Charlie Chaplin movie lots. She learned comic routines, observed the slapstick comedy of the Keystone Kops and of Charlie Chaplin, played innumerable small roles, and eventually became a master in verbal comedy in the mid-1930s.

Joan Crawford's childhood was an unusually difficult one. Her father disappeared when she was a baby, and her mother married a vaudevillian. The family moved to Oklahoma where they lived for six years when another disruption occurred: her mother divorced her step-father and married for a third time, now moving the family to Kansas City. By 1920, at the age of twelve, Joan Crawford (whose real name was Lucille Le Sueur) was an awkward, insecure, overweight girl. She began dancing at fifteen in an effort to overcome her shyness and embark on a career in show business. The story from this point on sounds like a Hollywood script. She won an amateur dance contest, moved to Chicago and then to Detroit, where a Shubert recruiter saw her and offered her a job in the chorus line of a Broadway musical. A contract with MGM in 1925 was the beginning of her movie career.

Judy Holliday's parents separated when she was six in 1928, and Doris Day's parents divorced when she was twelve. In all of these cases, these women were raised by mothers alone, and the model for adult womanhood was that of a woman supporting her family and making decisions. The spunk and initiative later demonstrated by these actresses was a combination of inborn instinct and learned behavior. From their mothers, they learned how to be autonomous women. The role modeling that occurred enabled them to pursue the line of work they wished for themselves.

Daughters of movie stars have a particular burden to bear. They often find themselves in the shadow of greatness and unable to stand firmly in their own place. Liza Minnelli and Jane Fonda are exceptions to this rule. Despite difficult childhoods, they carved their own inimitable niches in Hollywood history. Fonda's mother committed suicide when she was twelve, but her father remarried a woman nine years older than she. Jane Fonda has said that her stepmother, Susan Blanchard, is "the woman I love best in the world."[19] Liza Minnelli lived alternately with her mother, Judy Garland, and her father, Vincente Minnelli. By the time she was a teenager, she displayed a maturity that startled many adults. In her relationship with her mother, it was not always clear who was the child and who was the mother. "The kind of childhood I had can make you or break you," she once observed. "I've had knocks, but I'm not sure it's not better to have them when you're young. At least it teaches you how to handle them when they come later."[20]

Certainly, many daughters of stable families do not achieve movie stardom, nor do they become independent women. Most girl children of divorced parents do not succeed in Hollywood, and most movie stars' children fail to imitate their parents' careers. But among the stars, these parental models emerge as frequent and striking. More significant, independence was emphasized in the raising of these stars, no matter which family pattern prevailed. In other words, the ingredient that most women movie stars shared was that of self-confidence, confidence bred in childhood by supportive parents or a supportive mother. Rosalind Russell's father told her that a quitter never wins and a winner never quits; she never forgot that message. Bette Davis admired her mother's uncomplaining willingness to work hard for her daughters' educations and futures. Historically, strong women who distinguished themselves in public activities have come from households where encouraging fathers raised them to be independent or where mothers taught them self-reliance.

Another extremely important variable, of course, is the unique personality of the woman who becomes a successful movie star. She combines the strength derived from her family makeup, her talent, opportunities, and her personality. Many girls who were better-looking than Joan Crawford never got further than the Detroit dives where she began; few made it to the New York City dance halls. Many daughters of parents divorced in the second decade pf the twentieth century or the 1950s hurriedly married their high school sweethearts at eighteen to avoid their mothers' experience. The rare combination of circumstances, individual determination, and good fortune allows some to succeed. Most fail. However, among the winners, one is struck by the preponderance of daughters raised by single mothers.

One additional example of an orphan who enjoyed fame and fortune in Hollywood is Barbara Stanwyck. Ruby Stevens (her real name)

Movie star Barbara Stanwyck, an independent Eve, stands in front of a CBS radio microphone in the 1940s.

was born in Brooklyn in 1907. She was orphaned at four and raised by an older sister. After finishing elementary school, she worked as a bundle wrapper, telephone operator, file clerk, and pattern cutter. She became a dancer and, at the age of sixteen, toured with the Ziegfeld Follies. While dancing in an Atlantic City nightclub, she received a small part in a Broadway play and in 1927 was on her way to Hollywood. Throughout the 1930s and 1940s, she made innumerable movies, becoming one of the most popular and best-paid actresses of the day. Early in her career, she demonstrated an iron will that could also be detected in her screen portrayals. She told one magazine writer how she dealt with wily Hollywood producers who reneged on promises made: "I originally came to Hollywood with a written contract and a verbal understanding that I would be paid more money if I proved popular with movie fans. For many years I had had such verbal agreements with New York stage producers, and I never experienced difficulty. But when my motion pictures were successful and I reminded my employers of my verbal agreement, I was told that 'I had a contract and must live up to it.' I answered by keeping quiet until I was needed for a picture, then refusing to do that picture. I won the subsequent court fight and my salary was raised."[21] One of Stanwyck's favorite quotations is, "It isn't life that matters, it's the courage you bring to it."[22]

Hollywood produced more women survivors than it did victims. Those women who achieved stardom did so because their personalities and backgrounds combined to create determined, hardworking, ambitious women. In every description of the greats, mention is made of their unerring professionalism, their willingness to work long hours, and their uncomplaining devotion to their profession. Producer Jerry Wald was taken aback the first time he worked with Joan Crawford; he expected a temperamental star and instead he met a serious and hardworking actress. He later noted that on the set of the film *Mildred Pierce,* she "was on time every morning, . . . never complained how late we worked at night, . . . knew her lines and . . . was not only willing but positively humble about doing what she was told."[23]

Contrary to the myth of the unpredictable and temperamental movie star, most of the really successful women stars were serious about their craft. Bette Davis rebelled only when she hated the innocuous parts she received; it was in the interest of her integrity and sense of art that she questioned the studio bosses. Similarly, Katharine Hepburn was known for her expertise on the set; she knew everyone's lines as well as the cameraman's angles, the director's perspective, and the best lighting for herself. Carole Lombard demonstrated great knowledge of the mechanics of filmmaking. Elizabeth Taylor's seriousness on a set was frequently mentioned by her coworkers. All of these women defied the stereotype of the spoiled child/actress who selfishly kept the cameras waiting and pouted when her favorite chair was missing. Press agents dreamed up such stories for many stars and gloated when they came across someone who fit their preconceived image. Self-confident women do not behave childishly.

If many of these movie stars came to Hollywood with the personalities and life experiences that prepared them for the competitive movie business, how did they manage their personal lives and their careers simultaneously? How did they become the first group of women professionals whose every move was conspicuously observed by eager fans? Did they become models for other career-minded women? Did their lifestyles encourage other women to think that wifehood, motherhood, and career could be successfully combined in America?

The answers reflect the power of cultural values. Journalists have gleaned one message from the stars' many marriages, for example, while contemporary feminists create a far different interpretation. Pop culture commentators alongside the quick-analysis journalists have often, understandably, described the private lives of the stars as luscious but unnatural, because stars, being exceptional people, live lives unlike everyone else's. They are admired and envied. But those feelings are balanced with the comforting knowledge that stars experience divorce, alienated children, drug problems, and fading looks. Until recently, when single moms have become more common among the stars as well as among the fans, the preservers of the status quo (and journalists were in that category) understood that the best way to maintain traditional sex roles in America was to point out the failures of independent women. In pre-1980s America, where the rhetoric proclaimed one marriage per person for a lifetime with the woman devoting herself to the success of that marriage via her full-time commitment to being a wife-mother, the much-married movie star appeared neurotic, irresponsible, selfish, and unhappy.

From a feminist perspective, the stars' frequent marriages could suggest the healthy desire to remain happy, to feel deserving of happiness; rather than be martyrs or self-sacrificers, women stars assertively ended bad relationships and sought new ones. Being financially independent, they did not have to endure unhappy marriages. The generations before the 1960s, however, married their new lovers rather than just live with them; Elizabeth Taylor is the most prominent example. The stars remained products of the same cultural value system as the majority. Public success already was theirs, and they aggressively sought personal happiness too. Women movie stars, with few exceptions, may have lived feminist lives, but they often were unconscious of its feminist meanings.

While our culture has always assumed that men have careers and marriage simultaneously, only recently has that possibility come into being for women. As recently as the 1960s, women with careers outside of the home were considered anomalous. And what could be more irregular than successful women movie stars? Most of the women I have described loved their work, a particularly unwomanly quality. They believed that they were entitled to personal happiness in addition to professional success. In their interviews and memoirs, these women often revealed an uneasy awareness of how difficult it was for women to be careerists, wives, and mothers.

These earlier generations of women movie stars were the vanguard of the 1970s and 1980s women's movement; they were the pioneers in demanding female self-identities. Rather than be judged on the accomplishments of their husbands or children, they required assessment of their own work. They had strong senses of self as achieving, creative women. Bette Davis was one of the most self-conscious and thoughtful writers on the tortuous subject of being a woman professional and a wife-mother. Her autobiography, *The Lonely Life,* was so titled because she expected to spend her old age alone. But she also insisted that she would never do it any differently. Davis had four marriages; she was widowed once and divorced three times. She said, "When a woman is independent financially and eclipses her husband professionally, the man suddenly finds it necessary to be a nineteenth-century lord and master. He falls back on symbols that are insupportable to the self-supporting wife. My mistake was to attempt the duality. I couldn't be both husband and wife and I tried."[24]

Davis, a thoroughgoing careerist, never dreamed of abandoning her career; that would have been like denying or erasing an essential part of herself. Yet she wanted, as most women did and do, a husband and children. Davis tried to have both but concluded that, given the traditional attitudes of most men in her day, it was not possible. When she became a mother for the first time at the age of thirty-nine, she rejoiced and told gossip columnist Hedda Hopper, "You know, Hedda, I've wanted Barbara for so many years I can't tell you. I used to think it was awful I hadn't had her when I was twenty-one. But now I realize how perfect it is to have her at my age. When I was a youngster, I was struggling so hard to get somewhere. Now I've got the time to enjoy her."[25]

She later told writer Rex Reed,

> If I had to do it all over again, the only thing I'd change is
> that I would never get married. But then I wouldn't have my
> kids and without them I would die. But my biggest problem
> all my life was men. I never met one yet who could compete
> with the image the public made out of Bette Davis. . . . I am
> a woman meant for a man. I get very lonely sometimes at
> night in this big house. . . . There's nothing glamorous about
> that. . . . I was a good wife. But I don't know any other lady
> in my category who kept a husband either, unless she
> married for money or married a secretary-manager type
> where there was no competition. That's a price I've paid for
> success, and I've had a lot of it.[26]

Bette Davis never whined nor complained. She shrewdly commented, rather, on the impossibility of finding autonomous men in this culture. That was not her flaw, her failure, but the men's and the culture's. Davis charted a new course as a career woman/wife/mother. She tried to combine the best of both genders, but she failed to surmount powerful cultural values and perceptions. Husbands, an old social type in America, have a difficult time accepting a new social type: career wives. William Grant Sherry, the father of Davis's daughter, was a mediocre artist who could not endure remaining in the background of this strong-willed star's life. Husband number four, actor Gary Merrill, remained her husband for ten years, her longest marriage; with him, Davis adopted two more children. At the beginning of that marriage, she displayed her realistic, yet hopeful attitude toward marriage when she told a reporter, "Now, really, I'm too old for romance stories. That's kid stuff. Let's just say I am wonderfully happy. I feel that this is a good marriage."[27]

Bette Davis often shared her thoughts with her fans. At the end of World War II, she discussed what working wives should do after the war in *Motion Picture* magazine, particularly those women who had no formal career; her remarks did not apply to women who had combined career and marriage successfully. She said, "I am talking here only to those war-working wives who plan to continue working after their GI husbands come home from the war—women who never have tried the experience of combining a career and homemaking, but who are intrigued now with the idea, women who have found a business life stimulating and exciting as well as financially productive, yet know nothing of the problems, obligations, and threats it will involve when combined with homemaking."[28] She advised such women to consider the prospect seriously: "You always can quit a job, but you cannot always recapture a marriage!"[29]

Within her discussion, however, Davis spoke out firmly against the general male domination of women: "Have you observed that the talk is always about what women should or should not do, never about what men should be prepared to face or accept?" Though outspoken, Davis still acknowledged the separate spheres for the sexes when she proclaimed, "No husband should be expected to come home from his own full day's work to run a vacuum sweeper or clean up the kitchen."[30] Ostensibly, a woman who worked used her wages to hire domestic help—or she ran the vacuum cleaner when she returned from her job. Still firmly planted in traditional culture, Bette Davis moved tentatively into unknown territory when questioning male superiority and women's rights, but she did not make the leap into autonomy for women. "The wife with a job must not allow or want her husband to think of her, or treat her, like another man in business. She must be a wife, first, last and always, as far as he is concerned. Otherwise, she is an idiot and deserves to lose him."[31]

A woman must never put her work before her home, reminded career-oriented Davis; yet, reflecting her considerable inconsistency on this subject, she had claimed earlier in the interview that "(t)he accident of sex has nothing to do with human rights and justice in an enlightened world." Proclaiming that women should have rights equal to men's was followed by utterances such as, "She must be prepared to give her free time to the wants and pleasures of her children and

Bette Davis poses alongside her costar, Leslie Howard, in the movie *The Petrified Forest.*

husband, regardless of how exhausted she may be from the day's labors." She concluded by saying, "For no matter how great a career and success, without a home a woman cannot be happy. But I still say she *can* have both!"[32] How that noble goal was to be accomplished remained unanswered.

Given the high divorce rate in this country, women movie stars foreshadowed a trend that has overtaken all Americans. Being women, their behavior was unusual, but being financially independent (also unusual), they were able to initiate divorce proceedings and remain self-determining. Much-married Joan Crawford (once widowed and thrice divorced) frequently discussed her personal life with magazine interviewers. Like Bette Davis, she sought the harmonic blend of personal and public success. Her first marriage to Douglas Fairbanks Jr. taught her a great deal about the royalty of Hollywood, lessons a poorly educated young woman appreciated. Second husband Franchot Tone introduced her to the literary classics. With husband Philip Terry, she adopted a child. When that three-year marriage ended, gossip columnist Louella Parsons asked Crawford if she was going to give up on marriage and devote herself wholeheartedly to career. She replied, "I can't say I'll never marry again, Louella, because—I get too lonely. I love my children, little Christina and Christopher, but I am a woman who does not like to be alone. Perhaps," she smiled, "I'll marry an Oscar who can't talk back. But seriously, when and *if* I marry again, I want a man who will say, 'We are *not* going to live in your house. I will give you a house, and you can have it any way you want, but it will be our home, not yours.'"[33] Crawford's fourth husband, Pepsi-Cola chief Alfred Steele, fit the bill; their four year marriage ended with Steele's death in 1959.

Neither Bette Davis nor Joan Crawford fell apart due to their personal trials and tribulations. Though both freely acknowledged their desire for a compatible male, their work provided security and useful activity when their personal lives proved unsatisfactory. Movie magazine interviews are highly contrived sources of information; the false intimacy created is precisely that. Yet the repetitive themes of many articles suggest the essential truths articulated. Thoughtful and successful women movie stars such as Davis and Crawford had many opportunities to consider their lives, their roles in American society, and their contrasting position to mainstream women. They understood how they were like all American women and how they were

Joan Crawford, the female Horatio Alger of 1930s and 1940s movies, looks thoughtful in this 1947 photo.

decidedly different. Acknowledging loneliness, a very human trait, bridged the gap between the stars and their fans.

Another good example of an actress who truly valued the traditional womanly roles, and lost them—yet survived—is Barbara Stanwyck. While married to Frank Fay, she told an interviewer that "I would rather be Mrs. Frank Fay than anything else. I don't care what people say or think. Frank and I understand each other. I want two children, a little boy with red hair like Frank's and a little girl. What do a lot of pictures matter in the face of that?"[34] Unfortunately, she never had the little girl, however, the Fays adopted a little boy. The marriage, though, ended in divorce after seven years.

In a remarkably candid 1937 interview, Stanwyck described her marriage to Frank Fay as having been one in which she totally submerged herself to his wishes, his needs, and his inclinations. And when the marriage ended, she was immunized from future subjugation. "I know what it is to have no life of my own at all. Even in little, inconsequential things. I know how it feels to move a chair in the living room and have *him* give it one look and, hastily, put it back again. You lose your life for love, this kind of love, though you are living. And this is what I'd advise girls not to do, to *try* not to do.... I know that I have reached the stage where I wouldn't place my whole trust in any man. Not unreservedly. This is no aspersion on the male sex or any member of it. I just don't think it's in them." She continued,

> I do trust women. I really believe that women are capable of
> disinterested friendship, of undivided loyalty, of keeping
> faith. . . . For my advice, for what it's worth, is for girls to
> have their own lives, to have vital interests, to build such a
> wall of interests around their hearts that, while love may
> find a chink in the wall, it can't completely capture the fort.
> To me, right now, there's such romance in living my own life
> as I wish to live it, that I can't believe it's dangerous. And
> even if it were . . . life is always dangerous, however you live
> it.[35]

Stanwyck's second and last marriage to romantic idol Robert Taylor lasted from 1939 to 1951. Taylor left her for a younger woman, and by most accounts, Stanwyck was very hurt and upset by the divorce. Her work occupied her mind and time, thereby dulling the

Barbara Stanwyck and Henry Fonda in *The Lady Eve*.

pain. After movies no longer provided good parts for her, Stanwyck turned to television and acted successfully for a number of years in the popular series "The Big Valley." After retiring from acting, Stanwyck participated in many charitable endeavors.

When Carole Lombard married Clark Gable in 1939, fan magazines assured their readers that home and family meant more to Lombard than her hard-won career. While she kept working, writers proclaimed that all Carole ever wanted was a loving husband, a warm fire, and children. While Lombard's actions belied her alleged words, she obliged one reporter by saying, "I'd just like to let 'Pa' (Gable) be the star, while I stay home and mend socks and mind babies."[36] She never did. Her life ended in a plane crash in 1942. But during the three years of their marriage, Lombard made more serious movies than before, suggesting a deepening of her talent and a change from her famous screwball comedies of the mid-thirties. Fans wanted Carole Lombard to be just like the girl next door, yearning for the same dreams and goals as she did. While Lombard undoubtedly viewed personal happiness with a loving man high on her list of wishes, it did not preclude her interest in her career.

Rosalind Russell, married to the same man her whole adult life, appears as an anomaly in much-married Hollywood. She once admitted that she had no logical explanation to the longevity of her marriage but went on "I do know that a woman should learn early that everything in her marriage is not going to be her way. It's not enough to like men, as I do, and to want to be liked by them. In this life we have to carry our weight. A woman should exhibit qualities her husband will want to brag about when he is off with the boys, even if it's just running the house economically, or wearing a dress attractively or being a good cook."[37] "We have to carry our own weight" appears to be a key principle to Russell. Self-esteem based upon accomplishment in any area is necessary for women and men.

Katharine Hepburn is the only representative of this group who continued to act into old age. While her only marriage was a brief one, she had a long-term relationship with actor Spencer Tracy. This subject remained private, however, and was never discussed in the fan magazines. Until her old age, Hepburn assiduously avoided interviews. In a much celebrated interview with Dick Cavett in the 1970s, she claimed that a professional actress could not and should not marry. A husband and children are a full-time career. Hepburn never discussed her eight-year marriage to Ludlow Ogden Smith in the late twenties, nor her relationship with Tracy. Her self-defined image remained that of an independent woman, a fully absorbed careerist. Hepburn argued for the scrupulous separation of roles. While men are not faced with performing both domestic tasks and professional ones, they can ignore their husbandly and fatherly responsibilities without consequence. Women do not have that luxury. Thus, according to Hepburn, the decision is simple for a woman: become a career woman or a wife-mother.

Elizabeth Taylor has sought to combine personal and professional happiness in her tumultuous and intense life. She has borne three children, been married eight times (twice to actor Richard Burton), been widowed, and survived high-risk surgery. She has won two Academy Awards, been photographed innumerable times since the 1940s, and made an impressive number of films over a long career. She, like the generation of stars that preceded her, has been a survivor in the difficult world of filmmaking. Taylor's thoughts, as quoted in the endless articles about her, reveal a woman of above-average intelligence and wit who has learned how to endure public exposure and private pain.

In recent years, Taylor has become an AIDS crusader, raising money to increase public knowledge and awareness of the disease. Like Jane Fonda, she has used her celebrity to gain a public hearing and public sympathy for a cause that concerns her. Clearly, all of the stars described in these pages came to terms with their fame; they understood its advantages and its disadvantages. While Bette Davis and Barbara Stanwyck were the most explicit and conscious commentators on the immense difficulties faced by successful women stars, all of the famous women experienced the multiple tugs on their time, affections, and money. All understood the extreme risks they took every time they confided in someone, every time they gave their love and trust to a man. Their personal failures only underscored their deep commitment to values they shared with most other American women.

Within the confessional literature of the movie magazines are multiple layers of information. We recapitulate the history of show business through the biographies of stars such as Barbara Stanwyck and Joan Crawford, we learn how stressed movie stars cope with many demands, and we see how images are made and remade. In trying to explain themselves to their fans, the stars often explained themselves to themselves. They ordered their lives and created harmony out of chaos, rationality out of irrationality. In so doing, they glossed over failures, condensed despairing experiences, and always emerged with a happy ending.

But the most sustaining evidence of their testimonies and confessions is their lives, their continued presence on the screen, and their enduring impressions on our consciousness. Women movie stars as a group offer us an admirable portrait of interesting, independent Liliths who coped with the dilemma of living full public and private lives long before most of us even articulated the problem. Unwittingly, perhaps, they have been the vanguard of the women's movement. Their successes and failures, writ large because of their fame, offer us a looking glass into the false and true starts of all women forging their own adult lives in modern America.

5

Child Stars

To the surprise of many, child stars prospered in 1930s Hollywood. Despite (or perhaps because of) the insecurities of the Depression, Americans eagerly went to the movies to see six-year-olds and ten-year-olds sing, dance, and act their way across the screen. The fact that adults had not figured out how to solve the most knotty problems facing them made them anxious to escape into the child's fantasy world where all came out all right in the end. Fathers and mothers took their families to the children's movies and, by many accounts, seemed to love watching children as the stars of the film as much if not more than did their children. Contemporary newspaper pictures of lines of adults waiting to see the latest Shirley Temple movie attest to her popularity—among adults. Fathers were often photographed holding their daughters' hands as they waited in line. Film critic Jeanine Basinger saw Shirley Temple's role as that of Daddy's little helper, the surrogate wife and mother to the needy father.[1]

Child stars Peggy Ann Garner and Margaret O'Brien enjoyed success, as did Mickey Rooney and Freddie Bartholomew, but no one was more popular and loved than Shirley Temple. She became the superstar in the field. The little six-year-old with her wide smile, bright eyes, and curly hair endeared herself to a whole generation of moviegoers.[2] The peculiar attraction of Shirley Temple cannot be exaggerated; however, though she will be the focus of this chapter, she was joined on the screen by other little children as well as teenagers because the appeal of young innocents was so powerful during this period.

The hopefulness, natural optimism, and cheerfulness of children acted as a buoy to the nation's spirits, and the children's movies flourished—a phenomenon unique to this period. One could argue that the child star, Shirley in particular, was the quintessential Mary, the sweet, pure innocent in child form, untouched by all of the travails of the depression. In contrast to characters in the Disney films such as Snow White, which were animated characters taken from fairy tales, Shirley and her cohorts were real live children whose film experiences could offer comfort and support to both children and their parents.

Because the family has always been seen as the anchor of American society and children are the critical future of the family, it makes sense that during the depression when normal life was threatened, Hollywood responded with a spate of movies that featured energetic children who displayed faith in life and the future. Shirley Temple acted in a complex manner to become the supreme example of the genre and to rise above it as well. No other child star came close to her popularity. In her movies, everyone else was an accessory to the star, a supporting player. As scriptwriter J.P. McEvoy wrote, "Hollywood is lousy with talent—children who can sing, who can dance, who can act, who have curls, dimples and little round legs. But there is only one Shirley."[3]

She was born in Santa Monica, California, on April 23, 1928, though her mother Gertrude later shaved a year off her age to make her appear even younger. Shirley had two older brothers, and both parents doted on their cute little girl. At the age of three, she was learning to dance—tap, tango, and rumba—at the Ethel Meglin Dance Studio in Santa Monica.[4] A talent scout chose Shirley and eleven other children to play in a series of one-reel spoofs called *Baby Burlesks.* The little children were dressed up in adultlike costumes with heavy make-up in stories that parodied adult adventures, melodramas, and comedies. She made eight of these films, working eleven-and-a half-hour days and earning ten dollars a day. Shirley Temple's discipline, her ability to take direction, and her sweet personality were already evident and distinguished her from all of the other children.

With her mother's words, "Sparkle, Shirley," in her ears, she appeared in Twentieth Century Fox's–1934 *Stand Up and Cheer* and sang

"Baby, Take a Bow." By all accounts, the movie was forgettable, but Shirley Temple's appearance evoked considerable comment. Fox put her under contract, and in that year, at the age of six, she made three additional movies, averaging four movies a year for the next five years.[5] Temple quickly displayed a professionalism unusual in such a young child. As one interviewer observed, "Shirley is apparently one of those extremely sensitive children who is so highly tuned to the feelings of others that she requires no heavy handed discipline."[6]

So many reporters wrote about her and so many photographers took her picture that she soon became an experienced hand at granting interviews. When asked in a 1938 interview if she tired of this constant attention, she answered, "I don't mind at all. It's part of the job."[7] The numerous writers throughout the 1930s all commented on her self-assuredness and her unspoiled nature. Note was taken of the fact that Shirley received thousands of gifts on her birthday and thousands of fan letters every month. She took all of it in stride, though she once asked her mother why people screamed "I love you, Shirley" at her. Her mother answered that they enjoyed her movies, and that was that.[8]

Some people credit Shirley Temple with saving the Fox studio; others think she saved Hollywood during the depths of the depression. (What a contrast to those who blamed Mae West for bringing censorship down on Hollywood.) Both views are overstatements, but the economics of a Temple movie reveals her impressive box office power; while the film cost two hundred thousand dollars, a goodly sum for that era, her movies grossed between one and one and a half million dollars. Further, Shirley's movies always came in under schedule, and childhood illnesses seemed to evade her. Her life was carefully regulated: for three hours each day, in a red and white trailer on the movie lot, Shirley Temple did her classwork, supervised by a public-school teacher. Her amazing ability to remember her lines, and to learn the lines of everyone else as well was often commented upon. The constant media attention contributed to her continued success. By 1936, after just two years of intensive filmmaking, her face appeared daily in about twenty different venues—ads, newspapers, and magazines.[9]

News that Shirley Temple's IQ was 155, genius level, did not surprise her many fans or her coworkers; that explained her retentive ability and her bright intelligence. Actor Adolphe Menjou, who appeared with Shirley in *Little Miss Marker,* said that she frightened him because "she knew all the tricks."[10] When another eminent actor, Lionel Barrymore, forgot his lines during a scene, Shirley quickly supplied them. In *The Littlest Rebel* (1935), a Civil War film, her multiple talents were on full display. The film opened with Temple as the daughter of Virginia planters hosting a birthday party for herself. She offered each of her child guests cake and ice cream, and when one of the servants whispered to her that they had no more ice cream (and the fat little boy next to her wished some more), she thought quickly, cleaned the cake off of her plate, and gave the remaining ice cream to the servant to give to the boy.

During the course of the film, Shirley had to be the brave little soldier when her father went away to war. Later, she asked President Lincoln to pardon her father after he had been captured by the Union Army. She sat on the great man's lap while explaining her plight to him and shared the apple he was slicing, one piece for Abe and one for Miss Virgie. When Lincoln mistakenly took two pieces in a row, she reminded him that that piece belonged to her. Temple's spunk, her independence, and her audacity were clearly demonstrated, much to the delight of the audience.

In *The Little Princess* (1939), one of Temple's last films as a child (she was an "old" eleven years old at that time), Miss Minchen, the school headmistress, asked little Sara (our heroine) for an explanation for her rebellious behavior. Sara replied, "Yes, Miss Minchen, as soon as I can think of one." Temple, as Sara, said this with candor and pluck, but not cheekiness; from her lips, the words did not sound rude, dangerous, or impossible. They sounded sensible, funny, and refreshing, precisely the qualities adults expected and desired of movie children. After all, it was sweet Shirley speaking. In this movie, like all her others, Shirley confidently presented herself as spunky, perky, and exuberant, a powerful force in any and all environments.

In *The Littlest Rebel,* as in five other movies, Bill "Bojangles" Robinson, the great African American tap dancer, appeared with Shirley. He was Uncle Billy, the loyal slave-servant who stood by the family during the difficult days of the Civil War. Shirley established a friendly and personal relationship with him throughout the film. He accompanied her to Washington to see President Lincoln, and held her hand as is appropriate for an older, wiser man walking with a little child. Race differences did not appear to matter, though Uncle Billy was a

Child star Shirley Temple offers comfort in *The Little Colonel* to Lionel
Barrymore.

slave; in fact, when the war broke out, Miss Virgie (Shirley) asked him about slavery and he answered: "I don't know what it means myself." Of course, white audiences were comforted with this response. But despite the obvious will to erase differences and to project an image of unity during the dark days of the depression, Shirley conveyed the impression of truly having treated the slaves, including Uncle Billy, as equals, not as inferiors.

She developed a similar relationship in *The Little Princess* with a servant girl who lived at the boarding school; when Shirley's fortunes changed (it was assumed that her father was killed in the war and the family assets lost), she was assigned the attic as her residence, next door to the little servant girl. Because Shirley had always treated her with kindness and affection, they became close companions and collaborators. Class and race differences disappeared in her universe, a truly desired fantasy. Shirley judges people as they were, not as they were labeled by society. Her natural vivacity and interest in everyone was clearly seen. This was an important reason why audiences loved her. She faced adversity with cheerfulness, she included everyone in her world, and she wished for good fortune for all.

Shirley Temple's film characters occupied an interesting space between childhood and adulthood. At times, her behavior accurately demonstrated her little-girl status; at other times, she imitated adults by taking command of a situation. When doing so, she often defied authority and questioned established practices, but paradoxically, she did not appear to be a danger to society or an anarchic force to be contained. She was not a subversive child, merely an assertive one, interested in justice. While goodness looked in danger of losing out to multiple evil forces, Shirley stood for the good and triumphed.

Shirley Temple appeared the embodiment of adult ideals, not adult realities; while depression America was suffering, though still committed to capitalism, rugged individualism, and optimism, Americans continued to express belief in the American way. Shirley provided examples of family hope amidst sorrow; she provided faith in a perfectible society, and pointed to a better future. She could speak frankly, cut through the formal and the artificial dross, and act decisively. Her ability to ameliorate a difficult situation made her a heroic figure.

The child star's persona captivated the American public. Audiences were enthralled by her ability to cope, to adapt, to survive, and to surmount all crises, all catastrophes, and all tragedies. Her resistance to adult authority was always justified and seen as a necessary step toward resolving whatever crisis she faced. No less a personage than President Franklin D. Roosevelt commented, "It is a splendid thing that for just fifteen cents, an American can go to a movie and look at the smiling face of a baby and forget his troubles."[11] As a female child, she reassured both women and men in the audience that family life would continue, that little girls would not threaten the power structure, and that ultimately, the father figure in the movie (and life) would prevail.

Darryl F. Zanuck, the head of Twentieth Century–Fox Studio, often wrote memos regarding the scripts of Shirley Temple movies. He fancied himself an expert on how to use the child most effectively. In April 1938, he advised the writer and producer of a soon-to-be-made Temple film, *Just Around the Corner*, that the script should have Shirley asking a lot of questions. "Shirley," he went on, "is most effective when she asks the kind of questions to which there are no answers one can give a child, like 'Why is the Depression?'"[12] Temple's open and intelligent face and her sincere voice effectively captured her natural curiosity and her child's demeanor. The naive question may typify a child, but adults could not come up with an intelligible answer for themselves either.

During Shirley Temple's glory days and since, many commentators have wondered whether Mrs. Temple was a pushy mother, a show business mother who pressured her little girl into the movies. In recent times, with the new awareness of child abuse, the topic reappears. In the more innocent thirties, the question was framed not as abuse, but rather, as officiousness, unnecessary meddling, and denial of a child her childhood. As writer Gladys Denny Shultz observed, after spending time with Shirley and Gertrude on the movie set and at home,"Many children have been ruined by excessive mother love under such circumstances. The story of Shirley Temple is the story of a mother who turned her anxiety and her absorption . . . into a helpful thing for the child, who did not make her great love an excuse for indulgence."[13]

J.P. McEvoy, who wrote one of Shirley's movie scripts and spent a lot of time with her on the set, also claimed that Mrs. Temple was not a typical stage mother and that "Shirley has been kept unspoiled."[14] Finally, in her 1988 autobiography, which she dedicated to her parents, Shirley Temple stated emphatically that her mother was only a positive influence on her and that she loved to perform. Rather than being forced into a disciplined regimen, she reveled in it. Or so she claimed. In a time when abusive and overambitious parents were much in the headlines, Temple chose not to join the chorus of adults who blamed their parents. In sharp contrast to the daughters of Joan Crawford and Bette Davis, who wrote unflatteringly of their mothers, Shirley Temple preserved only pleasant public memories of her childhood.

In the 1930s, Shirley Temple's incredible fame and fortune was due at least in part to three new features of American life: a low birth rate, thereby increasing the value of the fewer children born; the parental desire to preserve the innocence of the child; and the formation of a national culture, thanks to the radio and movies. Shirley Temple's name and face were immediately recognizable to millions of people who went to the movies regularly. She became a nationally known figure. No matter where they lived, people could see a Shirley Temple movie. Her sunny smile was plastered on billboards on the roads of America, and her face appeared on the covers of magazines regularly. She connected with audiences of all ages and classes. Temple's fame rivaled that of pop culture heroes such as Charles Lindbergh and Greta Garbo. In her nineteen-year career, she earned more than three million dollars, a majestic sum for the period (or for any period). More important, her movies from 1934 to 1940 kept Americans happy as they watched a precious symbol of childhood succeed in every venture. With Shirley around, there would always be a happy ending.

The ideology of child as savior offered a powerful additive to the mix that led to Shirley Temple's success. An innocent child can navigate through the corruptions and catastrophes caused by adults. The precious child, who could also save the situation, as Shirley did in every movie, became a dynamic combination. In the crowds that gathered to see a Shirley Temple movie, there were more adult men than women, more adults than children. How could a little girl inspire such love and such a following? Why did mothers all over America style their daughters' hair into exactly fifty-six curls, just like Shirley Temple's? Why did her polka-dotted dress become the fashion setter of the period and start a children's fashion industry? Why, in other words, did Shirley Temple, rather than any number of other child stars, become the fabulously successful Shirley Temple?

Contemporaries labeled Shirley Temple unique; she was immediately placed, by publicists and fans alike, in a category all her own. It was assumed that Shirley was inimitable. Her sweet, self-assertive personality always conveyed a sense of optimism and a ready smile to everyone around her, thereby capturing the public's imagination and heart at precisely the moment they needed an inspired and hopeful symbol. The joining of movies, publicity, the depression, and particularly the rise of the children's movie genre enabled someone, and in this case the someone was Shirley Temple, to engage the movie audience. It is not easy, or even possible, to identify the precise reasons why she and only she would inspire the popularity she did. Other stars shared many personality traits, but few rivaled Temple's success. Elizabeth Taylor came onto the scene as a lovely twelve-year-old near the end of the decade, but achieved her greatest fame as an adult star. No other five-or six-year-old gave Temple serious competition.

Shirley Temple was a symbol of the importance of the child in American culture. This was her greatest achievement and her great power. Children are our future, and in that sense, they are our last chance, our concrete evidence of accomplishment. They are our immortality. This idea is not tied to any time period or any particular problem. It is a universal view held by adults in all cultures, but it had particular resonance during the depression. The innocence, freshness, and hopefulness of a child inspires adults to act decisively and to persist when necessary. In Temple's case, she combined the qualities of a child with the audacity, intelligence, and drive of an adult. Her problem-solving abilities rivaled any adult's; her willingness to tackle extremely difficult problems may have been motivated by a child's naïveté, but her ingenuity appeared adultlike.

A little girl, rather than a little boy, possessed the endearing qualities necessary for adulation: Her audacity could and would be tamed, unlike an obstreperous Huck Finn type. Little girls, little mothers, remain anchored to the home, to the tried and true, even when they temporarily venture away. A female child, then, had the power to assure everyone's future in a way that a boy child could not. Shirley always stood for order, the home, and family values. She brought husbands and wives together, she reconciled adult differences, and she used the female qualities of negotiation, compassion, and understanding to do so. A cute little boy who acted rebelliously would have been viewed as a social threat to the audience, to both mothers and fathers, who feared the unbridled energy of boys. Girls were not to be feared, only loved.

Shirley Temple, though surrounded by many other child stars, moved away from the pack of little girl stars and distinguished herself as the indubitable first and only child star to be the top box office draw and the top choice of the motion picture exhibitors from 1935 to 1938. Exhibitors competed for every Shirley Temple movie because they knew that they would be assured of a good audience that week. Temple's cuteness, her talent, and her lovely personality offered audiences the child everyone wanted, while her child's wisdom offered answers to parents. Her rebelliousness was always presented for a good cause so that the social order was never threatened.

All of her movies blended into one. It was the sameness of the plots, the sameness of the Temple persona, that drew audiences to her films. *New York Times* film critic Frank Nugent wondered "why they bother with titles, or with plots either for that matter. . . . The sensible thing would be to announce Shirley Temple in *Shirley Temple* and let it go at that."[15] The plots, characters, and settings of her movies were irrelevant. Nugent, however, missed the point. It was precisely the predictability of the plots and the certainty that little Shirley would succeed that kept audiences coming. What was important was the power of Shirley Temple's personality; she was the ultimate problem-solver. In an uncertain world, the Shirley Temple world was predictable, knowable, and desirable.

Little Shirley reformed criminals, got drinkers to quit, and reunited husbands and wives. No social problem was too tough for her. She never lost her spunky nature or her cool demeanor. She assured her viewers that all would be righted in an off-balance world. Shirley Temple's movies confirmed one of our most wished-for fantasies: all human problems have solutions as long as everyone displays goodwill and determination. The individual makes a difference and the child individual, given her innocent nature, could aid corrupt adults. Error could be erased and replaced with goodness; common sense could surmount adult deceit and machinations.

In *The Little Princess,* for example, the movie took place during the Boer War in the late 1890s, and Shirley (Sara) had to stay in an English boarding school (her mother is dead) while her officer-father went off to fight the Boers. She had to be a "good soldier" while he was away and do her father proud. We could count on Shirley to do just that. The 1930s audience watching a movie about the 1890s easily transferred the human qualities displayed by our young heroine to their time and circumstance. Similarly, the Civil War setting of *The Littlest Rebel,* seemingly far removed from the depression, was really quite close in mood. Everyone could rely on Shirley to show them the way to withstand the many travails they faced in difficult times. The perfect fantasy world created in a Shirley Temple movie appealed enormously to movie audiences, especially to adult men in the audience, who were needy and eager for simple solutions to unemployment, family tensions, and a personal sense of failure.

Shirley's ever-present smile, her bouncy walk, and her active nature exuded self-confidence to a doubtful audience. If adults could recapture the child in them, if they could remember their innocence, their goodness, and their cooperative spirit, then they could repair the damage of their lives. The child's qualities of faith, loyalty, and trust in loving adults offered guidance and emotional comfort to troubled adults. For children watching her movies, her success and her effectiveness surely appealed. Adults listened to Shirley Temple; they took her advice. Children had to feel enormous satisfaction to know that at least one child had the respect of adults; one child, if she were imitated, could influence a parent, a teacher, or another adult.

Perhaps, children made fun of Shirley's eternal goodness and her eternal success. Certainly, both adults and children could see her as the contrast, the counterpart, to their lives and hopes. They may have felt that Shirley was too good, too pure, too successful. They may have relished their difference. They could have taken pleasure in their rebelliousness and carved out their separate identities from the pure model of Shirley Temple. The kids in the audience could have had it both ways: they could have dreamed about a world in which they were the heroines/heroes and everything always came out to their satisfaction while departing from conventional behavior to defy the too-good image of the Shirley Temple character. Adults may have imagined themselves in the decisive central role played by Shirley and relished the successful outcome.

While film critic Frank Nugent complained about the sameness of all of Shirley Temple's movies, he failed to grasp the rich and paradoxical nature of her persona. She was innocent, yet wise; a child, yet responsible. Temple's movie character embodied both childish and adult qualities, the ideal and the real traits of both children and adults. She could be disobedient, yet ultimately justified in her actions, the ideal fantasy. She could have a temper tantrum, a typical childish action, followed by an ingenious adult behavior. She could be frank, but also calculating and cunning. It is precisely the versatile array of human qualities that Shirley displayed that made her enormously appealing to large and diverse audiences. In this sense, she was everyperson, child and adult.

The father-daughter connection was a primary one in all of Shirley Temple's movies. Mothers were often absent. Shirley may have had to reform her irresponsible father or father figure in the movie, but the basic bond of love and affection was always evident. Daughters can correct their fathers in ways that sons cannot. Sons and fathers are often competitors; daughters and fathers are always loving companions. Fathers needed bolstering in the 1930s, and what better place to receive it than from a loving daughter? Wives can be worriers, pessimists, and fatalists, but daughters are eternally supportive, optimistic, energetic, and hopeful. Daughters give aid without analysis, comfort without criticism. Shirley Temple's heroines appealed to adult men enormously. The lines of adult men waiting to see Shirley Temple movies, often with their daughters at their side, attested to her influence.

Mothers might have enjoyed taking their children to her movies to show them how to behave. Or they may just have loved the sheer radiance of her personality and, by imitation, hoped that their offspring would act accordingly. So mothers bought Shirley Temple clothes and Shirley Temple dolls and Shirley Temple cut-outs for their daughters. And mothers curled their daughters' hair like Shirley Temple's. Over the years, Shirley Temple granted 163 licenses for products bearing her name and face. Children played with the dolls, wore the polka-dotted dresses, imitated her hair style, and participated in a behavior that has continued: fans demonstrating their loyalty to their favorite star by purchasing whatever goods are identified with the star. In the 1930s alone, more than one and a half million Shirley Temple dolls were sold. Today they are collectors' items selling for $595 to $925, depending on their condition.[16]

The commodification of Shirley Temple is, of course, a phenomenon that our generation knows only too well. The familiar faces of celebrities appear on billboards, commercial products, and television commercials. The quick saturation of the consumer market with Shirley Temple paraphenalia ensured her success, while the close identification of the star's persona, attitudes, values, and behavior with a variety of products guaranteed her, her family, and the manufacturers and producers financial profit. Though child labor laws existed in the 1930s, movie stars were given special exemptions; Temple's movie studio provided a tutor, but school became a secondary consideration to her film career. Shirley Temple, unlike other child stars, never lost her freshness and her sunny disposition. Like the adult image of the womanly Mary, she remained pure forevermore. Her parents did not exploit her, and she seemed to make the transition from star to citizen with greater ease than most in her situation.

The Temple phenomenon reached across the globe during the 1930s and continued to have an effect on girls growing up a generation later. Twelve thousand of her photos were sent out each month in answer to requests from all over the world. Hawaiian crowds greeted Shirley Temple when she visited in the 1930s, and African American activist Angela Davis's mother curled Angela's hair into fifty-six curls when she was growing up in the 1940s.[17] Actress Shirley MacLaine was named after her as were many, many not-so-famous children. Fan clubs, which became a major fact of celebrityhood in the 1930s, formed all over the world for Shirley Temple admirers. In 1968, when Shirley went to Czechoslovakia as a United States representative to an international meeting, she met members of the original Shirley Temple Club in Prague. According to one estimate, nearly four million people belonged to her fan clubs worldwide. The 1990s have seen a renaissance of interest in Shirley Temple with her dolls and cut-out books reappearing. The perennial need for children to play with dolls and possibly to identify with a child doll, may explain her return. But Shirley Temple could never regain the status she once occupied. The 1930s was a specific historical time with specific needs. Sound movies gave Americans the exciting opportunity to witness a singing, dancing six-year-old darling whose presence always turned a catastrophe into a happy ending, the essential wish of all Americans. She tap-danced with Bojangles Robinson and sang the "Good Ship Lollipop." She wore navy uniforms and catapulted sales for children's clothing.

Her stardom did not survive the 1940s, but neither did her childhood. She was seventeen years old when World War II ended and she announced her engagement to Jack Agar, a soldier. During the war, she had visited USOs to much acclaim and answered letters from servicemen. To raise money for the new world organization, the United Nations, she donated seventy-five of her movie dresses for an auction.

Shirley Temple did her part for the war effort, dutifully maintained her cheery persona through depression and war, and now made the transition to private citizen. Though she made a few films as a young adult, she never repeated the spectacular success she had enjoyed as a child star. Like silent screen star Mary Pickford, audiences wanted their child stars to remain children; they would never accept them in mature, adult parts. Temple retired from filmmaking at the age of twenty-one.

As an adult, Shirley Temple Black (she divorced Agar and remarried) became active in public life. With her second husband Charles Black, she had two more children and remains happily married at this writing. Through her activity in the Republican Party (she ran unsuccessfully for Congress in 1967), she received a number of presidential appointments: first, as the first woman delegate to the UN (1969–70); then, as ambassador to Ghana (1974–76); and then, as chief of protocol (1976), the first woman to hold that position. In 1989, President Bush appointed her ambassador to Czechoslovakia, a country she had visited during its difficult days in 1968. By the early 1990s, Shirley Temple Black had spent twenty years in diplomacy, more than she had spent in Hollywood. During President Reagan's years in office, she cochaired the ambassadorial training seminars and, in 1989, received an honorary Foreign Service Officer award from the State Department, the only nonprofessional to attain that award.[18]

In 1992, two television documentaries were made on Temple's career, evidence of her enduring fame. Further, writers with different perspectives have explored her 1930s films to illuminate their respective theses. A child star ignites curiosity and questions. Critic Bret Wood, for example, looked at the *Baby Burlesks* in an essay on the Lolita syndrome and argued that all of the children played "seasoned trollopes," though he grudgingly acknowledged that none of the later Shirley Temple movies were vulgar. But, he asserted, "there is evidence of sensual exploitation and significant elements of sexualization at the hands of various studios."[19] This judgment, it seems to me, is more reflective of a 1990s mentality than of a 1930s worldview.

Revisiting Shirley Temple's films for present purposes rather than to recreate the period in which they were made is a good example of bad history. Other writers have gleaned different messages from the movies. Film critic Jeanine Basinger saw Temple's films as "woman's films. She is the center of the universe in them, and her concerns are always related to love, family, choices, and other usual things."[20] This general appraisal, of course, placed the emphasis on Shirley as a little mother, a prototypical female fulfilling woman's traditional role in life. The child as child disappears, overtaken by the child as female because she performs functions similar to those of adult women. Though I have already suggested that only a little girl could successfully appeal to both adult men and women during the depression, the little girl part cannot be overlooked. The novelty and the familiarity of a little girl solving a family crisis, talking to President Lincoln, and behaving as the stoic through every travail was what made the persona so powerful and effective. And we can never forget the consistently charming personality of Shirley Temple. Watching her movies at the end of the 1990s (and Twentieth Century–Fox has made that easy by releasing all nineteen of her movies on video) remains an enjoyable experience.

In 1990, Gerald Early, an English professor at Washington University in St. Louis, sat down with his two daughters (ages seven and ten at the time) to watch Shirley Temple movies. He explained, "The project appealed to me because I felt I could share something with my children while exercising parental control."[21] Early, an African American, was appalled by the fact that his daughters admired Shirley Temple's hair enormously. While he tried to lecture them on how blacks were treated in 1930s Hollywood, the girls laughed at the clowning of Stepin Fetchit and were charmed at Shirley's antics. After they watched all of the movies three times, his daughters announced that they wanted to straighten their hair. Linnet, the ten-year-old, answered her father's objections by saying, "I don't think I am Shirley Temple or a white girl, but I want to look like a girl, not like a boy."[22] Their mother supported their decision because she had straightened her hair and believed that it was a form of self-expression. White girls, Mrs. Early reminded her husband, changed their hair color, texture, and style all the time.

Influence is difficult to determine, measure, and control. But the above example offers compelling testimony to Shirley Temple's enduring effect on an unexpected audience. A whole new generation of children and adults are being and will continue to be introduced to Shirley Temple. It is safe to assume that Temple's movies, the cut-out dolls, and future computer games featuring Shirley Temple will be with us in the next century. Audiences will extract new and unexpected meanings from her determinedly cheerful movies, but all will be attracted to her optimism, her good humor, her Mary innocence, and her sense of self—qualities that children and adults need in every generation.

6

Minority Women in Popular Culture

Stereotypes are familiar features of popular culture. Performers are labeled according to the color of their skin, their ethnic background, or their occupation. In a sense, the triad of images assigned to women, of Mary, Eve, and Lilith, is one form of stereotyping. Women performers offer viewers only a few different but predictable varieties. The very definition of a stereotype is that individuals are more often portrayed as a group member than as a unique individual. Gangsters always appear as crude and cruel, and they always behave callously; mothers sacrifice themselves to their families (until very recently); and children on television usually exhibit innocence, rebelliousness, and unconscious wit.

In 1930s movies, for example, African American women were usually mammies or silly, childlike characters, never responsible and mature women and never romantically involved. These distinct images had to be carved out for them because the Eves and Liliths among African American women actresses would have been too threatening to white society of the time. A beautiful Lena Horne, for example, had a very bad time in 1940s Hollywood because no producer would cast her beside a white man in a romantic role; nor could she star alongside a handsome African American man. The prevailing wisdom of the period was that white audiences, who constituted the overwhelming majority of moviegoers, would not watch a romance between two African Americans. It took many years to break down this stereotypical way of thinking.

Rigid typecasting is usually packaged within accepted and expected formulas, which, because they too are predictable, function as another layer of stereotype; melodramas, westerns, gangster films, romances, and horror films all have conventional and predictable formats. Ask any fan about the general plot of a melodrama or about the expected ending, and you will witness an accurate prophesy. Genres have story lines, characters, and settings that are as rigid and certain as is each stereotype. A whore with a heart of gold and a muscle man as heroic destroyer are tried-and-true formulas that live in each time period of popular culture. Therefore, conventional images of people are encased in stereotypical stories and formulas. Predictable characters are framed by predictable and accepted settings and plots.

In the introduction to this book, I suggest that a woman entertainer represents two texts—her biography and her work—while she operates in two contexts—the genre within which she performed and her contemporary culture. The genre, in this sense, also functions as a stereotype. There are unexamined assumptions about who can star in what kind of vehicle. Women stars, based upon their physical characteristics and personalities, are cast accordingly: a breathy, buxom Marilyn Monroe may be placed in a comedy but never in a tragedy. Monroe's sexy body doomed her to playing the Eve, albeit the sweet, funny Eve. Innocent looking women, by contrast, become Marys in melodramas or comedies but never Eves in any genre. African American women in the movies, until very recently, could not even enter these conventions. As already suggested, Lena Horne, a beautiful light-skinned singer and actress in the 1940s, had a frustratingly brief career in Hollywood because filmmakers feared a racist reaction if they placed her in a romantic part. Moviegoers in the American South would not attend a movie featuring an African American woman (or man) in the romantic lead.

Genre and stereotype go hand in hand. The viewer follows the predictable script with the formula genre providing the expected plotlines. The star operates within this comfortable framework. This is not necessarily a criticism; rather, audience members gain enormous pleasure from the very predictability of the heroines functioning as stereotypes within the formulas. Though the romance always has misunderstandings and miscommunications as the essential core of the story, the fan can be assured that all difficulties will be overcome by story's end. It is this certainty that keeps viewers coming again and again to witness the same story. Surely this delicious paradox is appreciated by the fan. It is the sameness, the certainty of outcome, that ensures loyalty to the genre.

Similarly, adventure stories guarantee a male hero saving a vulnerable heroine, a theme audiences never tire of. A woman blues singer, by definition, will sing of faithless lovers and heartbreak. By joining the blues club, performer and viewer agree to the terms of the contract. The narrative of the song, the TV domestic comedy, and the melodramatic movie shape every character's role. Much of the world of popular culture is based upon these assumptions. Just as any building requires a sound foundation, so too does the sturdy world of entertainment. Unconventionality upsets the universe, questions its underpinnings, and challenges established authority—not a desirable state of affairs for the suppliers of popular culture. Paradoxically, audiences crave diversity within this yearning for order. Thus, most generic material offers a few (though predictable) variations within each dominant stereotype. The paradox of change within sameness seems to capture the persistent need for certainty along with the counter need for novelty. Women's roles as sweet young things (Marys) may also contain dashes of boldness; sexual temptresses (Eves) may occasionally win the good guy; and independent women (Liliths) can succeed or fail depending upon the circumstance. Underlying the variety, of course, the women are still ruled by the men and the patriarchal authority system is undisturbed.

Minority women, however, are given less maneuverability, less room to explore the limited stereotypes available to women. Historically, minority women have had far fewer possibilities for artistic expression. If white women stars are bound, minority women stars are bound and gagged. Hollywood producers during the golden years of the thirties, for example, placed all African American women in roles as mammies or as tragic mulattas.[1] Hispanic and African American women fell under the dual stereotype of minority peoples and women. As described in earlier chapters on African American women entertainers, all minority women suffered from the general portrait of their racial group while experiencing the added burden of being women.

Hispanic women were and are a particularly problematic group for Hollywood image makers. They are on the other side of the "other," more foreign than African American women and more recent arrivals onto the American scene. In the 1930s, when American movies were exported to Latin America and more Mexicans came to California, Hollywood and Washington, D.C., wanted Latin actors and actresses to appear on the movie screen for obvious commercial reasons. President Franklin D. Roosevelt introduced a good neighbor policy toward Latin America and Hollywood took notice. But the parts available to Latinos were limited and predetermined. The men were generally characterized as "Latin Lovers" (Cesar Romero and Gilbert Roland come immediately to mind), while the women became either singing/dancing machines or screechy lovers. They sometimes offered comic relief, simply because their English was accented.

The career of Lupe Velez is a case in point. Born Maria Guadalupe Velez de Villalobos in San Luis Potosi, Mexico, on July 18, 1909, Velez came to California in the twenties, working as a salesgirl and then a dancer before she appeared in her first film in 1927.[2] The following year, in a real life script that rivaled Hollywood's, she attracted a great deal of notice for her performance in *The Gaucho*. MGM signed her to a five-year contract. She seemed, at least for a brief time, the classic Horatio Alger heroine: the poor but talented young woman who made good. In an early interview in July 1928, she appeared as a very sweet, self-confident but naive newcomer. Reporter Gladys Hall quoted her words, illustrating her accented English. When asked if she were awed by Hollywood, she was quoted as saying: "Why I be ascurt of anything?" and later, demonstrating her directness and honesty, "Why I not say so when so it was?"[3]

On the silent screen, Velez portrayed the attractive Latin lover; her flashy eyes and attractive figure became her chief assets. Typical of white Americans' stereotypical characterizations of Hispanic women, Lupe Velez was portrayed as earthy, sensual, and fiery. Her essence defined her. She was pure instinct. Because the films were silent, her voice and accent played no role in her performance. Rather, her exaggerated movements of eyes and body expressed her peripatetic manner. With the advent of sound movies, audiences could hear the spirited but accented words of Velez. Just as Desi Arnaz's Cuban accent was viewed as comical on television, so Velez's Mexican accent became the basis for jokes in her movies.

Lupe Velez's limited success in Hollywood was no accident. Nor was the timing for her arrival. As suggested, studios were interested in selling their movies around the world, including in Latin America. However, moviemakers, confident in their cultural superiority, never recognized the obvious insult of placing Latin stars in predictable roles. One could argue that stereotype shaped all scripts and stars, so why should Hispanics be an exception? A quick rebuttal, however, would note that the image of Latins narrowed the lens even further on their possible portrayals. The simple assumption was that chauvinistic Latins would run to see any movie starring a Latin. So Gilbert Roland played the romantic lead in numerous movies while Hispanic women stars occupied three dominant roles: sultry Eves (Dolores del Rio), comic relief (Carmen Miranda), or screechy women issuing malapropisms in heavily accented English (Lupe Velez).

Velez's portrayals combined aspects of the Eve with the comic; she was attractive and popular and insofar as she portrayed a sexy lady, she fit the traditional Eve image. However, Velez became the butt of jokes in many of her movies because of her misuse of English. Her accented English and her scripted malapropisms became grist for the humor mill. Examples of Velez movies in the thirties include *Kongo, Hot Pepper,* and *Strictly Dynamite.* The *New York Times* film critic, Mordaunt Hall, described Velez's portrayal of Pepper as someone "who displays a good measure of audacity, recklessness and extraordinary vitality."[4] In the 1939 movie, *The Girl from Mexico,* Bosley Crowther of the *Times'* wrote about the frantic pace of the movie, which he blamed on Lupe Velez. "Lupe pepping it up, flinging madly about in all directions and screeching like a parrot"[5]

The frenetic pace in many of Velez's movies, though clearly evidence of the narrow vision of the producer and director, was blamed on Velez's performance—as though Latin women were congenitally incapable of acting in other than a rhumba-styled fashion. Latin American music, first popularized in thirties movies became a regular feature, with all Latins dancing the tango, the rhumba, and the mambo. The image of constant motion, both the body and the mouth moving, reinforced the view that, Lupe Velez, was pure instinct, animal energy ever on display. This narrow characterization ultimately trapped her.

From 1939 to 1943, Velez made a series of six "Mexican Spitfire" movies for RKO. In *The Mexican Spitfire's Baby* (1941), for example, you hear Lupe, known as Carmelita in the movie, say things like "I have too much appetite to be hungry," and "You keep my business out of your nose." She is the comic relief, the foreigner whose fractured English is always a source of humor. But, like Gracie Allen, her malapropisms often revealed interesting and thought provoking truths. In one scene, the aunt said, "We are living in a fool's paradise." And Carmelita replied, "We can move." ·

When she wasn't corrupting the English language in this series, Lupe was screaming undecipherable words. She was hot-tempered, short-tempered, and ill-tempered, according to this portrayal. She was, in short, the stereotypical Latin woman. Carmelita was married to an Anglo but seemed decidedly out of place in his world. She was the classic "other," the marginal woman who was both desirable and repugnant to her Anglo lover. While her difference was seen as exotic and appealing to her husband, it also made her unsuitable for respectable "American" society. The husband, played by Buddy Rogers in this movie, seemed uncomfortable relating to her, as if she were a bomb about to explode. Yet the marriage persisted, despite its turbulent quality. And the silly plot was resolved happily after mistaken identities were corrected and marital balance was restored. ·

After six pictures with the same characterization, Lupe Velez must have felt frustrated and bound to a very limited image. Her 1933 marriage to Johnny Weissmuller, Hollywood's Tarzan, ended in divorce in 1939. An unwanted pregnancy led to her suicide on December 14, 1944. She was thirty-five years old. Lupe Velez's brief career in Hollywood and her tragic end demonstrate deep personal problems and frustration with the narrow range offered her in the movies. The stereotypical roles available to her, the lack of progress in her professional life, and an unhappy personal life resulted in a premature death.

The small imaginations of screenwriters and the accepted prejudices of the moviemakers made Lupe Velez and her sister Latin actresses unable to shape their own images or even to operate in a broader universe of traditional Eves, Marys, or Liliths. You don't see a Hispanic Hepburn or Russell; nor do you see a Latin carry on Mary Pickford's tradition. (Ironically, Velez adored Pickford and said that she had helped her adjust to 1920s Hollywood.) Velez had no control over her films because she was under contract to a studio and had to play in the movies assigned. More significant, even as a free agent, she would have had no greater choice of roles.

The unwritten but powerful rules that shaped movies and American society prevailed. Anglo-Americans, the major purchasers of movie

In a typical Hollywood pose, Lupe Velez shows off her pet cheetah.

tickets, liked to laugh at Spanish Americans speaking English. Latinos did not join in the laughter. The 1930s and 1940s were not far removed from vaudeville, slapstick, and crude ethnic humor. Labeling immigrant groups and highlighting their weaknesses received an amused response from multiple audiences. However, while 1910–19 vaudeville made fun of all newly arrived immigrants, 1930s Hollywood cast its narrow eye primarily on Latinos and African Americans.

Lupe Velez fit the stereotypical bill for her cultural group. As a woman, she combined physical beauty and accented English with an assumed shrillness. Presumably, the Latin woman was a fount of boundless energy who was either dancing or shouting the whole day long. It is depressing to note that in 1995, Rosie Perez, a young Hispanic actress, reprised the Lupe Velez persona in a movie called *It Could Happen to You*. As the wife of the hero, she screamed her way through her role, offering a very unsympathetic and single-note characterization. Probably, Perez had never heard of Lupe Velez, but unwittingly she was reinforcing that negative stereotype. The screenwriters' cultural universe did not admit complex or diverse roles for Latin women, nor had it changed substantially since the 1930s.

Watching *The Mexican Spitfire's Baby* in the late 1990s is a painful experience. The highly exaggerated style of Lupe Velez's performance becomes a grotesque caricature. Did Velez know that she struck such an extreme pose? Was she a participant, a self-creator of the parody? Her gestures seem more befitting her silent film experience than sound movies. The only consolation is that all of the participants in the film acted in a gross and hammy manner so that no one was immune. Leon Errol's dual role as her uncle and an English duke was equally ludicruous, and the mistaken identity premise of the movie was laughable. Similarly, Buddy Rogers's extremely dense persona did not elicit admiration. In short, the Anglos looked equally silly. But the sameness of Velez's roles in every movie she made rises above the silliness of this particular film. It speaks to the larger issue of how persistent stereotypes can be, how vital they remain, and how difficult it is to remove them from public consciousness.

Lupe Velez's poor reception in Hollywood was shared by other Spanish speaking actresses. Carmen Miranda, who appeared in fourteen movies during the 1940s and early 1950s, usually wore elaborate headgear made up of bananas, apples, and oranges; she had to navigate with this unwieldy fruit basket on her head. In *Weekend in Havana,* for example, she was Rosita Rivas dancing with harvest baskets on her head. In *The Gang's All Here,* Bosley Crowther noted that she "wiggles at random but keeps her skyscraper hats firmly balanced."[6] When she wasn't dancing with heavy weights on her head, she was being "peppery" in her performance. In true stereotypical fashion, the Latin woman was always moving at a fast pace, smiling from cheek to cheek, and offering comic relief to the Anglo stars of the production.

Dolores del Rio, a beautiful, sultry star whose "ebony eyes" were often referred to in the film reviews, was presented as a decorative object, a lovely vision who allured men and provided the male audience with a visual delight. In a Busby Berkeley musical, *In Caliente,* a man sang, "Muchacha, at last I've gotcha where I wantcha, muchacha."[7] This tortured lyric, which trivialized both English and Spanish, aptly illustrates the oversimplified and plain silly manner in which the Hispanic woman was presented. Del Rio's roles were always the same; the locale and costume changed but her basic persona as the tempting Eve never did.

Though more familiar, the story regarding African American women stars in Hollywood is no better. As Donald Bogle, Thomas Cripps, and others have pointed out,[8] the mammies, the sirens, and the tragic mulattas dominated Hollywood's depictions of black women since sound movies started in the 1930s. The tragic mulatta is a particularly interesting example of an "acceptable" image for African American actresses. The mulatta, light-skinned with a white ancestor in her past, was doomed to failure as she straddled two worlds, accepted by neither. Often, she yearned to be white, only to be discovered by suspicious whites; passing into the white world was not to be.

Ethel Waters, one of America's great African American entertainers, could be a successful blues singer, but when she went to Hollywood, the only role open to her was that of the classic mammy. A fattened up Louise Beavers, another great actress, could fill that role too, but no screenwriter imagined a larger universe for black actresses. The terrible irony of portraying black women as mammies to white women's children was lost on the moviemakers. African American filmmakers, though few in number, often followed the stereotypical treatment of black entertainers. One critic, writing in *Crisis,* the journal of the National Association for the Advancement of Colored People (NAACP), lamented the fact that "the films produced by Negro companies fail miserably because their producers simply ape white movies."[9]

The career of Pam Grier offers a tantalizingly different image of a black woman on screen, a strong Lilith/Eve. Born on May 26, 1949, she represents a later generation and presumably a different time in race relations. Grier spent her early years in Winston-Salem, North Carolina, where her father was an Air Force mechanic. The family moved to Europe when she was five years old.[10] They lived on various military bases for the next nine years. Upon their return to the United States, the Griers settled in Denver. Pam Grier said later that her experiences in Europe gave her a different perspective on race and sex relations in America. "Society has not had a tremendous effect on how I accept myself."[11] Her mother once told her, "Use your own strength and no one will ever be able to take advantage of you. When you allow someone to take advantage of you it is another form of slavery."[12]

While participating in a beauty contest in Denver, she met the man who would become her agent, Dave Baumgarten. Her first job was as a secretary at American International Pictures, run by Roger Corman. In 1972, she won a part in the movie, *Black Mamma, White Mamma* and the positive public response led to a series of films that joined other so-called "blaxploitation" films. This subgenre of action movies starred African American heroes and heroines who were always violent avengers of criminals and determined eliminators of the bad guys. Grier described her role in these movies this way, "So all you see is *bang, bang, bang,* shoot 'em-up, tits and ass, *bang, bang, bang,* shoot 'em up, tits and ass."[13] Though she mocked her movie image, she really was breaking new ground—an attractive African American woman as sexy adventurer.

The initial success of this new subgenre ensured many examples of the same essential story. With Fred Williamson or Richard Roundtree as the male lead, Pam Grier became the female counterpart of the macho destroyer of all evil. For a few years, from 1972 to 1976, moviegoers saw Grier, a tall (5'7"), statuesque, brown-colored woman, exude confidence and strength in her very appearance. Posters announced her role in this way: "Meet the Godmother of them all— Coffy—and she'll *cream* you!"[14] In that film (1973), which defined this miniboom of black woman as Lilith, Grier played a nurse, Coffy, whose sister was hooked on drugs. Grier was bent on revenge and revenge she got. In an action film much like the multiple Clint Eastwood and Charles Bronson offerings on the same theme, our heroine destroyed enemy after enemy. By film's end, she had killed nine bad guys.

Throughout, she justified her actions by noting that no one else was eliminating the scum and she felt as if she were in a dream when she pulled the trigger. Coffy's world was surrounded by corrupt cops and corrupt politicians. White cops were on the take, as was her lover, a black politician who posed as an idealist. The only potential hero, a black policeman, was blown away by the bad guys. Coffy had to assume power and control in this decadent world with no visible heroes. She had to fill the vacuum, take charge, and bring purity out of the dirt around her. Pam Grier effectively fulfilled the audience's need for a moral catharsis. The formula of this film was so successful that it was quickly followed with imitators; Grier starred as Foxy Brown and Sheba, Baby, roles in movies that grossed millions and ensured her an audience for the role some called "Super Bitch."

Grier, a very attractive actress with a beautiful and athletic body, used her sexuality to attract and entice the evildoers. As a traditional Eve, she snared them into her nest, only to destroy them. She was an independent Eve, however, a woman who knowingly took the law into her own hands in order to cleanse the world. In a desperate world, where the police were often corrupt, the unspoken rationale for her behavior was that vigilante justice was the only justice available. She was a superwoman, not a superbitch, who stood for the only law and order around. At the end of *Coffy*, Grier walked the beach at night alone, uncaught and seemingly untamed. She was not subject to anyone's system of justice; because the establishment's law system collaborated with the drug dealers, she was obligated to create her own law and become the judge and executioner.

In interviews, Grier defended her role as superavenger, arguing that blaxploitation movies provided work for many African American actors and crew.[15] In the 1930s, W.E.B. DuBois, the editor of the NAACP magazine *Crisis*, had criticized Louise Beavers for playing black maids in Hollywood movies, thereby perpetuating that negative stereotype. Beavers responded that she would rather make a thousand dollars a week playing a maid than ten dollars a week being a maid. In both cases, the women actresses took the pragmatic point of view, arguing that working and providing work for many African American entertainers and crew were worth more than standing on principle.

Grier's movies, in which she played essentially the same role: *Foxy Brown* (1974); *Sheba, Baby* (1974); and *Friday Foster*(1975), appealed to the same fantasy needs served in the white Eastwood and Bronson movies. The plots were the same, with Grier as Foxy playing the typical male role of avenger. Fans were assured that cool Foxy could level a wrestler-shaped male as well as a karate-expert woman. Some movie critics, however, were critical of her role. Alan Ebert, for one, complained that her character lacked "essential humanness." He also said, "Although many Black women probably secretly fantasized being a Pam Grier *type*—one who took no shit from 'the man'—still many others were embarrassed to think the image of the Black woman at that particular time in history was wrapped up in Pam Grier."[16]

Grier herself noted in an interview that she was hurt to think that women could confuse the film image with the real woman: "Why would people think I would ever demean the Black woman?"[17] In the various interviews that Pam Grier gave to magazine reporters in the 1970s and 1980s, she sounded like a highly intelligent and opinionated person. In the interview with Ebert, for example, she commented that men should not treat her like her fictional character Coffy and that she had no problem separating out her film persona from the real one. "Sex," she said while discussing everyone's favorite subject, "isn't something to be taken for granted. I need to feel good about me, about the man I am with, before sex can feel good."[18] In a 1988 interview, she noted, "Well, society is on its own and I'm on my own."[19]

Grier recognized the fact that her visibility in the public arena, her high profile, made her a reluctant spokesperson for black women in film. But she felt uncomfortable playing that role. "I have paid my dues," she said. "I no longer want to be political. I want to work."[20] Grier was unwilling to criticize Hollywood and its treatment of African American performers because she believed that that was the equivalent of biting the hand that feeds you. She also thought that even her macho movies offered her black sisters a positive role model. She had observed black women in movie theaters slapping their boyfriends on the arm and saying, "Hey, man, the next time you give me trouble, I'm gonna give you trouble the way Pam Grier does. It makes me feel real good."[21]

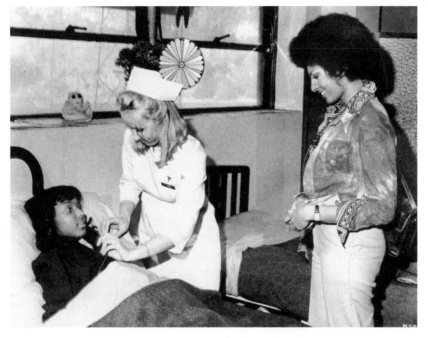

Action heroine Pam Grier (right) shows a softer side in this scene from *Coffy*.

After the novelty of a few Pam Grier movies wore off, however, she lost her market appeal. Charles Bronson and Clint Eastwood stopped making the destroyer movies only when Arnold Schwarzenegger bested them at their own game, destroying more cars, buildings, and people than they had. Fans did not tire of the male action hero but sought other examples of male stars acting out that predictable theme. In contrast, the female action hero is seen as a cute gimmick, good for a few times out but not an enduring genre. In the women's liberation seventies, Angie Dickinson could be a policewoman on television and Pam Grier could destroy drug dealers in a quartet of movies, but the type did not continue into the Reagan eighties.

Neither Linda Hamilton nor Sigourney Weaver, while attractive avengers, could perpetuate the powerful woman wielding mighty weapons for long. Though Pam Grier reprised the role in 1996 alongside Richard Roundtree in a movie called *Original Gangsta,* in which she played a kung fu avenging mother, it is doubtful that this will start a return to the old genre. Grier, however, may benefit from the popularity of thrillers and adventures; in 1996, she made a sci-fi thriller with Jack Nicholson called *Mars Attacks* and in 1997 starred in *Jackie Brown.*

A powerful woman, and a black woman at that, adept at karate and skilled in the use of lethal weapons, served as a novelty but may have posed too great a threat to the mainstream audience. Such an image qualified more as a nightmare than as a desired fantasy. Pam Grier's stardom could only have been a temporary phenomenon, a flash across the screen that offered a breathtaking vision of a beautiful and powerful woman who could not be controlled by men. She outwitted and outgunned them all, too frightening a prospect to continue nourishing. Grier's brief moment of glory may have been Hollywood's experiment with women's liberation gone awry. The male critics, black and white, must have rustled uncomfortably in their seats during *Coffy,* an experience they never wished to repeat.

Tamara Dobson, a black actress who fit into the tough independent persona, played Cleopatra Jones, a special agent of the government with unlimited power to destroy the bad guys, in the movie of that same name. Cleo had the authority to blow away the drug dealers and to eliminate millions of dollars worth of poppie fields. At one point, she told the cops, "My jurisdiction is from Ankara to Watts Tower." Cleo was skilled in karate and appeared, like Coffy, to be invincible, above the law. She was truly a masculine nightmare come true. But again, the genre of black female superagent never blossomed.

Audiences, screenwriters, producers, and directors shared the limited vision that awesome physical power, expert use of weaponry, and sheer audacity were all qualities reserved for men only. Black women such as Pam Grier and Tamara Dobson were the exceptions that proved the rule. Similarly, minority women as a category could occupy only the restricted stereotypes originally designed for them. Any change in the accepted universe would cause chaos, questioning, and uncertainty, undesired qualities in an ordered world. The comfort provided by stereotypes undermines any opportunity for positive change. The resistance to innovative, imaginative, and novel treatments of minority women is strong; the greater impulse for pseudostability and comfort prevails. At least in the fantasy world of the movies, the ending is predictable as long as the cast of characters remains the same.

A further obstacle faced by African American women actresses is the white monopoly on the definition of female beauty. Light-skinned mulattas, because they look more like white women, have a better chance at a Hollywood role than dark-skinned African American women. Pam Grier, an astute commentator on this issue, once told an interviewer, "just because they (black actresses) may have a big nose, thick lips and big behinds, they're not accepted as part of Americana."[22] At century's end, though there are a greater variety of colors and shapes both in the movies and on television, the svelte star still prevails. Oprah Winfrey, Rosie O'Donnell, and Roseanne, all television stars, are the exceptions to the rule.

The dearth of opportunities available for minority women in popular culture is particularly acute; however, the problem can also be seen in the number of opportunities to portray mainstream women. While a small ray of light shone in the 1970s when movies focused on women's lives (a brief nod to women's liberation), the trend quickly disappeared and Hollywood returned to its usual mode of operation: women were either ignored or stereotyped. In 1995, for example, three of the five women nominees for the Academy Award played prostitutes in their award-winning roles.[23] The more things change, the more they stay the same.

Minority women's predictable status in popular culture only underlines the general problem. Though women's lives have changed radically during the course of this century, most particularly in the last thirty years, the men who control the movie studios, the record companies, and the television networks choose to rely on traditional stereotypes. They do not wish to share airtime or screen time. Though loss of power and authority is clearly one of the fears, the larger fear or rather the larger weakness is a lack of imagination. Few executives or few writers, male or female, portray credible women in a variety of human roles.

Creators of popular culture are extremely conservative, governed by the bottom line and afraid of negative backlash. When they venture to include women, they do so in such a way that the men remain the dominant figures. On the new television medical shows, for example, there is one woman doctor, perhaps, but the overwhelming majority of the medical staff remains male. If an African American is included, it is a male before it is a female. Latinos remain the most underrepresented minority group on mainstream television, and they remain invisible in mainstream movies.

While stereotypes are to be deplored, ironically, they offered minority actors and actresses job opportunities in the golden era of Hollywood. As already noted, black actress Louise Beavers preferred playing a maid to being one. Pam Grier would probably express the same sentiments. When one lives in a universe of limited possibilities, one takes whatever roles are available in order to work. A fine actress like Beavers brought dignity to her portrayal of a maid as did many of her cohorts. Similarly, the many actresses who played whores often gave the role distinctive qualities. Stereotypes were stretchable; they may have had boundaries around them, but within the territory, there was room to maneuver.

In this sense, we have come full circle. While I began this chapter defining and implicitly criticizing stereotypes, I end this discussion expressing more positive views on the subject. For women to appear in popular media, and that, after all, is the first goal, it may be necessary to operate within preexisting images. The challenge then is to redefine and reshape the stereotype according to the actress' values, talents, and interests. The Eve as whore has been played in many different ways over the years by a variety of actresses of all colors and backgrounds. When Barbara Stanwyck, for example, who frequently played whores in 1930s movies, spoke, walked, and acted, the viewer knew that she not only accepted her fate but transformed it into one of dignity and courage.

If given the opportunity, a minority actress can transpose a stereotypical image in a film or a television program. Gaining the attention of the audience by first introducing herself within a knowable universe, she can then redefine the stereotype according to her understanding and personality. Unfortunately, Lupe Velez could not rise above the narrow image offered, her whereas Pam Grier made the woman adventurer a distinctive role. The challenge that still remains at the end of the century, just as it was at the beginning, is to allow minority actresses to enter the world of pop culture performance. After they have entered, their possibilities can be various and exciting. But the door must first be opened.

7

Women Comics

For the first time in entertainment history, funny women became accepted performers on twentieth-century stages. Privately, women have laughed and caused others to laugh throughout history, but publicly, humor was men's domain. As Mae West and other bawdy women entertainers effectively demonstrated, women have senses of humor. During the nineteenth century, women wrote humorous prose and poetry, and though many were popular at the time, their reputations did not survive in the way that Mark Twain's did.[1] Western culture, until recently, has ignored women comics preferring to imagine women as humorless and incapable of creating or understanding humor.

In this century's theatrical comic tradition, particularly during the early days of burlesque and vaudeville, men dominated. Women were nowhere to be found. No wonder. The humor was physical, crude, and vulgar, behavior outside the accepted realm for women. Slapstick humor was men's business. Falling on a banana peel, a typical source of guffaws, was decidedly unladylike behavior. The close connection between American cultural values about women and popular culture is nowhere more evident than in the treatment of women in comedy. But as popular theater grew, women became participants, first as the butt of male humor, as the second banana in a duo, and eventually as solo performers with a variety of comic poses.

This chapter will survey examples of women comics in various media. Their images will vary, depending upon the type of humor they practice; women comics can appear in many guises—as Marys, Eves, and/or Liliths. Their presence in the twentieth century attests to the expansion of show business opportunities for women and to the constant search for novelty and new personalities and acts. Further, as society becomes more tolerant, more permissive of what is acceptable behavior for women, the words Sophie Tucker sang to a few can receive a larger audience. Boundaries still exist, of course, and the saltier words of Joan Rivers cannot be aired on network television. But the emergence of this new type of woman entertainer, the comic, is testimony to the growth of women's roles and repertories in entertainment.

The nitwit, for example, a rather unflattering image for women comics, was a Mary. It was an early, permissible form of woman comic. The nitwit often acted childlike, naive, and dizzy. It was no accident that she was often a blonde, allegedly ethereal and out of touch with reality. The nitwit always needed an adult in the form of a male hero to rescue her from her self-made disasters. This comic type, of course, harmonized with accepted attitudes; women as Marys were dependent upon men and often childlike. However, no sooner had this type been created than it was subverted. In an about-face variation, the nitwit outsmarted everyone by her canny logic. From silent film star Constance Talmadge (1899–1973) to radio and TV goofball Gracie Allen (1906–64), the nitwit became a successful comic persona for women.

A beautiful blonde with an elegant face and figure, Talmadge's beauty was compromised by her distracted persona. She played the cute flirt whose seemingly innocent advances always got her into trouble before she was saved by the hero and taught the proper lesson. In the 1923 film *Dulcy*, for example, she made her husband's prospective client engage in rigorous exercise only to discover that he hated athletic activity. Talmadge blended coquettishness with distractedness in her portrayals. She teased men but always acted as if there could never be any adverse consequences to her behavior. In *Her Sister from Paris* (1925), she played a twin who forgot that she was masquerading as her sister and got herself into ridiculous situations. In a role where she was a hapless bandit, *Venus of Venice* (1927), Talmadge entered a fashionable dining room in stolen clothes and sat down next to the woman whose clothes she was wearing. Talmadge's pretty face and absurd actions offered audiences the unexpected contrast that evoked laughter.

In an article she wrote for *Motion Picture* magazine in 1927 called "The Tragedy of Being Funny," Talmadge said that comedy was a very serious business requiring careful preparation and thought: "And in the comedies that I do, which might be called sophisticated stories of modern life, one can't just dash on and be funny. There are subtle shades of humor that have to be caught by the camera, which actually only captures fifty per cent of what the human eye takes in."[2] Talmadge characterized her humor as "refined clowning" and displayed both self-consciousness and an articulate awareness of her actions. According to her view, all human situations are potentially comic; it is the art of the comedian to exploit the humorous possibilities. In a sense, the literary Talmadge contradicted the nitwit Talmadge she portrayed on the screen, though the nitwit persona served her well.

While Constance Talmadge had to display her silliness largely through facial gestures in silent film, sound movies and radio gave nitwit comics rich verbal opportunities. Perhaps the queen of radio nitwitdom was Gracie Allen. Born in San Francisco to a family of vaudevillians, she left school at fourteen and went into show business with her three sisters. In 1923 she met George Burns, whom she married three years later. They formed an act and toured the vaudeville circuit. Eddie Cantor brought them to radio in 1932, and the following year they got their own show, which became one of the best-loved radio programs of all time. Burns and Allen remained on the radio for seventeen years and in 1950 moved to television. Gracie retired in 1958 and died six years later.

Gracie Allen came to personify the ingenuous, sweet woman who marched to her own idiosyncratic tune. Her unpredictable responses to situations always left audiences laughing. George Burns always played the straight man. He fed her the opening lines that resulted in her illogical and unexpected witticisms. Gracie once said to George, "Why, if you don't believe me when I'm telling you the truth, when I'm not telling the truth you might think I was lying."[3] Many of the funny stories concerned Gracie's family, who seemed to be as crazy and unpredictable as she was. In one routine, Gracie told George that she was going to send her brother Willie, who was joining the army, a yo-yo in case he went to Egypt. The following dialogue ensued:

George: I don't understand.
Gracie: Well, you know how lazy he is. He always wants to

Gracie Allen and her husband George Burns became a very popular comic duo, thanks to Gracie's screwball humor.

play with a yo-yo, but doesn't like to move it up and down.
George: I still don't understand.
Gracie: Well, they ride camels there, don't they? and they
sway up and down all the time, so all he'll have to do . . .

The wit of Gracie Allen depended on preserving her naive persona. Only Gracie understood her very special logic. Her angle of vision remained fresh and unique. Another example of her perspective can be seen in the brief interchange Gracie had with Eddie Cantor on his 1931 radio show, "The Chase and Sanborn Hour." Cantor said he wanted to be president of the United States.

Gracie: You can't be president of the United States. My
father told me this morning that he is going to be the
president of the United States.
Cantor: Your father?
Gracie: Yes. My father said, "Gracie, if you can get on the
Chase and Sanborn Hour, then I'll be president of the
United States."

On another occasion, George asked Gracie, "Did you ever hear silence is golden?" Gracie replied, "No, what station are they on?"

Gracie's humor often relied on confusion about words. When George complimented her and called her a wizard, she said, "I'm a wizard?" George wondered aloud whether she knew the word's meaning. "Yes," she answered, "a snowstorm." This, of course, led to further puns on "blizzard" and "lizard." George asked whether something unusual had occurred to Gracie when she was a baby. Gracie had the last line (and the laugh): "When I was born, I was so surprised I couldn't talk for a year and a half." In sharp contrast to the humor of the bawdy woman such as Mae West, the nitwit is innocent, sweet, and charming precisely because she is untouched by worldliness. Though the nitwit is clearly out of fashion today, and for good reason, she occupied an important place in the pantheon of women comics.

A variation of and a refinement on the nitwit type is the screwball, a form that flourished in 1930s movies. The screwball uses idiosyncratic verbal wit with physical comedy, such as making facial grimaces and tripping over her own feet. No one was more identified with this image in Hollywood movies than Carole Lombard (1908–44). (On early television, of course, Lucille Ball was the queen of the genre.) As already noted in the chapter on women movie stars, Lombard came to Los Angeles with her mother and two older brothers when she was seven. At the age of fifteen, she played a lead opposite Edmund Lowe in *Marriage in Transit*. A precocious teenager, she astonished veterans with her ability to ride horses in the cowboy movies and to exchange witticisms with tough and experienced men.[4]

After recovering from an automobile accident in 1925, she returned to moviemaking at Mack Sennett's comedy unit where she learned a great deal about slapstick technique. She made the transition to sound movies and by the mid-1930s, was known as a skilled practitioner of madcap comedies. Among her most notable films were *Hands across the Table, Twentieth Century,* and *My Man Godfrey.* The latter film, made in 1936, is a fine example of the genre.[5] Set in the early days of the depression, the movie featured rich people participating in a treasure hunt as part of a charity event. Lombard played a spoiled socialite who went to the nearest Hooverville (temporary housing set up by unemployed tramps and named disparagingly after President Hoover) to find a treasure. She brought back a homeless man, won the prize, and convinced her father to hire him as their butler. "Can you buttle?" she asked him. The man, Godfrey, became their man and as expected, Lombard fell in love with him, behaved like a silly nitwit throughout, and got what she wanted in the end. When she was not riding a horse into the family library, she was following Godfrey around, nearly driving him crazy with her continuous flow of nonsensical talk. True to 1930s comedies, however, Godfrey was not really a tramp but a Harvard-educated man down on his luck; thus, he was a suitable marriage partner. The rich family was portrayed as eccentric, while Lombard always looked lovely and lovable while practicing her antics.

The domestic comic is perhaps the most popular humorous role available for women and reflects an enduring social image of women. Set in the home, the allegedly natural place for women, and centered on family life with its potential for multiple mishaps, the role is a surefire comic situation. After all, home life isn't, according to this perspective, momentous or as significant as business life, school life, or any other life. Therefore, women's activities in the home are easy comedic targets. Their words can get them into trouble, a variation of the screwball image; or their behavior can be misconstrued and have disastrous consequences that require a husband's skill to mend. It is the trivial nature of domestic life, according to unspoken cultural opinion, that makes domestic comedy possible, indeed probable. In the American cultural lexicon, the home is either a funny place or, in melodrama, the site of emotional land mines. Domestic comedy also preserves the woman's image as essentially Mary, not as sexy Eve, or as independent Lilith.

African American maids on radio programs were one example of the domestic comic. Beulah brought laughs to "Fibber McGee and Molly" and "The Beulah Show." Critic Frank Wertheim called Beulah "a happy-go-lucky maid."[6] Hattie McDaniel, the movie star who won the Academy Award for her role in *Gone with the Wind,* became the radio Beulah in the fall of 1947. The good-hearted mammy became the easygoing domestic comic. Beulah laughed easily and made fun of herself. "I been bendin' over a stove for fifteen years now. (Laughs) The job is new, but the position ain't."[7] In the 1990s, that line would be more rueful than funny. Beulah always behaved congenially to the white family she worked for. On television, two other great African American actresses have played Beulah, the juiciest role available to them: Louise Beavers and Ethel Waters.

Mary Tyler Moore contributed to this genre first by playing the sweet wife on "The Dick Van Dyke Show," and then playing Mary Richards on "The Mary Tyler Moore Show." In the latter program, Mary worked in a newsroom that seemed like a home. All of her co-workers became members of her extended family, and the humor of their personalities and situations made for one of television's most popular and enduring shows. From 1961 until 1966, Moore played Laura Petrie, Dick's wife and mother to son Richie. While Van Dyke, joined by Carl Reiner, Morey Amsterdam, and Rose Marie, were the focus of the show, Moore projected a sweet, wholesome image, and while some humor emerged from her indecisive nature, the ensemble offered multiple opportunities for laughter.

But it was on "The Mary Tyler Moore Show," first premiered in the fall of 1970, that Moore came into her own as a comic actress.[8] Mary began as a traditional Mary, but during the show's seven-year run, she grew into a Lilith. Moore played a thirty-year-old associate producer in a television newsroom. Supported by a superb cast including Ed Asner as her boss, Lou Grant; Valerie Harper as her neighbor, Rhoda; Cloris Leachman as another neighbor, Phyllis; Ted Knight as one of her colleagues; and Betty White as Sue Ann Nivens, the Happy Homemaker for the television station, the newsroom became a substitute family for the group. Audiences identified with Rhoda's efforts to lose weight and find a husband, they laughed at Ted's constant bunglings and arrogance, and they enjoyed Lou Grant's gruff demeanor. Phyllis's pomposity and Sue Ann's pretentiousness gave Mary and Lou the opportunity to express witty and wry observations.

The domestic comedy style of Moore allowed her to be both subject and object in the humor of each episode. She shared her self-doubts, her fears, and her ignorance with her colleagues and her audience. Mary displayed a healthy ability to make fun of herself and to be empathic to the foibles of others. She overcame her diffidence toward Mr. Grant, though she was the only one who called him Mr., got the courage to ask him for a raise, and gradually became more self-confident. Each episode was a masterpiece of comic timing and clever dialogue. In 1977, Moore decided to end the show while it was still successful. Harper, Leachman, Knight, and Asner all went off into other situation comedies created for them, a sure testimony to the popularity of "The Mary Tyler Moore Show."

As historian Paula Fass has noted, "Mary is neither mother nor whore, although she is both supportive and sexually attractive. She is a pal."[9] Mary Tyler Moore's characterization of Mary Richards combined the best aspects of the traditional Mary and Eve images with the newer independent woman. Domestic comedy is interactive, relying upon the combined talents of all the participants. The genius of Moore was in being a distinctive personality while not an overpowering one. The humor arose out of daily living, with each cast member featured at different times. The other women in the cast often exhibited some of the tried-and-true features of comic women: Sue Ann as the nitwit, Rhoda as the self-deprecator, and Phyllis as the sharp tongue.

Beulah and Mary are major representatives of the domestic comic genre, but they hardly encompass the form. Isabel Sanford as Weesie, on *The Jeffersons* is another fine example. Television lent itself to the domestic comic formula, particularly in the years when the sets had small screens and the living room was the primary venue for watching. The interior space of the home, the woman's domain, became the perfect setting for humorous takes on domesticity, a sign of the culture's less than admiring view of women's place. On daytime television, the

Isabel Sanford and Sherman Hemsley starred in *The Jeffersons*, a popular situation comedy show that depicted a middle-class African American family.

melodrama, or soap opera, became the dramatic counterpart to the evening domestic comedy.

Silent comedy and television have been two venues congenial to women as physical comics, an atypical and unusual image. The need for gross physical gestures as well as grace and speed in silent comedy gave women talented in that area an opportunity not seen on the vaudeville stage. Women such as Marie Dressler (1869–1934) could shove men across the stage, throw frying pans at them, and receive blows in turn. Dressler relied on her stoutness, her dark, menacing eyes, and her gruff manner to create laughter. She once said, "I was born homely and for fifty years it has been my lot to make my living on the stage where the first requisite for a woman's success is supposed to be a face that's easy on the eyes."[10] Since her face and figure did not conform to anyone's standard of beauty, she simply made a face, exaggerated her homeliness, and made everyone laugh.

Dressler's persona was usually that of the hapless woman whose yearnings for romance were thwarted. In the Broadway show, *Tillie's Nightmare,* which was later made into a series of movies, she played a drudge who lived in her mother's boarding house and dreamed of a better life. Her fantasies for happiness were viewed as comedic material; when Tillie dreamed of marrying a rich man, going on a yacht, or flying an airplane, the audience laughed uproariously. One contemporary commentator called her a "burlesquer in thought, word, and deed."[11] In films with Mabel Normand and Charlie Chaplin, and later with Wallace Beery, she became a rough and tough brawler who loved to drink. With Beery in *Min and Bill* (1930) and *Tugboat Annie* (1933), this older couple fought and made up, fought and made up. Audiences knew that Min would defend Bill against all outsiders, but they also knew that in her efforts to reform him she would beat him up every chance she got. The humor was physical with objects flying around the room.

One of Dressler's colleagues in the Mack Sennett comedy unit was another physical comic—Mabel Normand. Dressler described her as "vivaciously pretty and mischievous as a monkey." Normand (1893–1930) was the young, athletic variety of physical comic. She was one of the great pantomimists, clowns, and farceurs of silent film. In sharp contrast to Dressler, Normand was slight of build, graceful, and ever in motion. She threw the first cinematic pie into Fatty Arbuckle's face

Marie Dressler's physical comedy made her a favorite with audiences in the early 1930s.

and was considered an equal to Charlie Chaplin in the eleven comedies they made together. At the age of sixteen, Normand went to the Biograph Studio in New Jersey where the famous director D.W. Griffith was in charge. With no stage experience whatsoever, she began making one-reelers for him, one of the few film stars to do so.[12]

At the Biograph Studio, she met Mack Sennett, the film comedy director with whom she made most of her successful movies. In 1911, she appeared in Sennett's *The Diving Girl,* in which she wore a daring costume consisting of full-length black tights. Normand played an adventurous woman who, against the wishes of her cautious uncle, did high dives; during the course of the comedy, she was locked up for her risk taking, only to escape and repeat the feat, thereby providing comedic material for all to appreciate. As an actor in moving pictures, Normand fell into water, flew an airplane (she was the first woman to do so in film), and paraded around in her bathing suit. She was as active as her male companion, running from Keystone Kops, avoiding physical disasters, and looking appealingly helpless when necessary. She behaved like the good sport and the girl next door. She was always willing to laugh at herself as well as at someone else.[13] In a decade of silent film, she made 150 movies.

Television also allowed women to engage in physical humor. The small screen, viewed in the intimacy of the home, resembled the silent film screen and exaggerated the need for dramatic physical gestures to communicate a comedic point. Lucille Ball became the top woman comic in American popular culture for good reason: she successfully combined physical comedy with screwball and domestic comedy on the most pervasive form of entertainment—television. The small screen became the medium most congenial to slapstick women, and Ball became the undisputed queen of television comedy, dominating the field for twenty-five years.

From "I Love Lucy" (1951–57) to "Here's Lucy" (1968–74), she divided her humor between gross hammings and nitwit capers. Lucille Ball regaled generations of television audiences with her sweet deceptions of Desi (her real life and television husband), her awkward efforts at getting and holding a job, and her elaborate conspiracies to fool Desi, usually concocted with the aid of her friend and neighbor, Ethel Mertz. Critic Diana Meehan called Lucy's characterization a "mischievous child-woman," thus capturing her nitwit, screwball, Mary features.[14]

On the set of *Jinx*, Mabel Normand displays the antic comic style that made her as popular as Charlie Chaplin and Buster Keaton during the silent screen era.

Born in August 1911 in Butte, Montana, Lucille Ball later recalled that she never laughed as a child and believed that comedians do not laugh.[15] Despite an unhappy childhood and a bad auto accident as a young woman, she became a dancer in musical theater in the 1920s and then went to Hollywood in the early thirties. In 1941, she married Cuban bandleader Desi Arnaz. "The only spectacular thing I ever did was eloping to Greenwich and marrying Desi. It happened so fast," she later recalled, "he had only time to grab a wedding ring in the ten cent store."[16] Their marriage, in exaggerated comic form, became the material for their very successful television show ten years later. Lucy spent three seasons on CBS radio as the female lead in the situation comedy "My Favorite Husband." On that show, she developed many of the comic mannerisms and themes that would become famous on "I Love Lucy." Her scatterbrained persona and easy ability to cry loudly every time something went wrong became part of her trademark.

The 1951 premiere of "I Love Lucy" featured Lucy and Desi (called Ricky on the show) as a happily married couple. Ricky was a bandleader, later a nightclub owner, and then a TV personality. Lucy constantly tried to inveigle her way onto Ricky's show. The couple lived in an apartment building where their next door neighbors were Fred and Ethel Mertz (played by William Frawley and Vivian Vance). In 1953, when the "real" Lucy became pregnant, this situation was written into the show, and when Desi Junior (Ricky Junior) was born, the show had the largest television audience in the history of the medium to that point. "I Love Lucy" never dropped below third place in audience ratings during its six-year run.

Viewers remained loyal week after week. President Eisenhower changed the date for his presidential address so that it would not conflict with Lucy; Marshall Field's department store in Chicago closed early on Monday nights so everyone could go home and watch Lucy. Viewers remembered their favorite episodes. In the summer of 1958, CBS asked people to send in the name of their favorite Lucy skit as they planned a special to include ten of the most popular. The audience response was so great that CBS ended up including thirteen episodes.

A constant theme on the show was Lucy's efforts to get into Ricky's nightclub and later, his television show. This repetitive theme suggests that Lucy was striving to become a Lilith, her own person with a career and an identity of her own. In one episode, she maneuvered

Lucille Ball as Lucy (second from right) is shown with her husband Desi (known as Ricky on *I Love Lucy*) and their nextdoor neighbors, Ethel and Fred Mertz.

A surprised Ricky looks at Lucy, a chick, and her latest fiasco.

her way onto his show to do a cough medicine commercial only to get drunk sampling the product. Because Lucy seemed more interested in show business than in domestic business, she regularly tried to impress Ricky with her domestic skills, usually with disastrous results. In another favorite show, Lucy decided to bake bread from scratch; she put two whole packages of yeast into the dough and ended up getting pinned to the far wall of the kitchen when the bread was released from the oven. Lucy was not above crushing grapes in her kitchen and getting grape juice all over herself. She never shrank from slipping and sliding, getting smudges on her face, grimacing, and generally using all of her dancer's and comedic skills to turn her attractive self into a harried, disheveled mess.

In 1960, Lucy and Desi divorced in real life, thereby ending one of television's most successful marriages. She returned two years later with "The Lucy Show" in which her children, Lucie and Desi, played roles; the show also included Vivian Vance and Gale Gordon (who played her sour-faced boss). In her next series, "Here's Lucy," she and Gale Gordon were featured. Although these latter two series were popular, they did not match the incredible success of the original "I Love Lucy" show. In the later situation comedies, she relied more on verbal wit than on the physical humor that had been so enormously effective. In some of her early skits, she had mimicked Charlie Chaplin, using her great facial expressions and dancer's body to create comic situations. The 1951–56 shows are still seen on late-night television and cable. Lucille Ball died in 1988.

Carol Burnett (born in 1944), a generation and a half younger than Ball, brought vaudeville to television. Combining the physical humor of Ball with the screwball humor of Lombard, Burnett remained a popular entertainer on prime-time television from 1967 to 1978. Using the variety show format, in contrast to the domestic situation comedy, Burnett surrounded herself with a talented ensemble of comic actors: Harvey Korman, Vicki Lawrence, and Tim Conway. Each week special guests joined them in skits spoofing current movies or old fairy tales. Burnett often sang as well. Her Cinderella character, for example, was a raucous woman with a hangover. She usually deemphasized her pleasant looks, making ugly faces, wearing silly wigs, slouching, and generally appearing as an awkward duckling. As one critic noted, "If she wears a wig, it is invariably snatched off, revealing her own flattened hair beneath. Every crafty thought, base motive . . . and trembling hope is so pitiably naked that it commands excruciating sympathy."[17]

Burnett wore baggy clothes, acted the part of a shrewish wife to Harvey Korman's portrayal of the prissy husband, and generally clowned around for a laugh. Just as audiences remained loyal to Lucy on Monday night, so they tuned in to Burnett's show every Saturday night. No gag, no indignity was below her. At the beginning of every show, coming forward as Carol Burnett and not one of her characters, she spoke directly to the audience. But after that dignified opening, anarchy took over. Burnett, as the quintessential physical comic, purposefully made herself ugly to exaggerate the humor. She grimaced, slouched, fell down, and generally downplayed her pleasant looks to exploit her comic persona.

While all of the comics described had the ability to criticize themselves and look objectively at subjective material, a separate group of women comics can be labeled self-deprecators, women who had the intelligence (a necessary quality for all women comics) to display their weaknesses center stage in their performances. These comics are both the subjects and objects of their work. Self-criticism is a distinctly modern form of humor, and the presence of women in this genre indicates society's willingness to consider women as coequal participants in discussions of human frailty. Self-deprecators can appear as solo artists on nightclub stages, or they can function within a domestic comedy setting. A good example of the latter type is Valerie Harper's role as Rhoda, first on "The Mary Tyler Moore Show," and then on her own television series, "Rhoda."

Harper's humor arose from her self-doubts, her obsessive interest in her appearance, and her dogged determination to get married. She emphasized her low self-esteem, allowing audiences to laugh at her announced weaknesses and vulnerabilities. Women fans could easily identify with the issues she raised, issues they understood only too well. Laughter arose from a sense of sisterhood and perhaps from gratitude that Rhoda said aloud what many women said only to themselves. And she said it in a funny way. When Valerie Harper left "The Mary Tyler Moore Show" in 1974 and began her own series, the opening statement describing herself said it all: "My name is Rhoda Morgenstern. I was born in the Bronx, New York, in December of 1941. I've always felt responsible for World War II. The first thing that I remember liking that liked me back was food. I had a bad puberty, it lasted seventeen years."[18]

As a solo self-deprecator and as an Eve because of her interest in sexual matters, Joan Rivers stands out. Since her first appearance in 1965 on Johnny Carson's "The Tonight Show," she gained popularity in nightclubs and made frequent appearances as host of his show. Rivers's willingness to discuss her small breasts, her inadequate love life with her husband Edgar, and her insecurities made her distinctive. Of course, she also used her wicked wit on others. She insulted actress Elizabeth Taylor in the late 1970s when she was overweight and occasionally took off against politicians and other vulnerable targets. She has said of her comic persona, "I love that woman up there because she's so common and so vulgar. . . . I do all that for shock values, and it really works . . . However, I wouldn't want to be that woman's friend. I wouldn't want her at my dinner party."[19]

Rivers's acerbic humor tested the limits of television's endurance. In this respect, she resembles the bawdy women entertainers and is a bridge to women satirists. She has noted, "You have to be abrasive to be a current comic. If you don't offend somebody, you become pap. I think ten percent of the people should just hate me . . . Humor is tasteless. These are tasteless times. . . . Truth is vicious, but why can't we say it. The question is—who is going to tell the emperor he's not wearing clothes? I think that's my job. I'm expressing what people think—and they love it."[20]

Rivers has always kept an extensive and elaborate card file on her material. She categorized all of her jokes according to subject and found that nothing was beyond the boundaries of her self-defined tastelessness. As a self-deprecator who also attacks everyone else, Joan Rivers also moves into the final category of women comics, the satirists. The best example of independent women in comedy, of Liliths supreme, can be found in this group, the rarest breed of humorist among women and men alike. Satire requires a particularly astute intelligence, knowledge and interest in social conditions, and a bold ability to translate critical opinions into humorous words. All of the women comics described possessed the intelligence essential to satire, but not all favored this form of expression.

Like self-deprecators, satirists can be found in situation comedy or as solo artists. An early practitioner of this genre was Fanny Brice (1891–1951) who performed her clever skits in the Ziegfeld Follies from 1910 to 1923. She created characters and situations that commented on the role of women and on cultural life in New York. As show business historian Robert Toll wrote of Brice's art, "Even in her satires and parodies, she was an eminently humane comedienne, sensitive to the feelings of people and the characters she laughed at."[21] Brice also wrote about her comedic style:

> If you're a comic you have to be nice. And the audience has to like you. You have to have a softness about you, because if you do comedy and you are harsh, there is something offensive about it. Also you must set up your audience for the laugh you are working for. So you go along and everything is fine, like any other act, and then—boom! you give it to them. Like there is a beautiful painting of a woman and you paint a mustache on her.[22]

Brice's ability to spoof popular people, ideas, and shows of her day endeared her to audiences. She had a lovely voice that she used in a conventional way in the first verse; but by the second chorus, she changed her tone, mood, and style. When she sang "I'm an Indian," for example, she dressed in costume as an authentic young Native American woman only to destroy the illusion in the chorus by assuming a Yiddish accent and becoming Rosie Rosenstein, a nice Jewish girl who somehow landed on an Indian reservation.[23] By stepping out of character, she shared with her audience the fact that she was performing and that she was more than the part she played. Brice's satire gently pointed out human weaknesses that she, as a human, shared with everyone else. She became everywoman, whose criticism was constructive, not destructive.

Brice began singing as a child at amateur nights in Brooklyn, where the voluntary contributions of the audience made her a rich little girl. In 1909, while performing in the musical comedy *College Girls,* she was seen by a Ziegfeld representative and was hired for the Follies. At the age of eighteen, she was on her way.[24] Brice's songs became seriocomic routines in which she created a whole story. "Second Hand Rose," one of her greatest hits, described the life of a young woman who always had to settle for used objects. Her father, a dealer in second-hand goods, provided the family's furniture and each member's clothes. The height of indignity, she revealed, was that the man she loved had been married before. Brice often portrayed herself as the hapless victim, a typical comic pose. She became the long-suffering woman. "Oy, How I Hate that Fellow Nathan" was a self-deprecating song in which she described a lover who treated her badly; though he promised to marry her, he told her the month but not the year. Nathan said he would lay down and die for her, but, she sang, he would not stand up and work for her.

Brice sang songs that simultaneously declared woman's love for a man while satirizing the male ego. She could spoof her own devotion in "Cooking Breakfast for the One I Love" or sing it straight in "I'd Rather Be Blue over You than Happy with Someone Else." She counseled her audiences to be brave and to take the good with the bad in "If You Want the Rainbow You Must Have the Rain." In other routines she made famous at the Ziegfeld Follies, Brice satirized the modern dance movement, evangelical preachers, and serious drama. She made fun of the Romeo and Juliet story and mocked doting mothers in "Becky Is Back in the Ballet."

In interviews, Fanny Brice maintained that she could be satirical because she never took herself seriously and never saw herself as above the audience. The same viewpoint was certainly shared by all of the women comics described in these pages. The critics loved Brice; they never tired of describing her as a skillful farceur and a marvelous mimic. Brooks Atkinson of the *New York Times* once wrote, "Fanny is in top form. . . . Toward the end of the first act she is Countess Dubinsky, who right down to her skinsky is working for Minsky, whereupon she performs a hilarious travesty upon the sinful fan dance."[25] Brice's career took a different turn in the 1930s when she went on the radio as a child named Baby Snooks. Through this persona, Brice continued her antic treatment of life. She became the screwball whose youth excused her witless and anarchic behavior. Brice's life and spectacular career were reprised by Barbra Streisand in the movies *Funny Girl* and *Funny Lady*.

Satire had few practitioners on early television. By the 1970s, however, Bea Arthur as Maude, a loud-mouthed, outspoken critic of everything, became a favorite. From 1972 to 1978, the "Maude" show dealt with controversial topics such as abortion, women's rights, racism, and sexuality. Her husband on the show, Walter, played by Bill Macy, was often the butt of her humor. Framed as a domestic comedy, the biting satire borrowed its style from "All in the Family," the pacesetter of the genre. Maude attacked rather than reacted to the humor of others. She appeared as a self-confident, mature woman who had opinions on all subjects. In a sense, Maude is either an example of the success of women's liberation or evidence of the nightmarish extremes to which women's equality led, depending on your point of view.

Bette Midler (born in 1945) offers us a good example of a comic Eve whose career links the past with the present. In the 1970s, no one brought the bawdy woman Sophie Tucker-Bessie Smith-Mae West tradition to life better than Midler.[26] Performing in open-air stadiums, her concerts epitomized the new freedom experienced by young women. She danced, ran, and stood on her head, tantalizing and pleasing her fans, much in the way Eva Tanguay had pranced across the vaudeville stage sixty years earlier. Beginning her career in the late sixties by working as a singer at the gay Continental Baths in New York, Bette Midler learned how to exaggerate, dramatize, and expand her persona. Dressed in vivid colors, furs and frills, black lace corsets, and gold lame pedal pushers, she delighted her audiences with her self-mocking manner. "I am a living work of art," she declared in a way reminiscent of her heroine, Sophie Tucker. Her dirty-lyric songs received uproarious responses. Making fun of macho men and their dubious abilities became standard features of her act. In the intimate setting of a gay bathhouse, of course, like the intimate 1910 nightclub, she could be as ribald and raucous as she liked. On *The Johnny Carson Show*, where she first gained national attention, she had to clean up her act. Later, on the concert stage, she returned to her bawdy ways.

Thanks to video recordings, later generations can witness "The Divine Miss M," as she modestly called herself and her show. In her 1979 show, for example, Midler presented many of her already famous personae, including Delores Del Lago, whom she called the lowest form of show business and the toast of Chicago. In her most recent concert tour of 1993–94, she repeated many of the same routines. Appearing in her mermaid outfit in a motorized chair, she tooted around the stage singing in a screechy voice. Interspersed with her songs (which consisted of blues, bawdy, and rock 'n' roll) was continuous patter. Her three black women back-up singers, she explained in her 1979 show, are called "The Harlettes"; they are a Greek chorus, but, she added, "These girls don't know shit about Euripides but they know lots about Trojans."

Midler made a successful transition to movies with her debut 1979 film *The Rose* which offered her an opportunity to portray an over-the-top rock performer. In 1986, she returned to her comic roots with two successful movies, *Down and Out in Beverly Hills* and *Ruthless People*. Midler occupies a rare position as a bawdy woman entertainer who moved into the respectable popular arena; as a comic whose wit and restless humor suggested bawdiness but did not explicitly state it, she could move into the mainstream. In this sense, she resembles Mae West and her unexpected popularity in movies. At the end of the century, Midler remains a favorite comic star at a time when filmic opportunities for women comics are rare. *The First Wives Club* (1996) reminded her fans as well as audiences who had missed her earlier movies that she still possessed the anarchic humor and sly grin that had made her famous in the 1970s.[27]

All types of women comics, be they Lilith-like satirists, self-deprecating Eves, Mary-like nitwits, screwballs, or physical clowns, share an appreciation of human frailty, of the delicate nature of cultural behavior, and of the need for reform through laughter. In the 1990s, women comics flourish in every venue and every genre. Comedy clubs, TV domestic comedy, and concert halls provide settings for Ellen DeGeneres, Brett Butler, Roseanne, and many others who ply this trade. It no longer seems strange, incongruous, or inappropriate to hear women practice every form of humor. They can be feminists who tell bawdy jokes, who relate stories in which they are the butt of the humor, and who poke fun at politicians. There are no boundaries to women's humor. In the postliberation era in which we live, the old stereotypes and categories appear as anachronisms, relics of a bygone era. Though the period in which women's humor was unrecognized was decidedly longer than the current liberated one, the sound of everyone laughing at women's humor is refreshing and welcome.

As a category, women comics offer a good measure of how far women entertainers have come in the twentieth century. While women performers began the century in limited roles, the stage, radio, the movies, and television offered them opportunities to redefine the stereotypes and create new ones. Eva Tanguay and her many imitators combined outrageous behavior with humor, knowing that a laughing audience is an understanding and tolerant one. Bessie Smith and Sophie Tucker sang the blues and funny bawdy songs. Mae West knew that a wisecrack was worth more than a dramatic gesture, and Mary Tyler Moore's sweet willingness to be the butt of some newsroom jokes endeared her to all. She made new values and behaviors about women professionals easier to accept, because the presentation was funny.

Women comics may be responsible for stretching the boundaries of good taste, for expanding women's expectations for themselves, and for making a place for all other women entertainers. People are willing to consider far more weighty matters when they are laughing than when they are crying. Finally, by finding humor in intimate as well as in common subjects, women comics are astute commentators on human frailty. In this sense, women comics, like women movie stars, offer their fans guidance in considering difficult life issues. If Lucy wanted a life outside the home, maybe the subject's serious implications would be analyzed after the laughter faded.

8

Change within Continuity

In the post–World War II period, women's lives changed dramatically. For women entertainers, it was a particularly perilous time; they had to preserve the old images while struggling with the new realities. The wartime Rosie the Riveter continued to work in large numbers in peacetime, and the percentage of American households with two-income earners continued to grow. Mothers, particularly those with older children, entered the workforce in the 1950s, and the momentum increased in the sixties and since. In the 1990s, married women with very young children are working, a relatively new phenomenon. The reality for most American women is two work lives: one at home (that has not changed) and one in the workplace.

While women movie stars, working women par excellence, were still highly paid and highly visible members of society, their roles continued in the tried-and-true tradition: they were usually Eves, sometimes Marys, but, new to the 1950s and since, rarely Liliths. Television women in situation comedies, one of the most popular formats, were most often wives confined to the domestic sphere. In an unusual twist, the actresses on the 1950s domestic comedy shows were professional women playing traditional mothers. TV actresses enjoyed financial success and lived as independent women while they portrayed dutiful wives and mothers. While earlier generations of movie stars played

Eve and Lilith roles alongside the Marys, the TV women were most often moms. Thanks to the multiple fan magazines available, Americans knew of the personal life of Dinah Shore while watching her faithfully every week. The magazine writers, never appreciating the irony, portrayed Shore as a dutiful wife and mother while acknowledging her as a competent professional on the small screen. The tensions caused by the enormous demands made on women stars professionally and personally were rarely discussed from a feminist perspective.

Television during the 1950s and most of the 1960s, particularly, reflected a desired world in which Mom stayed home while Dad was the sole breadwinner. "Father Knows Best" and its many clones reinforced this stereotypical view that, incidentally, never described the family lives of working-class white women or minority women. The world of mainstream television was largely a white middle-class one. Most households acquired a television set during that period and watched as the middle-class ideal of the nuclear family dominated the television screen. There were no widows, divorced mothers, or unmarried mothers on public view. Nor were there African American heroes on the crime-adventure shows or Latins as housewives. As in earlier periods, women entertainers had to fit their talents and interests within the preconceived molds available to them. If they were of the wrong color or ethnicity, they sang, danced, and acted in other than mainstream media.

"The Mary Tyler Moore Show," which premiered in 1970, offered a new image of women, a single career woman on her own. In the previous chapter, I discussed Moore's image on this show; its newness cannot be understated. All women had to be taken aback by the daring of Mary, moving to a new city, living alone, and working in the new industry of television. The rhetoric of women's liberation was heard throughout the land in the late 1960s, but most Americans still resisted its message. Because television reporters showed viewers student demonstrations on a regular basis and feminists appeared on the new talk shows, people often had the false belief that revolution was imminent. Traditional values die hard, and the screaming by young street protesters was matched, if not outnumbered, by dutiful students attending their classes. As a result, no change was seen on television.

Americans resisted new roles, new portraits, and new views about

Mary Tyler Moore played Mary Richards on the popular 1970s show *The Mary Tyler Moore Show.*

woman's adult destiny. Mary's engaging and nonthreatening personality played an enormously important role in introducing the growing audience to the single career woman. While Moore's fictional character lived a new kind of life, her moderate tone and style assured viewers that change did not have to cause drastic and extreme alterations in people's behavior. A sweet demeanor, as personified by Mary, could accompany a new lifestyle; this seemed to be the unspoken message, one of the subtexts of the show. And Mary's engaging personality made *The Mary Tyler Moore Show* a great and enduring success. The show's popularity offers an interesting example of cultural readiness for a somewhat new image of woman embodied in a star who evoked the desirable, more traditional image.

In the following pages, I am going to consider the careers of Dinah Shore and Mary Tyler Moore as examples of women whose images embraced the "old" and the "new" woman. Because they were able to exemplify both tradition and innovation, they won the hearts of America. Their careers, their texts, flourished within a cultural climate that was willing to consider new ideas on the subject of women, but only cautiously and tentatively. Shore and Moore represent two different generations of professional careerists, and in that sense, each faced a different set of challenges. But because women's roles and images have often been the anchor of a culture, their ability to capture both the old and the new made them enormously successful.

Both women's professional personae offered viewers an opportunity to observe the changes in women's lives while retaining the charm and "femininity" associated with traditional females in Western culture. The healthy schizophrenia that often characterizes American society is nowhere more evident than in the majority's wish to acknowledge new opportunities for women while clinging to old roles. Both Shore and Moore made the transition from dependent to independent woman gracefully and without fuss. Their many fans did not reject them or see them as threats to the status quo. Because they never gave up their old characteristics—their natural sweetness, charm, and willingness to cooperate rather than compete—they had long and effective careers in a changing period.

Shore's and Moore's temperaments were ideally suited to the cultural view of women, but paradoxically, their wills captured the modern woman's ambition, drive, and pursuit of personal excellence. Shore and Moore shared with many men the wish to succeed, to compete, and to excel. However, they couched these traditional male traits within conventional female personae. Both women's careers symbolized many of the changes women underwent in postwar America, though neither they nor most people could articulate the nature of the dilemma or recommend the best ways to solve it. In this sense, they shared with the women movie stars of the 1930s a new behavior while still espousing old values.

Shore and Moore became strong women while remaining sweet; they displayed independence while preserving a commitment to interdependence. Their sweetness may have been interpreted as dependence upon the kindness of men, but their steely natures emerged whenever a crisis occurred. Neither woman ever appeared as a shrinking violet or a helpless ninny. And though they became effective individuals, they stayed loyal to family values. Moore's persona on "The Mary Tyler Moore Show" was closely tied to her colleagues at the station, while Shore's many variety shows created a warm, homey atmosphere. They always linked themselves to others, avoiding the rugged-individual male image, thereby reinforcing the notion that as women, they were part of a community.

Dinah Shore, a generation older than Mary Tyler Moore, began her television career in the 1950s alongside Lucy's; yet her long career in many venues effectively demonstrates her ability to combine the best of the traditional and innovative modes available for modern women.[1] Born in Winchester, Tennessee, on March 1, 1917, to Anna (Stein) and Solomon Shore, she was named Frances "Fanny" Rose. She had a sister, Bessie, who was eight years older. A trauma at the age of eighteen months deeply affected Fanny. She suffered an attack of polio and was left with a paralyzed right leg. Her mother played a critical role in her rehabilitation, massaging her leg regularly and insisting on a rigorous exercise program. As a result, she overcame the disability and, as a young child, learned to swim, play tennis, and dance ballet.

When Fanny was six years old, the family moved to Nashville. The Shore family had been conspicuous in little Winchester where they were the only Jewish family. Nashville had a small but distinct Jewish community. The woman who became the famous Dinah Shore later told interviewers that she was extremely conscious of the fact that she came from a religious minority and always felt she had to be exemplary in all of her actions. When she graduated from Hume Fogg

Dinah Shore, as both singer and television host, had a long and successful career in show business.

High School in 1934, she was voted Best All-Around Girl in the Class. As a teenager, her strength and determination were already in evidence. At fourteen, without her parents' knowledge or permission, she got a job singing in a nightclub. Her dream for her adult career and her ambitious nature could not be subdued even at a young age.

Shore had to overcome another trauma as a young woman: the death of her mother when she was fifteen. She and her father lived with her older sister (who was already married) until she finished high school. Then Shore went to Vanderbilt University, a path only open to middle-class daughters of well-to-do fathers who encouraged intellectual development. Many southern women attended finishing school or married right after high school. Going to a liberal arts college, particularly in the 1930s, indicated the young woman's seriousness of purpose as well as her family's support. Shore majored in sociology. She headed the women's government club and she also became president of her sorority. Her leadership talent was clearly evident. During the summer of 1937, she went to New York City with her sorority sisters and fulfilled an ambition to sing on the radio. After her college graduation, she returned to New York and got a job singing on radio station WNEW. Dinah Shore never looked back. A career as a singer fulfilled a longtime dream.

Shore had a light but pleasant soprano voice. Her articulation was excellent and her smile and sunny disposition could almost be heard over the airwaves. In January 1939, she became a singer with the Leo Reisman Orchestra. Though the *Variety* critic who heard her was not overly impressed with her voice or style, audiences clearly had a positive impression. By this time, she called herself Dinah, the name of a song she had sung on the radio. In September 1940, she went on "The Eddie Cantor" radio show. The exposure she received in this venue launched her career. Cantor later recalled that Dinah Shore was not only the nicest person he had ever worked with but also the most hardworking. She learned more songs per show than anyone else had ever done and certainly more than could be sung on one program. Her great intelligence and diligence, though masked behind a sweet persona, always emerged in her work. Shore sang on "The Eddie Cantor Show" for three years.

In 1940, her recording of "Yes, My Darling Daughter" sold half a million copies. In 1944, her rendition of "I'll Walk Alone" was one of the year's biggest hits. During the war, she visited soldiers around the country, toured with the USO, and endeared herself to all Americans. While Betty Grable became the soldiers' favorite pin-up, Dinah Shore was the girl next door—loyal, patient, and ever pleasant. Only Frank Sinatra exceeded her popularity among record buyers. All in all, she had seventy-five hit recordings. From 1941 to 1961, she was voted the best pop female vocalist in the *Motion Picture Daily* Fame's annual poll in radio and TV. During the dark days of World War II, Dinah Shore reminded the soldiers and the workers at home that traditional American women remained loyal to their overseas sweethearts. She sang the popular "Don't Sit under the Apple Tree with Anyone Else but Me" and assured her audiences that fidelity remained a cherished value. American soldiers voted her one of their favorite entertainers.[2]

Dinah Shore displayed a calm demeanor and an assuring manner during difficult days. Her grateful fans never forgot that. On December 5, 1943, she married actor George Montgomery, and in 1948, gave birth to a daughter, Melissa Ann. That same year, she had her own musical variety radio show, "Dinah's Open House," a format that was reminiscent of the old vaudeville shows. Dinah would sing, greet guests who also performed, and engage in pleasant chatter. In an unobtrusive way, Shore was living the new social role for the modern post-1945 woman: she was wife, mother, and careerist. Like the 1930s movie stars, she was a highly visible and successful entertainer. During the 1950s, though she was clearly a pioneer, she never declared herself a feminist, nor did she ever say anything to suggest that her career was more important than her family. In this way, she was a calming influence and a reassuring one to all women.

In 1951, she made the transition from radio to television and appeared twice weekly for fifteen minutes. She had appeared in six movies, the most notable being *Up in Arms* with Danny Kaye but did not enjoy movie-making. Shore believed, rightly, that movies did not capture her intimate, friendly personality. The more personal television screen was far better suited to her style. Just as the small screen (in those days it was truly small) captured the comic anarchy of Lucy, so too did it show off the warmth and friendliness of Dinah Shore.

Throughout the "domestic" fifties, Dinah Shore combined a demanding professional schedule with childrearing and marriage. Popular magazines featured her sitting in her living room or on her patio. Reporters focused on her personal life, though one interviewer noted, "Dinah is a businesswoman, although she is certainly never ruthless."[3]

Another said that "it would be a mistake to underestimate her shrewdness and toughness in business dealings. Dinah has the best deal in the country on phonograph records."[4] Fans, however, were assured that home life took priority over work. True to the cultural universe that could not imagine a woman careerist investing more interest and energy in work than in family, the reporters all commented on how hardworking she was while assuring the fans that family came first.

Shore subscribed to the same ideology; in all of the interviews, she described her family life as her primary concern. In so doing, she convinced her fans that there need be no conflict between a heavy-duty professional and a rich personal life. Though she worked six days a week, fourteen hours a day, she preserved the fiction that both dimensions of her life remained healthy and intact. Shore's confident demeanor implicitly assured her audience that a happy marriage and a fulfilling career were not incompatible. In interviews, she explicitly said that she recognized that she was a woman in a man's world willing to defer to male judgment. She never announced a feminist message; her clear competence and independence was assumed, not expressed.

Dinah Shore's popularity in 1950s television helped to ensure the success of this new medium. Audiences enjoyed her nonthreatening and homey style. On her first show, which aired from 1951 to 1957 (the same years as the first Lucy show), Dinah sang and had guests who performed. In 1957, *The Dinah Shore Chevrolet Show,* a one-hour weekly musical variety show, came into being, and Dinah became even more famous singing her slogan song: "See the USA in your Chevrolet." The show remained high in the ratings for seven seasons. Appearing in living rooms each week, Shore created an important connection between the audience and herself. The musical variety format was reminiscent of the old vaudeville show, a tried-and-true American entertainment hosted by a popular American woman.

In 1954, while married to George Montgomery, Shore adopted a son, John David. But the marriage ended in divorce in May 1962, thus dashing her fans' faith that she could successfully combine family life and a career. However, as if to assure her fans that her family did, indeed, come first, Shore decided to retire temporarily from her weekly television show to spend more time with her children. She moved her family from Beverly Hills to Palm Springs, California, away from the constant media spotlight. Though she made TV specials and occasional guest appearances on other shows, her weekly exposure ended. The media respected her decision to place her career behind her family's welfare.

Shore's decision to drop out of the limelight while her career was flourishing endeared her to her public. She implicitly made the "right" value decision from the traditionalists' perspective: when a woman had to choose between career and family, there was only one correct decision. And Shore made it. She appeared occasionally in concerts and in Las Vegas, but stayed out of the public eye until 1970 when she returned to a new half-hour talk show called *Dinah's Place*. Shore's behavior also confirmed the fact that she shared with her fans the commitment to family over career for women. With her children older, Shore resumed doing what she did best: singing a pleasant song, talking to her celebrity guests, and hosting other acts. The fact that she was able to obtain and sustain a weekly show after having been out of the limelight for eight years is a testimony to her enduring popularity. The show lasted for four years.

In 1974, Dinah Shore left prime time to do an afternoon show called *Dinah!* Here she talked to her guests, sang, and expanded her repertory; she shared recipes and cooked with celebrity guests. As a pioneer in this format, Dinah Shore made her guests comfortable; her set looked like a family's living room and kitchen, the conversation was casual and informal, and audiences heard their favorite stars discuss ordinary likes and dislikes. Dinah never challenged or confronted people in an aggressive way; neither did she encourage her guests to reveal deep, dark secrets before millions of viewers. While some critics compared her unfavorably with Phil Donahue, another leader in afternoon talk shows whose style was far more confrontational, her fans remained loyal to her precisely because Dinah remained an oasis of civility during difficult times. The show was on the air until 1980.

Perhaps because Shore's public image of sweetness personified was so firmly entrenched, her much publicized affair with a much younger actor, Burt Reynolds, did not harm her career. Dinah Shore's unusual tenure on television—flourishing in the 1950s, nonexistent in the 1960s, and resurfacing in the 1970s—remains unique. Usually when a star leaves the public eye, she is forgotten forever. But Shore, ever adaptive and ambitious, returned and transformed her format from an evening variety show to an afternoon talk show. She built upon her strengths, also following her audience to a time when they would

In the 1940s, a young Dinah Shore projects a sweet, feminine demeanor.

watch her. Young mothers for example, in 1974 would be less likely to watch Dinah than their mothers would be. Her older audience kept the show viable for more than five years, no mean task. All in all, she had a longer television career than most did in a business where ratings and profitability led to quick series cancellations.

Dinah Shore remained active in the 1980s, playing tennis and golf and sponsoring a major women's golf tournament. In 1981, she did a multicity concert tour, the first in over a decade. But her performing days were nearly over. She retired to Palm Springs and, though she appeared occasionally at sporting and charitable events, she led a quieter life. In 1981, after all, she was sixty-four years old, an older woman by the standards of that era. Dinah Shore died of ovarian cancer just short of her seventy-seventh birthday on February 24, 1994.

While Mary Tyler Moore played the television wife Laura Petrie during the 1960s and took a back seat to star Dick Van Dyke, she came into her own the following decade. As already suggested, Mary and Dinah shared features of the new woman at the same time that they preserved aspects of the "old" woman. The television Mary was a single woman, around thirty, living in Minneapolis and learning her way in the world as a woman alone, a new role for more and more American women. Dinah was a mature woman (from fifty-three to sixty-three years old during the decade) who still retained her vitality, her interest in working, and her independence. Shore's continued presence on television acknowledged the aging of American women and the need for television examples of attractive, older women. Both women possessed sweetness and charm, a ready smile, and a pleasing personality. Both, in other words, seemed to naturally present themselves as nice women, not like the confrontational feminists who received so much airtime in the early 1970s.

Mary and Dinah, a younger woman and an older woman, showed American men and women how women could make the transition to new roles while remaining lovely. Dinah assured older women that growing old could be accomplished gracefully; her athleticism and slim figure kept her looking young for many years; her ability to attract a young, famous actor only endeared her to older women who fantasized about such things. Dinah's continued success in real life and on television offered hope for divorced and widowed women.

Dinah Shore's career also displayed a shrewdness that was hidden by her pleasant demeanor. In a 1956 interview in *TV Guide,* for example, she showed her understanding of the male domination of her industry: "Show business is a man's world. So is everything else, for that matter."[5] But she hastily added that the reason for this state of affairs, including the dominance of male performers on television, was that the audience consisted mainly of women—and they wanted to see men. There is no criticism in the situation, no feminist urging. Rather, she insisted that she liked things the way they were. She was a hostess, not an emcee. "My big problem in being the female star of an hour-long show is finding the right male stars I can 'bounce' my lines off without being the aggressor."[6]

Dinah Shore was very conscious of the clear role designations in our culture. As a well-bred southern lady, she knew how to negotiate in a male world while remaining a polite woman. Yet her ambition and her drive clearly existed in her determination to succeed in the difficult entertainment world. Though she had male associates who remained by her side throughout her long career, no one doubted who was in charge. Shore's nonthreatening nature surely contributed to her popularity with men and women. While publicly supporting the separate spheres ideology, she practiced egalitarianism. As an experienced fighter in the treacherous ring of show business for more than thirty years, Shore knew how to build bridges while steering her own course.

Mary Tyler Moore's public persona changed over time. While she portrayed a sweet Mary in the early years of "The Mary Tyler Moore Show," she became more assertive as the show continued. But even when Mary asked her boss, Mr. Grant, for a raise or when she auditioned for a spot on the air (she was an associate producer earning less than others in the same job), she did it with a smile and seemingly accepted whatever fate Mr. Grant decided upon. However, her smile became more forced when she failed, and the last laugh was usually on Lou. Because the show was a comedy with an excellent ensemble of characters, each bouncing off the other, everyone's human frailties became subject matter for laughter.

But, the Mary character's strength was also her weakness: her niceness often held her career back. She could not be aggressive, though she tried to be assertive. In a competitive newsroom, where most of the action occurred, this was extremely difficult. In sharp contrast, Dinah Shore always played herself, and her sweetness was always an asset, never a deficit. Mary walked the narrow line between polite ambition and outright competitiveness. Becoming a new woman, Mary seemed to be saying, did not require abandonment of civility and more traditional virtues. Yet it was easier to say than to do.

Audiences loved her willingness to make herself the butt of the humor and to bow diplomatically to failure. They identified with her confusions, and her difficulties. They too had to figure out how to negotiate the frustrating and unknown waters of liberation. Women had to create and shape new roles for themselves while preserving the traditional ones; men had to understand how to deal with new women. It was not an easy task for anyone. Mary Tyler Moore's depiction of a single woman earning her living and gaining support from her colleagues rather than from her family represented a nonthreatening portrait of the new world. If all career women were like Mar (as Murray called her), then the brave new world would be OK.

Moore's personal life, which she shielded from public view until recently (in 1995, she published an autobiography, *After All*), was the opposite of the innocence, the pleasantness, and the sweetness of her public persona. Born in Brooklyn Heights in 1937, the family, which also included brother John, moved to Los Angeles when she was eight years old. Her father George was a utilities company clerk, and her mother Marge was an alcoholic. At eighteen, Moore married a twenty-seven-year-old salesman named Dick Meeker, became pregnant right away, and gave birth to her son Richie just three and a half months after her mother gave birth to her third child, Elizabeth.

The marriage ended shortly thereafter, and Moore began working as a dancer. While her professional life improved and her second marriage to Grant Tinker was successful both personally and professionally for some years, Moore hid the fact that she was a secret drinker. In 1978, her sister died of an overdose of alcohol and Darvon, and in 1980, her son accidentally shot himself. Compounding the personal tragedies, her brother died after a protracted battle with cancer—he too had been a recovering alcoholic. Moore's marriage to Tinker ended in divorce, and she discovered that she was an insulin-dependent diabetic. Around this sorrowful time in her life, she met a man eighteen years younger than herself—the age of her deceased son—Dr. Robert Levine, to whom she has been married ever since.[7]

Moore continued working after leaving "The Mary Tyler Moore Show." Her role in the 1980 movie *Ordinary People* cast her as a cold, unsympathetic mother, a harsh contrast to her warm Mary. She was nominated for the Academy Award for her performance. Moore's efforts to return to series television, however, were not as successful. To date, she has been in five failed efforts. However, her share of MTM Enterprises, which produced her show and many others, made her a wealthy woman. When she and Grant Tinker sold the business in 1988, her share was reported to be $85 million.

For the last thirty years, public opinion polls have confirmed Americans' conflicting views about the roles of women and the work world. On the one hand, they support women's right to equal pay and equal job opportunity, and on the other, they uphold traditional family values. If the pollster does not ask how women can be expected to care for a home, a family, and a full-time job simultaneously, the difficulty is not revealed. Americans continue to embrace both sides of the paradox. When not forced to choose, they blithely assume that home and family can be upheld, maintained, and cared for while an adult woman works a forty- to fifty- hour week outside of the home. Neither role should be sacrificed.

Dinah and Mary Tyler Moore as Laura Petrie seemed to be doing just that in the 1950s, while the 1970s Mary character, because she was single, did not have to juggle family and career. While Dinah put in long hours on her weekly television shows, she always publicly expressed her devotion to her marriage and her family. The fact that she quit her show after her divorce from George Montgomery in order to raise her children quietly in Palm Springs did not go unnoticed in the press. In this sense, she followed society's expectations and value system: she placed her children above her career and thereby reinforced her fans' love for her. When she returned to network television a decade later, her children were grown. No one had to say it aloud, but the male heads of the studio and her admirers felt comfortable with Dinah for living according to traditional rules.

Mary's encounter with new values and new behaviors came in her television newsroom. She had to figure out how to make friends, date, and succeed in her profession, all on her own. Living in a new city only increased the potential tensions she faced. But Mary always smiled, retained her feminine sweetness, and deferred to her male betters. She was not confrontational in a decade when many feminists were; she was not vulgar, rebellious, or shocking. Yet her television life rep-

A young Mary Tyler Moore costarred as Laura Petrie, wife to Dick Van Dyke's Rob, on *The Dick Van Dyke Show.*

resented a new social type, a new set of experiences for more and more young women coming of age in the 1970s and for more newly divorced women as well. So Mary's fictional life interested many women. For married women who were full-time homemakers, the show offered vicarious opportunities to witness the life of a single career woman.

In real life, Dinah Shore and Mary Tyler Moore represented successful public women. Both women had divorced their husbands (Shore had a brief second marriage that also ended in divorce), reflecting a new social reality: more and more American marriages were ending in divorce. Was it women's increasing ambitions outside the home that caused this? The evidence was not, and is not, in on this subject, though many people probably believed that the multiple marriages of many women entertainers demonstrated the inherent tensions of living in two worlds simultaneously. So while audiences rewarded their performances, traditionalists could feel satisfied that even successful actresses and performers did not have it "all."

In the 1970s, multiple generations of women could cheer. Shore was in her fifties, while Moore was in her thirties. But women of all ages enjoyed seeing a healthy and vigorous Dinah Shore and a still young looking Mary Tyler Moore take on the multiple demands of a career. Fan magazines reminded their readers that these women were serious business women and serious professionals who devoted endless hours to their craft. Their personal troubles and tragedies made them more human, more vulnerable to their many fans. Shore and Moore can each be described as a modern Lilith-Mary combination. Their lives demonstrated their independence and competence while their images perpetuated sweet Mary, a long-standing favorite of Americans.

How popular culture represents change is always a tricky and intriguing phenomenon to observe. To win over an essentially conservative majority to a new role for women, television writers and producers seem uncannily able to recruit personalities who embrace elements of both the known and the unknown, the old and the new. Dinah Shore and Mary Tyler Moore, women who had long and successful television careers, fit the bill. Dinah accompanied viewers through the seemingly predictable 1950s, while Mary helped viewers through the bewildering 1970s.

Contemporary and future viewers alike will find many redeeming virtues to admire in each woman's work. Shore's unflappable charm and warmth enabled her to draw out the best qualities of all her guests, no mean feat. In an age when talk shows dominate, there are few Dinah Shores around. Civil conversation, a Shore specialty, is also absent in the more contentious and confessional 1990s. Similarly, Moore's way of meeting every challenge with humor offers valuable lessons for women embarking on a new career or a new life phase. Popular television personalities probably remain the companions and guides for untold numbers of viewers. They could not do better than to watch old Dinah Shore or Mary Tyler Moore shows.

In the second decade of the twentieth century, audiences laughed and roared at Mae West and Eva Tanguay performances; they saw these performers as separate, different, and possibly unrelated to their own lives. By the 1930s, movies brought fans into the lives of fantasy figures while depicting working-class problems. Audiences knew of Joan Crawford's real-life troubles as well as her movie melodramatic crises. Television audiences in the 1950s and 1960s watched fictional characters who mirrored their lives, anticipated their concerns, or confirmed their wishes and fears. The dynamic interactions between the stars, their personal and imaginative stories, and the media that presented them continue to engage large numbers of viewers. The messages viewers bring away from the cultural lessons taught remain diverse. The impact the women stars had and have, however, continues to be great. Thanks to video, audiences at the end of the twentieth century can watch Mae West's as well as Katharine Hepburn's 1930s movies. They can listen to Bessie Smith sing the blues, and they can watch Mary on television channels that broadcast old reruns regularly. The past, the present, and the future women stars coexist and continue to influence multiple generations of viewers.

Epilogue

Where Are We Now?

Americans are accused of being ignorant of their history, but entertainers, fans, and the reporters who cover them are often extremely aware of past performers in their field, historical examples of excellence, and noted award winners. Bette Midler named her daughter Sophie in loving memory of Sophie Tucker, whose routines she cheerfully uses, while rocker Janis Joplin openly acknowledged her debt to Bessie Smith and Billie Holiday. Tina Turner is often called the "Mae West of Rock 'n' Roll." The TV character Murphy Brown adores Aretha Franklin's singing and fractures "A Natural Woman" in her ardent desire to imitate her. Franklin appeared on *Murphy Brown* and sang the song, written, incidentally, by a major woman composer and singer, Carole King.

Links exist between the generations of women entertainers; knowingly or unknowingly, they share a past through the genres they work in and the images they project. Continuity, however, can be seen as a strength or as a weakness. If the images and themes that endure display women performers at their best, it is a strength. If the images remain dreary and predictable, however, that limits women's opportunities in show business and suggests that the majority culture has not rethought its views of women. Like a defective recording that keeps repeating the same sound, Hollywood producers often stick to the old images of women. But even within the negative, as I have suggested, there are bright spots—outstanding women performers who reshape the old images, bawdy women entertainers who continue to tweak convention, and TV domestic comics who make us laugh.

At century's end, the bawdy women are just as outrageous, if not more outrageous than those in 1900. Since the women's liberation days of the late 1960s and 1970s when the subject of women's sexuality received a public hearing, women performers say and do things in a public venue that Sophie Tucker and Bessie Smith could do only in the small space of a nightclub. However, while social attitudes have loosened considerably—witness the high percentage of couples living together without marriage, the late marriage rate, and the extensive use of birth control—there is still a closed-mouth attitude toward public discussion of sexual matters. The rise of a vocal Christian Coalition, with its strong disapproval of contemporary culture, gives someone like Bette Midler or Madonna a lot of material for their shows. Cable television provides an outlet for the more salacious comics today. Hollywood, which produces movies and television shows, waxes and wanes in its treatment of women on screen, sometimes offering them multiple juicy parts and other times, most notably during the heyday of women's liberation in the early 1970s, ignoring them. Rather than face a controversial subject, the conservative and commercial response was to avoid it like the plague. Betty Friedan, a leader of the women's movement, described television's image of a woman in 1964 as a "stupid, unattractive, insecure little household drudge who spends her martyred, mindless, boring days dreaming of love."[1] The serious topic of women's roles was one Hollywood did not want to address.

The business of show business, of course, is always a major reason for the reluctance to treat women equitably. As the cost of moviemaking has skyrocketed and contestable issues divide and decrease potential audiences, producers seek the tried-and-true formulas over risky or controversial subjects. If male adventure films are the blockbusters, that genre dominates. Conversely, melodramatic movies, traditionally women's films (or in current parlance, "chick" films), are seen as less popular and are therefore less likely to be made. Movies that explore women's views and choices are even more dangerous. According to the market researchers, women will go to movies starring a man, while men will not go to movies starring a woman, a clear example of a gender divide.

A brief survey of singers, movie stars, and television stars of the 1980s and 1990s enables us to take the pulse of women entertainers in the contemporary period and determine the prevalence or the disappearance of Eves, Marys, and Liliths. How well have women performers been doing? Let us begin with popular music, a subject treated earlier when I looked at the lives and careers of blues singers, white and African American, and at the career of Dinah Shore. The blues, quintessentially women's music because of its preoccupation with love lost, became the framework and the foundation for pop music's most important new style in the last half century—rock 'n' roll. Rhythm and blues merged with other musical forms to create a louder, faster, and harder sound, with lyrics often displaying the same concerns as the blues, although from the male perspective.

One of the best examples of a woman blues singer who screeched her way onto the rock scene was Janis Joplin (1943–70). While women rockers, as writer Martha Bayles wrote, "are a distinct minority,"[2] Joplin captured the attention of other rock performers and attracted a substantial audience of admirers. As the lead singer of the group Big Brother and the Holding Company, Joplin sang "Big Momma" Willie May Thornton's song "Love Is like a Ball and Chain" at the 1967 Monterey Pop Festival. The song brought her quick fame. In her brief career, she screamed the blues with raw emotion to loud and fast musical rhythms. Joplin's presentation was crude and rude, and the fans loved her.

Joplin's success, like that of Madonna a generation later, was based on the unusual nature of her performance. Women singers, like American women generally, were expected to sing ladylike songs in the mode of Dinah Shore. Bawdy blues singers remained on the fringes. Her Lilith-Eve image made Joplin join hands with bawdy women singers of an earlier time. She sang lyrics like "Love's just draggin' me down," but didn't lament her condition; rather, Joplin shouted for recognition, understanding, and change. In the sixties, she was often compared to the great African American blues singer Aretha Franklin, a singer whom she greatly admired.

Like Mae West and Bessie Smith, Joplin unapologetically cried for sexual satisfaction and for respect from men. She drank Southern Comfort liquor on stage and used the public forum to discuss her latest love troubles. In her second album, *Cheap Thrills* (1968), her lead song, "Turtle Blues," included the words, "I'm a mean, mean woman." She went on to say that she treats men the way she wishes and that her needs are of primary interest to her. Contrary to the traditional image of the self-sacrificing, long-suffering woman, Joplin projected a strong, assertive, often vulgar woman who was "in your face," a new concept and expression of the sixties. Her constant screaming led one reporter to ask her whether she feared losing her voice; her response was, "When I can't sing, I'll worry about it then. Maybe I'll have babies."[3]

In a documentary on her life and career, Joplin said that she believed in honesty, to be "true to myself, to the person on the inside of me . . . to not bullshit myself."[4] Her audience knew of her personal troubles and, like fans of earlier generations, they removed the boundaries between the spheres. Fans had read articles about Joplin's unhappy childhood in Port Arthur, Texas; her escape in 1962 to San Francisco; and her participation in the drug subculture of the Haight-Ashbury section of the city. She sang about the glories of free sexual activity, drug taking, and rock 'n' roll. A love affair gone wrong became material for a song and a performance.

In October 1970, after four short years of performing, recording, and hard drinking and drug taking, Janis Joplin died of an overdose of drugs and liquor. She was quickly seen as a martyred casualty of the rock scene to be joined by male rockers such as Jimi Hendrix and Jim Morrison. Whether she was self-destructive, willfully leading herself into oblivion, remains an open question. But it is beyond dispute that Joplin's music, first heard and appreciated in the small but growing youth culture of San Francisco, gained a following among the teenagers in the Baby Boom generation. It is also clear that one reason she is remembered is that she was exceptional, a glaring standout from the male-dominated drinking, drug-taking world of rock music. Imagine a woman singing dirty lyrics and gyrating and twisting her body to loud music. Janis Joplin left a dubious legacy and few imitators. By singing the blues, albeit with her own aggressive signature, she not only upheld, but also broke the traditional categories regarding women and popular music.

Joplin was a blues-singing woman in a rock 'n' roll world, openly acknowledging to a growing public that while love and romance remained women's concerns, the independent woman's rendition had a decidedly hard edge to it. Joplin combined the old and the new: words that centered on romance and man troubles connected her to the past, while the sound and the style of rock suggested a new and bold stance. Joplin sang as her own person, free to share her fears, her hopes, and her troubles with her fans. She merged the personal and the public, the traditional and the revolutionary, presaging the confessional world of contemporary culture. Openly displaying weakness and vulnerability became the watchword of 1980s and 1990s daytime talk show television. Janis Joplin was one of the unwitting precursors to this trend.

The electric guitars and highly amplified instruments of rock music, meanwhile, became the exclusive domain of men, who allegedly are more capable of understanding, working, and playing complicated mechanical instruments. The sound of rock is aggressive and the messages communicated are similarly abrasive. The Rolling Stones wrote songs that demeaned women and viewed them as objects. "Yesterday's Newspaper," a Stones song, compared women to yesterday's newspaper, something to be used (read) and discarded afterwards. Male rock groups proliferated while the number of lead women rockers remained small. Cultural boundaries prevailed; women folk singers could play banjo or guitar, but acoustically enhanced instruments belonged to men. Similarly, men seemingly had a monopoly on aggression, brashness, and vulgarity.

One of the mighty exceptions to this rule is Tina Turner (born in 1940), who began in rhythm and blues with her husband, Ike Turner. After she left him in 1976, she became a rock and roller in earnest. Some years later she said, "I never wanted to do all that moaning, begging and pleading. I always preferred rock to r & b."[5] Her song, "Let's Stay Together," became a hit in 1983, and her album, "Private Dancer" (1985), went triple-platinum and won her two American Music Awards for Best Female Vocal, Pop; and Best Rock Performance, Female.[6] Turner is a high-energy performer with a beautiful, athletic body that she displays with confidence. In the 1990s, she remains active and as energetic as ever. Though she now lives in Europe, she continues to tour the world.

Though everyone has their favorite singers, two other African American contemporary singers who deserve mention are Aretha Franklin (born in 1942) and Whitney Houston (born in 1963). Franklin, an outstanding rhythm and blues singer, is of the same generation as Tina Turner, while Houston, an enormously successful pop singer, represents the younger generation. The two share a common heritage as daughters of gospel musicians. Franklin's father, the Rev.

Singer Whitney Houston demonstrated her great talent as a concert performer, a recording artist, and a movie star.

C.L. Franklin, was pastor of Detroit's New Bethel Baptist Church; he had a gospel caravan with Aretha as the featured singer. Houston's mother, Cissy Houston, is minister of music at the New Hope Baptist Church in Newark, where Whitney sang in the choir.[7] In the late 1960s and 1970s, Franklin's record albums sold more than one hundred million copies worldwide, and she won all of the honors in her field. Similarly, beginning in 1984, Houston has been a best-selling singer with songs such as "Saving All My Love for You" becoming number one on the pop charts. Neither are rock 'n' rollers. Rather, they connect to the older traditions of women singers: Aretha Franklin is a latter-day blues singer like Billie Holiday, and Whitney Houston can be compared to the white pop singer Dinah Shore.

Rocker Janis Joplin acts as a transitional figure, from the traditional pop and rhythm and blues singers, to the popular blues-rock singers of the sixties and since. The women in this latter group are few for the reasons already noted, but when they appear, they are often very popular and successful. Part of their success may be because they are rare, treasured by their admirers as fragile creatures in an alien, often hostile, world. They are Eves and Liliths in a male-dominated world. Who better epitomizes this persona than Madonna, a parodist, self-parodist, and extremist who first achieved public notice in 1983 with her first album, in which she declared her audacity.

Comparisons to Mae West are inevitable. Both stars enjoyed discussing sex and, in Madonna's case, acting out sexual scenarios in her music videos. Emerging precisely when MTV was catching on with the growing youth audience, Madonna's dancing, singing, and acting of her sometimes bawdy lyrics assured her a following. While critics often wondered whether Mae West was in danger of making fun of herself, Madonna openly declared that humor was her weapon in the sexual wars and that sexual attractiveness was a form of power. "If people don't get the humor in me or my act, then they don't want to get it. If ten-year-olds can get it and laugh, then an adult surely can."[8] Madonna aggressively displayed her assets and insisted on her own self-worth.

However, in contrast to Mae West, whose prime audience was energetic college men, Madonna appealed to teenyboppers, little eleven- and twelve-year-old girls who imitated her dress, exposed their belly buttons, and wore fingerless lace gloves. In her first tour in 1985, Madonna's audiences were often 60 percent female, unheard of for rock concerts.[9] The preteeners also wore Christian crosses as pieces of jewelry, offending many traditionalists in what became the first of a long line of affronts to social mores. Indeed, Madonna's distinctive identity was based on the flaunting of all social values. Pushing the envelope over the edge became her most noted characteristic.

Feminists were not sure what to make of her. As writer John Skow noted, "Some feminists clearly feel that Madonna's self-parody as an eye-batting gold digger . . . is a joke too damaging to laugh at."[10] But Camille Paglia admired Madonna's audacity and her willingness to poke fun at all social values and all stereotypes. "Madonna," she claimed, "has a far profounder vision of sex than do the feminists. She sees both the animality and the artifice."[11] Paglia admired Madonna because she was willing to sing and talk about all subjects and unapologetically appear in any costume she chose. Acting out a variety of poses becomes the ultimate example of free expression, in Paglia's view, a feminist goal.

Born in Bay City, Michigan, on August 16, 1958, Madonna Louise Ciccone grew up in a family of six children. Her mother died when she was five and her father remarried. As the oldest girl in the family, Madonna clashed with her stepmother, particularly when more children came and she was expected to assume many household tasks. "I really saw myself as the quintessential Cinderella," she later said.[12] Madonna has described her early life as one in which she was always comfortable with herself and her body. She liked boys and felt uninhibited around them, which she attributes to the fact that she grew up with older brothers. Her forwardness, however, was often misinterpreted in high school, and she often heard others call her "slut." "I didn't fit in and that's when I got into dancing."[13]

From 1985 to the early 1990s, Madonna's record albums (nineteen to date) and worldwide tours (four from 1985 to 1993) made her a frequent subject for newspapers and magazines. Her 1986 song, "Papa Don't Preach," in which she told her father that she was pregnant and planned to keep her baby, caused a stir; the music video in which she acted out the lyrics became very popular. While moralists decried her sexual promiscuity, and Planned Parenthood representatives lamented the message she sent to young women, Madonna reveled in the attention and the publicity generated by the song. Record sales skyrocketed and the album containing the song "True Blue" became a best-seller.

Singer and actress Madonna reinvented herself many times during the 1980s
and 1990s, beginning as a classic Eve, and becoming an independent Lilith.

Not content with just concertizing and recording, Madonna made her movie debut in *Desperately Seeking Susan* (1985) to critical acclaim; the free-spirited personality was in full view on the big screen, and though the role appeared to be very close to her personality, the film gave her a bigger and different audience than she had known before. Few of her subsequent movie roles, however, enlarged upon her success. Madonna's performances in *Dick Tracy* (1990) and *A League of Their Own* (1992) did not receive good notices. Her 1991 documentary, *Truth Or Dare* described life on tour; in 1996 she returned to the movie screen in the musical *Evita* which, despite a blizzard of publicity, was greeted with mixed reviews.

Known as an astute marketer of her persona, Madonna wrote a book called *Sex* in 1992 that displayed her body in graphic sexual poses with multiple partners of both sexes. Perhaps she overstepped the boundaries because the controversy did not produce a blockbuster. Critics panned the book as prurient and in extreme bad taste. It is not known whether Madonna knew of Mae West's 1926 play by the same name that also received bad reviews, but it is clear that Madonna continues to search for ways to create and recreate her successful image and remain a star. What pathways she will choose and how effective they will be remains to be seen.

An interesting and unique woman singer-star, Barbra Streisand (born in 1942), bridges the spheres of music and the movies. An overachiever, Streisand was a superstar while still in her twenties with record albums in the 1960s and 1970s that often sold millions of copies. First on Broadway and then in films, beginning with *Funny Girl* (1968) and *The Way We Were* (1973), she wowed her audiences and quickly developed a large and loyal following. Streisand won an Academy Award for *Funny Girl* and a Tony for her Broadway musical performance in the play of the same name. Songs like "People" and "The Way We Were" entered everyone's consciousness with continual playing over the years on radio stations throughout the country.

During the 1980s, however, while she continued to issue record albums and make movies, she experienced some bumps in her heretofore path of steady success. Her album *Emotion* (1985) was a flop and critics found many of her movies, particularly when she began directing herself in them, to be less than artistic giants. The gap that developed between her fans, who uncritically loved everything she did, and the professional critics, who found much of her work wanting, did not deter her creative output. Her movies, even if not well received, made money, particularly with the benefit of overseas audiences and video rentals. Her feminist supporters blamed insecure men in the Hollywood establishment for the negative reviews.

Such was the case with *Yentl* (1983), perhaps Streisand's most autobiographical film. The story featured a young Jewish woman in a small village in Poland who wanted to be a rabbinical student. Because of the orthodox prohibition on women studying the Torah, the Bible, she disguised herself as a young man to do so. Even though Streisand stretched credulity in her role as a young boy, her fans adored her portrayal as well as the musical score; her critics, however, pointed to her overweening egotism. In *The Prince of Tides* (1992), they were no kinder when Streisand starred as a psychiatrist and also directed the film. The recent *The Mirror Has Two Faces* (1996) received the same refrain: fans uncritically accepted every Streisand movie while detractors pointed to the film's weaknesses. Streisand's insistence on total artistic control was viewed differently depending upon the perspective: feminists argued that when male directors behave authoritatively, it is considered proper, but that when Streisand does, it is subject to ridicule.

Her fans insisted that detractors do not want a multitalented woman to express herself in so many arenas. Some critics wished she would just sing, while others recommended that she return to comedy. Pathologically afraid of live performances, Streisand had avoided concertizing for a quarter of a century, but in 1986, she allowed Home Box Office to tape a concert she gave in the privacy of her home for a political fund-raiser. It enjoyed good ratings when it was televised in December of that year. Eight years later, she ventured onto a stage for a series of live performances. In a multicity tour in 1994, she sang before sell-out crowds and experienced the adulation of her still large fan base. The compact disc and video of *The Concert*, as it was billed, became best-sellers.

In her movie roles, Streisand's image is often that of a Lilith, an independent woman trying to carve out her identity. Whether we look at the early feminist film *Up the Sandbox* (1972) (a box office bomb), *The Way We Were* (a hit), or *Yentl* (so-so), viewers face a woman who either has a clear sense of herself or is searching for it, and who does not assume that a husband is the definition of self. Except for her 1970s comedies, Streisand has chosen, quite self-consciously, roles that were committed to the search. As a professional career woman—a psychiatrist or, most recently, a college professor in *The Mirror Has Two Faces*—she captured the dilemma of many upper middle class and middle-class women today for whom career success, though much desired, does not replace the need for a lasting love relationship.

The Lilith, too, faces juggling career/job and home/family and Streisand's careful selection of movie subjects reflects her personal quest as well as that of many American women. In sharp contrast to the roles played in the 1930s by Katharine Hepburn and her cohorts, the 1990s Lilith wants satisfaction in both spheres of life. The male domination of the movie business with few women directors and producers, few women studio chiefs, and few women behind the camera, however, remains as the most telling signal that Hollywood has not changed its mind about independent women or about sharing power. Women scriptwriters in 1920s Hollywood held a greater share of positions than they do today. Barbra Streisand, then, as filmmaker, occupies a unique position and one that makes her all the more vulnerable to criticism. Her substantial clout only underscores her unique position in traditional Hollywood.

Meryl Streep (born in 1949) was quoted recently as saying, "There are great roles for young women in films but usually they are hookers who get sodomized."[14] The old Eve role is alive and well today and appears as *the* image available for women movie stars. But so few roles feature women at all that even those whp portray Eves have few opportunities. Hollywood no longer makes three hundred films a year; the golden years of the 1930s, when there were innumerable roles for women stars, are no more. The many variations of the three images have long vanished from the screen. Although the contemporary period has many worthy actresses, they usually must compete for the few roles open to them, with most a variation of the Eve image. Independent filmmakers and the major studios combined turn out less than half the number of films made in the 1930s.

Few Marys and Liliths are among those offerings. Actresses famous in the heyday of Hollywood filmmaking, but less well known today, like Jean Arthur, Rosalind Russell, Irene Dunne, Greer Garson, and Claudette Colbert, had their choices of roles each year. So did enormously popular stars like Joan Crawford and Greta Garbo. They may not have won Academy Awards, but they were rewarded by the fans with consistent popular support. In the 1990s, there are rarely

Meryl Streep, an A-list actress since the 1970s, has always portrayed variations on the Lilith theme in her movies.

more than five worthwhile roles for women; consequently, all of the women in these roles are nominated for the Academy Award in any given year. Rather than an embarrassment of riches, the Academy judges in the 1990s must search far and wide to find five movies starring women.

Meryl Streep is the leading A actress and is offered the rare Lilith part that allows her to exhibit her independence and intelligence. The list of actresses may be long but the roles available are few; newer talents have limited opportunities to gain experience in B movies because so few of them are made each year. Television and live theater are often the outlets for the younger generation of aspiring actresses. In the 1950s and 1960s, when a decent number of movies starred women, actresses did not deign to appear on television, a less worthy medium. But the table has turned today, and actresses have more opportunities on television and in off-Broadway plays all around the country than they do in movies.

Accordingly, a 1990s actress cannot acquire the corpus of films, the accumulated credits, that represents a long and worthy career in the movies. Unlike 1930s actresses, today's women in the movies have few credits gathered over long periods. Granted, Bette Davis was overworked, often appearing in four movies a year, and thanks to good health, Crawford, Hepburn, and Stanwyck enjoyed long careers that allowed them to make forty or more films. But today's movie actress is lucky to get a worthy role once every three or four years. The reasons are complex, but business considerations cannot be given all of the blame. If fewer movies are made only because of the high cost of film making, why not make fewer car-crashing thrillers?

That the melodrama and the romance, both quintessential women's movies, are eliminated as a viable genre is a cultural decision, one that reveals American values and attitudes. Young boys, one of the major groups of moviegoers, are generally interested only in action films; middle-class men and women in generation X spend their recreational dollars in a variety of ways with moviegoing only one of many options. Older Americans often watch videos or cable television. Going to the movies has become an expensive experience, and viewers may think that they can receive their fill of melodrama in the comfort of their homes; the genre is available on daytime television soap operas and on talk shows during the daytime and late night. The intimate television screen has brought women's troubles into the home and taken them off the big movie screen.

No longer does half of the American population go to the movies each week as they did during the depression thirties. With a far more segmented society, viewers have a cafeteria of choices on how to spend their recreational monies. Perhaps the personal and intimate trials of a Stella Dallas (one of Stanwyck's great tearjerkers) no longer play well on the big screen. Bigger and bigger disaster films with spectacular pyrotechnics have replaced the personal story. The infrequent moviegoer wants an eye-dazzling and awesome experience in the darkened movie theater. In the privacy of the home, with the lights on, they can cry with their favorite soap opera character. Similarly, they can hear eye-raising confessions of the most personal kind on TV talk shows, making Stella Dallas's troubles look trivial and minor by comparison.

The contemporary generation of movie stars, however, are as impressive as their 1930s predecessors. Meryl Streep, a seven-time nominee for the Academy Award (she won an Oscar for *Sophie's Choice*), is known for her wide range and her incredible ability to occupy a great variety of filmic characters. A graduate of the Yale Drama School, she represents a professional approach to acting and is a member of the "mature" generation of actresses who came of age in the 1970s. Her cohorts include Susan Sarandon (born in 1946) and Jessica Lange (born in 1949). They all made outstanding movies in the 1980s and 1990s (note table 2), but often, their roles were the only good ones available for women.

"There are not a lot of great roles for women out there," said film critic Jeanine Basinger,[15] and so the same stars compete with each other for the few good roles each year. As the earlier discussion of women movie stars in the 1930s suggested, of all dominant images of women portrayed on the screen, the Eves and Liliths were best represented. Innocent Marys were rare then and now. In the sexually liberated 1980s and 1990s, of course, it would be difficult to portray a virginal woman in need of male rescue; that would be naive in terms of sexual practice today and antifeminist in its stereotypical insistence on male heros saving the weak heroine. This cultural reality may be good evidence to support the view that the traditional Mary is gone forever.

But opportunities for Liliths are also rare. If Meryl Streep is the Katharine Hepburn of her generation, Susan Sarandon is the Bette

Davis. Sarandon, a five-time nominee for the Academy Award (and the 1995 winner for *Dead Man Walking*) often plays tough Eve-Lilith women, women who were educated in the school of hard knocks (*Atlantic City, Thelma and Louise*). Like Bette Davis or a Barbara Stanwyck, she must preserve her dignity and independence through continuous effort; no one gives her anything for free, nor can she rely on the protection of a man. Her good looks and sexy figure often get her into trouble, but she struggles for her freedom and autonomy. In *The Client* (1994), she played a mother who lost custody of her children because a traumatic divorce led to her excessive drinking. She got her life back in order, became a lawyer, and worked to save a young boy from harm.

While Streep and Sarandon qualify as the outstanding actresses on the current scene, they are joined by other actresses who play Eves. In sharp contrast to the Eves of the 1930s, those of the 1980s and 1990s are more jaded and often more corrupt. (Courtney Love in *The People vs. Larry Flynt* (1996) is a good example.) Bette Davis in the 1937 *Marked Woman* was a working-class whore who had few other occupational possibilities, but Sharon Stone in *Casino* (1995) and Mira Sorvino in *Mighty Aphrodite* (1995) do not appear to be class-bound; rather, each appears to have made a decision to use her body for financial gain because it is her most attractive asset. There is no moral consideration at all in their equation.

The whore with or without a heart of gold is a very old cinematic and literary image of woman. The fact that it has been so dominant in recent years speaks to the sterility of imagination in the scriptwriters and the larger culture. The Eve is viewed as a "juicy" part, one of the few open to women. Hollywood appears cautious, if not fearful, of portraying a woman careerist, albeit one in conflict over balancing her personal and professional lives—truly a subject of great interest to American women. While Hepburn, Russell, and many of their cohorts played aviators, reporters, lawyers, and doctors in the 1930s, Sarandon was a lawyer in one of the five films for which she was nominated; she also was twice a working-class woman, once a nun, and once a middle-class mother (*Lorenzo's Oil,* 1992).

Meryl Streep played the writer Isak Dinesen in *Out of Africa* (1985), an epic film that demonstrated Hollywood's ability to portray romance between an independent man and an independent woman. But the movie did not generate multiple imitators. It has remained sui generis.

Movie star Susan Sarandon has been a frequent Academy Award nominee.

In *Silkwood,* Streep was a working-class woman determined to expose the dangerous working conditions in a nuclear fuel plant; she was an actress in *The French Lieutenant's Woman;* and a survivor of a death camp in *Sophie's Choice.* Her versatility and talent qualifies her as a great actress but does not assure her good and frequent roles. The forecast for the near future is that she will reject more roles than she will accept and that her face will appear only rarely on the screen.

In recent decades, television has been kinder to women entertainers than has the movies.[16] Situation comedy, the genre most friendly to women, remains an essential part of the weekly TV schedule. In the 1996–97 season, for example, eight sitcoms featured women, the same number as twenty years ago during the Golden Era of television (see table 3). In both periods, there were only a few standouts; while *The Mary Tyler Moore Show* (1971-77), *Laverne and Shirley* (1976-83), and *One Day At a Time* (1975-84) all enjoyed long runs, most of the others during that period were short-term programs, typical of most television fare. Gaining an audience and keeping it for more than three seasons constitutes a long run in television history.

Murphy Brown (1988-1998) and *Roseanne* (1988-97) have each had runs of more than nine years, a testimony to their appeal to audiences. Because ratings drive survival for television, the success of a particular show suggests that viewers find the subject, the issues, and the characters meaningful. In this sense, television is a democratic, responsive medium; once a show loses its audience, it is yanked from the schedule. As long as the show endures, it connects with a significant number of viewers. As social critic Barbara Ehrenreich has written about *Roseanne:* "Since the entertainment media had not normally cast about for fat, loud-mouthed feminists to promote to superstardom, we must assume that Roseanne has something to say that many millions of people have been waiting to hear."[17]

A look at these two shows, which premiered in the same season, offers two radically different but equally important portraits of American women. Both operate within the situation comedy format with the home and the office as the center of action. The home, of course, remains the quintessential woman's domain. But beginning with *The Mary Tyler Moore Show,* the office became many women's second home. Classy Murphy and bossy Roseanne symbolize two rather new television types: Brown is an upper middle class professional white woman

Table 2. Academy Award Nominees (three times or more)

Golden Era of Hollywood Stars	Contemporary Stars

Golden Era of Hollywood Stars

CLAUDETTE COLBERT
1934 *It Happened One Night*
1935 *Private Worlds*
1944 *Since You Went Away*

BARBARA STANWYCK
1937 *Stella Dallas*
1941 *Ball of Fire*
1944 *Double Indemnity*
1948 *Sorry, Wrong Number*

INGRID BERGMAN
1943 *For Whom the Bell Tolls*
1944 *Gaslight**
1945 *The Bells of St. Mary's*
1948 *Joan of Arc*
1956 *Anastasia**

GREER GARSON
1939 *Goodbye Mr. Chips*
1941 *Blossoms in the Dust*
1942 *Mrs. Miniver**
1943 *Madame Curie*
1944 *Mrs. Parkington*
1945 *The Valley of Decision*

KATHARINE HEPBURN
1933 *Morning Glory**
1935 *Alice Adams*
1940 *The Philadelphia Story*
1942 *Woman of the Year*
1967 *Guess Who's Coming
       to Dinner?**
1968 *The Lion in Winter*
1981 *On Golden Pond**

BETTE DAVIS
1934 *Of Human Bondage*
1935 *Dangerous**
1938 *Jezebel**
1939 *Dark Victory*
1940 *The Letter*
1941 *The Little Foxes*
1942 *Now, Voyager*
1944 *Mr. Skeffington*

Contemporary Stars

JODIE FOSTER
1988 *The Accused**
1991 *Silence of the Lambs**
1994 *Nell*

SISSY SPACEK
1980 *Coal Miner's Daughter**
1982 *Missing*
1984 *The River*
1986 *Crimes of the Heart*

SUSAN SARANDON
1981 *Atlantic City*
1991 *Thelma and Louise*
1992 *Lorenzo's Oil*
1994 *The Client*
1995 *Dead Man Walking**

JESSICA LANGE
1982 *Frances*
1984 *Country*
1985 *Sweet Dreams*
1989 *Music Box*
1994 *Blue Sky**

MERYL STREEP
1981 *The French Lieutenant's
       Woman*
1982 *Sophie's Choice**
1983 *Silkwood*
1985 *Out of Africa*
1987 *Ironweed*
1988 *A Cry in the Dark*
1990 *Postcards from the Edge*
1995 *Bridges of Madison County*

*Denotes Academy Award winners

while Rosanne is a working-class unskilled housewife-worker. The workplace and the home get new images in these situation comedies. Both shows project new and familiar images to students of popular culture. Murphy and Roseanne are up-to-date versions of Liliths with a touch of Eve. Their overriding sense of independence and their comic perspective on life, however, supersede all other traits. Both characters star in comedies, one of the few acceptable genres in which women can shine. Verbal humor, perfected in screwball comedy movies and on the radio, has found a congenial home on television—from Gracie Allen and Lucy to Carol, Mary, and, beginning in 1988, Murphy and Roseanne. Men monopolize the crime shows, and buddy comedies often have both men and women in them, but the woman-centered sitcom remains a sure-fire formula. During the Reagan-Bush years, when some commentators believed that a negative reaction to feminism occurred, these two new shows offered a clear rebuttal. They openly confronted many of the unspoken issues that feminists and all women raised about their lives in the supposedly carefree 1980s.

Roseanne Barr (born in 1953), a housewife turned stand-up comic, began her routine by declaring, "Hi! I'm a housewife. I'm not gonna vacuum 'til Sears makes one you can ride on."[18] Her television character of the same name began as a brash comic and grew into a well-developed character. Barr (her maiden name, which she used for a while) has written about her life and her philosophy[19] giving credit for her comic approach to such predecessors as Mae West, Judy Holliday, and Lucille Ball.[20] But the major difference, she believes, between her humor and theirs is the fact that they had to achieve

Table 3. Women in Television Situation Comedies, 1970 to Present

Golden Years	Contemporary Period
The Mary Tyler Moore Show (1971-77)	*Murphy Brown* (1988-98)
Rhoda (1974-78)	*Roseanne* (1988-97)
Phyllis (1975-77)	*Ellen* (1994-98)
Maude (1972-78)	*Grace under Fire* (1993-97)
Laverne and Shirley (1976-83)	*Cybill* (1995-98)
One Day at a Time (1975-84)	*The Nanny* (1993-)
Alice (1975-84)	*Suddenly Susan* (1996-)
The Nancy Walker Show (1976-77)	*Caroline in the City* (1995-)

Roseanne (Barr Arnold) starred in one of the most popular television shows and brought a working-class woman's humorous perspective to millions of viewers.

their goals by clever indirection. Roseanne is direct, forthright, and open in her comedy.

The blunt-speaking working-class character that she brought to television in 1988 was a radical departure from all other personae in television domestic comedy history. She had no models to follow. Roseanne said, "I'm the first real mother on television."[21] Though that was an exaggeration, the fictional person Roseanne was unlike Lucy in every way; she was overweight, rude and crude, not particularly happy with her children, and struggling with her marriage, family, and work responsibilities. Although she sometimes made her husband, Dan Conner (played by John Goodman), the butt of her jokes, unlike Lucy, she never acceded to his authority. She was not the conciliator like Mary Tyler Moore, but the open confronter, the divider, and the trouble-maker.

Television audiences delighted in hearing the less-than-glamorous housewife-mother-worker speak her mind and ignore the consequences of her words. *Roseanne* was an immediate hit. For the first six seasons it was on the air, the show was always in the top ten. Taboos were overturned by Roseanne and private subjects received a public airing. Her personal life became public knowledge as well, and frequent magazine stories described her troubled family background (she said that she had been abused by her father, who vehemently denied it), her sixteen-year first marriage that produced three children, her divorce from husband Bill Pentland at the end of the first season of the show, her marriage and divorce from actor and producer Tom Arnold, and her frequent plastic surgeries.

As a stand-up comic in Denver, Roseanne Barr had experimented with comic styles and material before she developed the Domestic Goddess persona that she brought to television. Critic John Lahr wrote that "Roseanne's neurotic TV family was the first one to put America in contact with something resembling real life in the working-class world."[22] By her own admission, Roseanne is an angry woman who channels her anger into comedy. "If I hadn't found comedy, I'd probably be out killing people."[23] The show gave her the opportunity to express herself within a genre that audiences knew well and enjoyed. *Roseanne* took place in fictional Lanford, Illinois, where the Conners lived with their three children, thirteen-year-old Becky, eleven-year-old Darlene, and six-year-old D.J. As the children grew older, all of the social problems identified with teenagers became subject matter for the show.

Sibling rivalry and rebellious teenagers were always on view. Antimale jokes surely angered many men while women laughed at her audacity. Her fans watched as she lost weight and had extensive cosmetic surgery. Despite her popularity, Roseanne never lost her outsider status nor did she hide her disdain for the "establishment" in Hollywood. Nevertheless, in 1993, her peers rewarded her with an Emmy, television's award for best comedy actress, though the show never received an equivalent accolade. Her outspokenness and her willingness, even eagerness, to offend anybody and everybody kept her on the margin of the show business world. Battling with her network, ABC, and with declining ratings, Roseanne decided to make the 1996–97 season her last.

By contrast, Candace Bergen, the actress who created the hit show *Murphy Brown*, was a Hollywood insider. Born in Beverly Hills in 1946, she was the daughter of Frances Westerman, a model, and Edgar Bergen, the popular puppeteer whose partner, Charlie McCarthy, had a room next to Candace's. Her upbringing was a public affair. Walt Disney sent her presents every Christmas, and the children of Hollywood's elite were her playmates. Bergen described her life before her television show in a memoir called *Knock Wood* (1984). She attended the University of Pennsylvania during the turbulent sixties, dropped out, became a photographer then a movie star but never found personal satisfaction or professional acclaim for her work.

In 1980, she married French director Louis Malle; in 1985, at the age of thirty-nine, she had a daughter, Chloe, then stayed home for three years to raise her. In 1988, she was shown the script for the show and the character with whom she is now identified. Diane English, the writer and creator of *Murphy Brown*, said that she created a character "with fault lines and fissures."[24] Bergen, who is strikingly beautiful with blonde hair, a fine profile, and a good figure, appreciated the vulnerabilities of Murphy. Although wary of television, she warmed to the challenge of a tough character who required her to display her intelligence, quick wit, and great sense of timing.

The timing was right for Bergen and for American women, the primary viewers of the show. More and more women, particularly white middle-class women, were becoming careerists, reentering the workforce after divorce, and suffering from a variety of personal problems. The fictional Murphy Brown, as drawn by English, is a television journalist on a show called "F.Y.I.," a recovering alcoholic, and the survivor of many failed romances. Murphy's colleagues on the news show are her surrogate family. Unlike Mary on *The Mary Tyler Moore Show*, however, Murphy is not the self-sacrificer. Quite the contrary. She is a totally self-centered woman who thinks nothing of taking the last donut, ignoring the wishes of her dear friends, and turning a deaf ear to the problems of her colleagues, Frank Fontana, Corky Sherwood Forest, Jim Dial, and their producer, Miles Silverberg.

Just as *Roseanne* broke new ground, so did *Murphy Brown*. The show indulges in slapstick humor (Murphy is always hitting some guy) and political satire. The current headlines become topics for discussion on the weekly show. Murphy is a liberal Democrat and makes no secret of her disdain for the Reagan-Bush years. Whether the subject is free speech or pro-choice, Murphy and her cohorts have an opinion, usually a comic one. The blurring of the lines between television fiction and social reality, however, took over when, during the 1991-92 season, Murphy discovered that she was pregnant (from a lover she no longer saw) and, after much agonizing, she decided to have the baby and become a single mom.

In May, 1992 Vice President Dan Quayle gave a speech in which he criticized Murphy Brown for having a baby out of wedlock and considering it a "lifestyle choice." Feminist groups publicly defended Murphy's decision while conservative and evangelical Christian groups criticized it. What had been a provocative, but imaginative, scenario on a television show became part of a public debate on American values. "TV does blur the line between fact and fiction, but I'd hoped that the Vice President of the United States could distinguish between the two,"[25] said Bergen in response. The flurry of publicity that surrounded the episode lasted for months. CBS capitalized on the controversy by publicizing the next season's opener in October 1992, as the show in which Murphy would respond to the vice president.

In anticipation, advertisers paid dearly for the privilege of sponsoring *Murphy Brown*, and the special one-hour episode received one of the highest ratings for a television show; forty-four million people watched it.[26] In it, Murphy said, "Perhaps it is time for the vice president to recognize that families come in all shapes and sizes."[27] Bergen regarded this whole episode as "surrealistic."[28] The show continued

From 1988 to 1998, veteran actress Candace Bergen starred as a TV investigative reporter in *Murphy Brown.*

to enjoy large audiences for the next three seasons; since 1995 it has slipped and Bergen decided that the 1997-98 season would be the last. She and the show have been showered with awards with Candace Bergen earning three Emmys.

While both shows premiered in 1988, *Roseanne* was the clear favorite; *Murphy Brown* took three seasons to find an audience and reach number eight in viewership. Both shows had large audiences in the following two years, 1991-93. Clearly, the Dan Quayle incident boosted Murphy's ratings and gave her a loyal following that continued beyond 1992. The shows also shared another important component: They were produced by women—Diane English for *Murphy Brown* and Marcy Carsey for *Roseanne*. With her partner Tom Werner, Carsey also produced two other shows that premiered in the 1990s: *Cybill* and *Grace under Fire,* both starring strong funny women (note table 3). In 1996, Roseanne wanted to create a new spin-off show with the same character, but ABC declined her offer and no other network picked up the show. Consequently, she decided to end her long run as Roseanne Conner at the end of the 1996-97 season.

Television remains the best hope for women entertainers. Though the situation comedies will come and go with bewildering speed, given the short attention span of the audience, they will be on the schedule with great predictability. This fact alone supports two contradictory points: the cultural imagination of TV writers is limited, but women comics will have a better chance to succeed in show business than will dramatic actresses. In the 1960s, Madelyn Martin, the writer of *The Lucy Show* said of the relationship between women and comedy, "When you think of traditional figures of comedy—the short guy, the ugly one, the man with the big nose, the Negro or Jew or member of any minority group—comedy is a way of turning their misfortune into a joke. It's a way of being accepted—'Look at me, I'm funny' and 'Don't anybody laugh at me, I'll laugh first.'"[29]

The situation in the late 1990s is remarkably similar to that in 1964. Just as the best defense is an offense, so women comics can address all of the touchy issues regarding women before their critics do it in a familiar and comfortable setting for their audiences. In this sense, the old images have been transformed, and laughter covers a multitude of sins. So while we may lament the limited number and range of roles and images available to women, we can applaud their continued presence on the television screen. Further, the expansion of subject matter and the willingness to discuss a broader range of subjects on mainstream television reflects a greater openness in American culture.

Structural changes in how Americans amuse themselves, however, contribute to the static quality of women's images in popular culture. The segmentation of America has fractured the "woman's audience" into smaller and smaller units. Women of all classes, races, and ethnicities enjoyed a 1930s melodrama and laughed with Lucy and Ethel. Today, TV soap operas continue to attract women but in smaller numbers. The quantity of shows from which to choose is great, Spanish-speaking stations cater to their respective markets, and the proliferation of cable stations makes it difficult to create a shared cultural experience.

The cultural reason is as important as the economic one. The dearth of fantasy and dramatic roles for women is directly tied to the general fear and/or confusion about what women's roles, dreams, and hopes should be at century's end. Audience women today cannot watch a Joan Crawford overcome all odds and land a wealthy husband because that is no longer (or is it?) a woman's central dream. However, on melodrama, which is confined largely to afternoon soap operas, the latest pathology is dramatized and trivialized. A variety of feminist messages no longer occupy the public mind; indeed feminists don't always agree on one message. Therefore, it remains safer to take comfort in old formulas. An actress cannot find a movie or a television role that allows her to indulge in adventure/fantasy because these are still male territory. Sci-fi fantasy movies feature men and only men climb perilous mountains. Women continue to be rescued, but rarely do the rescuing. Pam Grier's exploits in 1970s movies have few imitators at the end of the 1990s.

Women's real lives are seen as too serious or too difficult to translate into either imaginative or dramatic scripts, and the only option, paradoxically, is to mock women's situations. Roseanne may make fun of her difficult working-class life but she cannot dramatize it. For fear of touching an open wound, Hollywood television producers and moviemakers avoid dramas, fantasies, and adventures that feature women. Rather than cause controversy while opening a public debate, filmmakers and television writers avoid the subject altogether, just as they ignored women's liberation issues in the 1970s. That is why women stars complain regularly about the few worthy roles available to them.

As I have argued throughout this book, the dominant formulas, be they melodrama, comedy, or the blues, have formed the outlines within which women entertainers perform. In this century some women stars, such as Lucy as the anarchic TV comic, have transformed the genre, and some, such as Mae West or Madonna, have operated on the margins building their celebrity from the outside in. But in all cases, they began with the familiar and shaped the format to their personality and talent. If the times favored them, such as the 1970s did for concert performers Janis Joplin and Bette Midler, they succeeded and built a following. If they appeared during a unique moment, such as Eva Tanguay did in vaudeville, they shone briefly but then lost their fame afterward. Enduring stars such as Dinah Shore and Mary Tyler Moore found their images to be comforting in both traditional and transitional periods.

Will women entertainers continue to find the times congenial to their various talents? Will more women scriptwriters, producers, directors, and editors emerge? Will television producers Diane English, Marcy Carsey, and their colleagues who have influence and power in television programming venture into uncharted paths? Will the current few women producers and directors around display a feminist consciousness and change the direction of popular cultural treatments of women? Perhaps most important, will women in the audience demand newer and bolder images of women in film, in music, and on television? Receiving an affirmative answer to all of these questions constitutes a major challenge.

In the late 1980s, women viewers insisted to CBS that their favorite women team of detectives, *Cagney and Lacey* remain on the air, and so they did for a few more years. Fans as consumers must join hands with like-minded creative types, male and female, to reshape programming or at least to open it to greater female talent, a mighty task. Given the durability of the old formulas, women entertainers will have to continue another long tradition: adaptability, survivability, and creativity in the face of formidable obstacles. The past century introduced memorable women entertainers to American audiences. Even a pessimist has to believe that the future will do no less.

Notes

Introduction

1. See Janice Radway, *Reading the Romance* (Chapel Hill: University of North Carolina Press, 1984).

1. Black Women Vaudevillians

1. The standard and most comprehensive works on early black vaudeville are Henry T. Sampson, *Blacks in Blackface: A Source Book on Early Black Musical Shows* (Metuchen, N.J.: The Scarecrow Press, 1988), and Sampson, *The Ghost Walks: A Chronological History of Blacks in Show Business, 1865-1910* (Metuchen, N.J.: The Scarecrow Press, 1988). Langston Hughes and Milton Meltzer, *Black Magic* (Englewood Cliffs, N.J.: Prentice Hall, 1967) is also a good reference.

2. George Schuyler, "Theatre," *The Messenger,* November 1923, 863.

3. Sampson discusses the life on the circuit in both of his books. See also Leo Harmalian and James V. Hatch, eds., *The Roots of African American Drama* (Detroit: Wayne State Univ. Press, 1991) for a sample of one act.

4. Edith Wilson's career is discussed in Derrick Stewart-Baxter, *Ma Rainey and the Classic Blues Singers* (New York: Stein and Day, 1970), 29-31; Allen Woll, *Black Musical Theatre: From Coontown to Dreamgirls* (Baton Rouge: Louisiana State Univ. Press, 1989), 132; and Edith Wilson, interview by J. Fred MacDonald, videotape, Northeastern Illinois Univ., fall 1973.

5. Sampson, *Ghost Walks,* 280.

6. In addition to the Sampson books, material on the life of the vaudevil-

lian can be found in John E. DiMeglio, *Vaudeville U.S.A.* (Bowling Green, Ohio: Bowling Green Univ. Popular Press, 1973), Marian Spitzer, "The business of Vaudeville," *Saturday Evening Post* 24 May 1924, 18-19, 125, 129-30, 133;, and in Charles W. Stein, *American Vaudeville as Seen by Its Contemporaries* (New York: Alfred A. Knopf, 1984).

7. Daphne Duval Harrison, *Black Pearls: Blues Queens of the 1920s* (New Brunswick, N.J.: Rutgers Univ. Press, 1988) is a good source for this subject.

8. One of the few sources to discuss the Whitman Sisters is Sampson, *Ghost Walks.*

9. Robert M.W. Dixon and John Godrich, *Recording the Blues* (New York: Stein and Day, 1970).

10. Dixon and Godrich, *Recording the Blues* discusses the recording business.

11. Sampson, *Ghost Walks,* and Sampson, *Blacks in Blackface,* 383 discuss Sissieretta Jones and her troupe.

12. Sampson, *Ghost Walks,* 268-69.

13. Sampson discusses Walker in both of his books and quotes from the critics.

14. Sampson, *Ghost Walks,* 290-91.

15. Ibid., 468-69.

16. Quoted in Woll, *Black Musical Theatre,* 97.

17. Theophilus Lewis, "Theatre," *The Messenger,* December 1923, 923-24.

18. Waters is discussed in Sampson, *Blacks in Boldface;* Sampson, *Ghost Walks;* Wall, *Black Musical Theatre;* and Harrison, *Black Pearls.*

19. Quoted in Woll, *Black Musical Theatre,* 132.

20. Larry Birnbaum, "Delmark Fortieth Anniversary Blues," *Down Beat,* March, 1994, 56.

21. David Hinkley, "Scat-Singing Pioneer Adelaide Hall Never Really Went out of Style," *New York Daily News* (reprinted by the Knight-Ridder/Tribune News Service, 19 November 1993, 1119K3115. Obituaries on Adelaide Hall include *Time,* 22 November 1993, 29.

22. Sampson in *Ghost Walks* discusses this subject.

2. Bawdy Women Entertainers

1. Douglas Gilbert, *American Vaudeville: Its Life and Times* (New York: Dover, 1940).

2. Quoted in Charles Samuels and Louise Samuels, *Once upon a Stage: The Merry World of Vaudeville* (New York: Dodd, Mead, 1974), 63.

3. Ibid., 54-55.

4. Quoted in Abel Green and Joe Laurie Jr., *Show Biz: From Vaude to Video* (New York: Henry Holt, 1951), 171.

5. Quoted in Allen Churchill, *The Great White Way: A Recreation of*

Broadway's Golden Era of Theatrical Entertainment (New York: E.P. Dutton, 1962), 209.

6. Quoted in Gilbert, *American Vaudeville,* 329.

7. Eva Tanguay, quoted in DiMeglio, *Vaudeville U.S.A.,* 81, from the *Dramatic Mirror,* 6 January 1915.

8. Samuels and Samuels, *Once upon a Stage,* 64. The New York Public Library's Clipping File has many positive reviews of Tanguay's performances.

9. Information on Sophie Tucker includes her autobiography, *Some of These Days: The Autobiography of Sophie Tucker* (New York: Doubleday, 1945), and Lewis A. Erenberg, *Steppin' Out: New York Night Life and the Transformation of American Culture, 1890-1930* (Westport, Conn.: Greenwood Press, 1981).

10. Biographical information on Bessie Smith can be obtained from a variety of sources including Larry Gara's sketch in *Notable American Women,* (Cambridge, Mass.: Belknap Press, 1971, vol. 3).

11. Quoted in Chris Albertson, "Bessie's Life," in *Bessie Smith: Empress of the Blues,* Clifford Richter, (New York: Schirmer Books, 1975), 9.

12. Doll Thomas's reminiscences can be found in Jeff Kisseloff, *You Must Remember This: An Oral History of Manhattan from the 1890s to World War II* (New York: Harcourt Brace Jovanavich, 1989), 304.

13. All of the musical examples in this section come from the record, *Bessie Smith: Empress of the Blues,* a compilation of 30 of her best-known songs. In 1983, Blue Angel Records released all 130 of her songs.

14. Pauline Kael, quoted in *Video Yesteryear* (New York: Video Publications, 1992), 79.

15. Rayna Green, "Magnolias Grow in Dirt: The Bawdy Lore of Southern Women," *Southern Exposure* 4 (1977), 29-33; and Nancy Walker, "Toward Solidarity: Women's Humor and Group Identity," in *Women's Comic Visions,* June Sochen (Detroit: Wayne State Univ. Press, 1991).

3. Entertainer as Reformer

This essay is a new interpretation of Mae West's career, but the basic biographical information is based upon the research I did for my book: *Mae West: She Who Laughs, Lasts* (Wheeling: Harlan Davidson Publishers, 1992).

1. Susan Sontag,"The Decay of Cinema," *New York Times Magazine,* 26 February 1996, 60.

2. Quoted in Green and Laurie, *Show Biz,* 169. Green was a veteran show business journalist and an intimate of Sime Silverman, the founder and reporter for *Variety* for many years. West discussed her early days in vaudeville in her autobiography, *Goodness Had Nothing To Do With It* (Englewood Cliffs: Prentice Hall, 1959).

3. DiMeglio, *Vaudeville U.S.A.,* quoting Harry Richman from *A Hell of a*

Life (with Richard Gehman) (New York: Duell, Sloan and Pearce, 1966), 40-41.

4. Mordaunt Hall, "She Done Him Wrong," *New York Times,* 10 February 1933, 12.

4. Woman Movie Stars as Role Models

This essay is an expanded and revised version of chapter 4 of my book *Enduring Values: Women in Popular Culture* (New York: Praeger Publishers, 1987).

1. Judith Mayne's study, *Directed by Dorothy Arzner* (Bloomington: Indiana Univ. Press, 1994) is an interesting study of the only woman director in Hollywood in the 1930s and offers a contrasting portrait of the problems of an independent director confronting the studio system.

2. Kirtley Baskette, "Hollywood Madcap," *The American Magazine,* October 1941, 2.

3. Garson Kanin, *Tracy and Hepburn: An Intimate Memoir* (New York: Viking Press, 1971), 60.

4. Ann MacGregor, "Katie's Hep!" *Photoplay,* April 1950, 77.

5. Rosalind Russell, "The Kind of Gal I Am," *Saturday Evening Post,* 29 September 1962, 30.

6. Baskette, "Hollywood Madcap," 2.

7. Dick Sheppard, *Elizabeth* (New York: Warner Books, 1975), 17.

8. Louella O. Parsons, "Sub-Deb or Siren?" *Photoplay,* March 1950, 76.

9. Ibid.

10. "Liz: Hollywood's Rarest Beauty," *Movieland,* April 1955, 30.

11. Ralph Edwards, "Queen Liz of Hollywood," *Photoplay,* December 1954, 102.

12. Gordon White, "Crying On the Inside?" *Motion Picture,* October 1955, 8.

13. M. Davidson, "Shirley MacLaine Sounds Off," *Saturday Evening Post,* 30 November 1963.

14. "Sweet, Hot, and Sassy," *Photoplay,* December 1955, 86.

15. Pauline Swanson, "Don't Be Unhappy," *Photoplay,* March 1950, 97.

16. Ibid.

17. Cynthia Miller, "No Greater Love . . . ," *Modern Screen,* December 1946, 44.

18. George James, "Blanche Sweet, Film Actress," *New York Times,* 8 September 1986.

19. H. Ehrlich, "Jane Fonda: Shining in New Roles," *Look,* 13 May 1969, 75.

20. Jane Quigley, "Interview with Liza," *Silver Screen,* July 1970, 40-41, 62-63.

21. Muriel Babcock, "Stanwyck, the Primitive," *Movie Mirror,* November 1931, 39.

22. Ibid.

23. Jerry Wald, "I Took One Look at Her," *Photoplay,* June 1947, 80.

24. Bette Davis, *The Lonely Life* (New York: G.P. Putnam, 1962), 186.

25. Hedda Hopper, "Welcome Stranger!" *Modern Screen,* August 1947, 104.

26. Rex Reed, "Bette Davis," in *Conversations in the Raw* (New York: New American Library, 1969), 17.

27. Liza Wilson, "That Old Magic," *Photoplay,* March 1951, 76.

28. Bette Davis, interview by Kay Proctor, "Should Working Wives Quit after Victory?" *Motion Picture,* August 1945, 36.

29. Ibid., 122.

30. Ibid., 123.

31. Ibid., 124.

32. Ibid., 124.

33. Louella O. Parsons, "You're Welcome, Joan," *Photoplay,* June 1946, 129.

34. Babcock, "Stanwyck, the Primitive," 111.

35. Gladys Hall, "Barbara's Advice to Girls in Love," *Radio Stars,* March 1937, 102-03.

36. "Will Carole Lombard's Marriage End Her Career?" *Motion Picture,* July 1939, 56.

37. Russell, "Kind of Gal I Am," 30.

5. Child Stars

1. Jeanine Basinger, *A Woman's View: How Hollywood Spoke to Women, 1930-1960* (Hanover, N.H.: Wesleyan Univ. Press, 1993), 282.

2. Besides viewing her movies, the best sources for Shirley Temple's life are Shirley Temple and the Editors of Look, *My Young Life* (New York: Doubleday, 1945) and Robert Windeler, *Shirley Temple* (New York: W.H. Allen, 1976).

3. J.P. McEvoy, "Little Miss Miracle," *Saturday Evening Post,* 9 July 1938, 11.

4. Temple's *Child Star: An Autobiography* (Boston: G.K. Hall, 1989) describes in loving detail her growing up years.

5. "Peewies Progress," *Time,* 27 April 1936, 36.

6. Constance J. Foster, "Mrs. Temple on Bringing up Shirley," *Parents Magazine,* October 1938, 64.

7. J.P. McEvoy, "Shirley in Wonderland," *Woman's Home Companion,* November 1938, 96.

8. Kristin McMurran, "Shirley Temple Black taps out a Telling Memoir of Childhood Stardom," *People Weekly,* 28 November 1988, 138-41.

9. *Time,* 27 April 1936, 38.

10. McEvoy, "Little Miss Miracle," 10.

11. Franklin D. Roosevelt, quoted in Geoffrey C. Ward, "America's Baby," *American Heritage,* March 1989, 12.

12. Rudy Behlmer, ed., *Memo from Darryl F. Zanuck: The Golden Years at Twentieth Century Fox* (New York: Grove Press, 1993), 17.

13. Gladys D. Shultz, "Mrs. Shultz Visits Shirley Temple," *Better Homes and Gardens,* September 1938, 71.

14. McEvoy, "Little Miss Miracle," 71.

15. Frank Nugent, quoted by Norman J. Zierold, *The Child Stars* (New York: Stein and Day, 1965), 75.

16. Judith Izen, "Composition Shirley Temple Dolls Produced by Ideal," *Antiques and Collecting Magazine,* April 1996, 58-60.

17. Angela Davis, *Angela Davis: An Autobiography* (New York: Random House, 1974), 96-98.

18. Michael Ryan, "As Ambassador to Prague, Shirley Temple Black Watches a Rebirth of Freedom," *People Weekly,* 8 January 1990, 38-40.

19. Bret Wood, "Lolita Syndrome," Sight and Sound, June 1994, 34.

20. Basinger, *A Woman's View,* 284-85.

21. Gerald Early, "Black Like . . . Shirley Temple?" *Harper's Magazine,* February 1992, 33-34.

22. Ibid.

6. Minority Women in Popular Culture

1. See Donald Bogle, *Toms, Coons, Mulattoes, Mammies, and Bucks* (New York: Viking Press, 1973) for a good discussion of this subject.

2. Biographical material on Velez can be found in *Current Biography,* 1945, and in the *New York Times* obituary, 15 December 1944.

3. Gladys Hall, "Whoopee! Lupe!!" *Motion Picture,* July 1938, 101.

4. Mordaunt Hall, "Hot Pepper," *New York Times,* 23 January 1933, 9.

5. Bosley Crowther, "The Girl From Mexico," *New York Times,* 8 January 1939, 31.

6. Bosley Crowther, "The Gang's All Here," *New York Times,* 23 December 1943, 26.

7. Mordaunt Hall, "In Caliente," *New York Times,* 27 June 1935, 16.

8. Donald Bogle's book, *Toms, Coons, Mulattoes, Mammies, and Bucks* originally published in 1973, remains, along with Thomas Cripps's *Slow Fade to Black* (New York: Oxford Univ. Press, 1977), and Dan Leab's *From Sambo to Superspade* (Boston: Houghton Mifflin, 1975) the best treatments of the general subject.

9. Loren Miller, "Uncle Tom in Hollywood," *Crisis,* November 1934, 336.

10. Jamaica Kincaid, "Pam Grier: The Mocha Mogul of Hollywood: Interview," *Ms.,* August 1975, 49-53.

11. Judy Dothard Simmons, "Sexual Ease," *Essence,* December 1988, 105.

12. Ibid., 53.

13. Ibid., 53.

14. Louie Robinson, "Pam Grier: More than Just a Sex Symbol," *Ebony,* June 1976, 33.

15. Ibid., 42.

16. Alan Ebert, "Pam Grier: Coming into Focus," *Essence,* January 1979, 104.

17. Ibid., 107.

18. Ibid., 108.

19. Simmons, "Sexual Ease," 105.

20. Ibid., 107.

21. Bob Lucas, "Pam Grier: Why Are Black Women Fading from the Films?" *Jet,* 6 November 1980, 61.

22. Ibid., 60.

23. The three in 1995 were Elizabeth Shue for *Leaving Las Vegas,* Mira Sorvino for *Mighty Aphrodite,* and Sharon Stone for *Casino.* Only one American actress was nominated in 1997—Helen Hunt—and she won.

7. Women Comics

1. See the introduction and Nancy Walker's essay, "Nineteenth Century Women's Humor" in Sochen, *Women's Comic Visions,* for an extended discussion of this subject.

2. Constance Talmadge, "The Tragedy of Being Funny," *Motion Picture,* August 1927, 102. See also DeWitt Bodeen, "Constance Talmadge," *Films in Review,* December 1967, 613-30.

3. Gracie Allen routines can be found in Joe Franklin, *Encyclopedia of Comedians* (Seacaucus, N.J.: Citadel Press, 1979), 46; and Arthur Frank Wertheim, *Radio Comedy* (New York: Oxford Univ. Press, 1979), 200-03. All of the examples in this chapter were taken from these sources.

4. The entry in Alan S. Downer, *Notable American Women,* vol. 2 (Cambridge, Mass.: Belknap Press, 1971), 425-26 provides the biographical information on Lombard.

5. My discussion of the film is based upon multiple viewings of it. The *New York Times Film Review* is a good source for film descriptions, though nothing replaces viewing the movie.

6. Wertheim, *Radio Comedy,* 238.

7. Ibid.

8. In the following chapter, Mary Tyler Moore will be treated more fully.

9. Paula S. Fass, "Television as Cultural Document: Promises and Problems," in *Television as a Cultural Force,* eds. Richard Adler and Douglas Cater (New York: Praeger, 1976), 41.

10. Marie Dressler, quoted in William Cahn, *A Pictorial History of the Great Comedians* (New York: Grosset and Dunlap, 1970), 122.

11. Lewis C. Strang, *Prima Donnas and Soubrettes of Light Opera and Musical Comedy in America* (Boston: L.C. Page, 1900), 182.

12. Wallace Evan Davies's essay on Normand in *Notable American Women,* vol. 1 (Cambridge, Mass.: Belknap Press, 1971) is a basic source as is the two-part essay on Mack Sennett by Robert Giroux in *Films in Review,* December 1968 and January 1969.

13. The reviews of Normand's films in the *New York Times* summarized the plots and the comic style of the movies. See also Kalton C. Lahue and Terry Brewer, *Keystone Kops and Custards: The Legend of Keystone Films* (Norman: Univ. of Oklahoma Press, 1968).

14. Diana M. Meehan, *Ladies of the Evening: Women Characters of Prime Time Television* (Metuchen, N.J.: Scarecrow Press, 1983), 21.

15. There are many sources on Lucille Ball. One of the early ones is Herb Howe, "The Lady That's Known as Luci," *Photoplay,* March 1947, 56-59, 84-86. Another is Eleanor Harris, *The Real Story of Lucille Ball* (New York: Farrar Straus and Young with Ballantine Books, 1954).

16. Howe, "The Lady That's Known as Luci," 86.

17. Cahn, *Pictorial History,* 187.

18. Quoted in Vincent Terrace, *The Complete Encyclopedia of Television Programs,* 1947-79 (So. Brunswick: A.S. Barnes, 1979), 831.

19. Richard Meryman, "Can We Talk? Why Joan Rivers Can't Stop," *McCalls,* September 1983, 63.

20. Ibid., 64. Another good source on Rivers's earlier career is Lee Israel, "Joan Rivers and How She Got That Way," *Ms.,* October 1984, 109-14.

21. Robert C. Toll, *On with the Show: The First Century of Show Business* (New York: Oxford Univ. Press, 1976), 323.

22. Fannny Brice, quoted in Cahn, *Pictorial History,* 67.

23. Brice's record albums capture her comedic style. Among the ones I listened to are *Fanny Brice* (Audio Fidelity Records, 1968) and *Fanny Brice/ Helen Morgan* (RCA Victor LPV-561, 1969). A recent biography, *Funny Woman: The Life and Times of Fanny Brice* by Barbara W. Grossman (Bloomington: Indiana Univ. Press, 1991) also has useful information.

24. Norman Katkov's biography, *The Fabulous Fanny: The Story of Fanny Brice* (New York: Alfred Knopf, 1953) offers a good summary of her early life.

25. Quoted in Katkov, *Fabulous Fanny,* 237.

26. "Divinely unpredictable, no-holds-barred Bette Midler is the strongest woman to hit stage or screen since Mae West." Molly Haskell, "Women in the Movies Grow Up," *Psychology Today,* January 1983, 18.

27. In 1997, Midler said: "I think I've finally realized the key to comedy. I think it's about freedom." Quoted in Cindy Pearlman, "Oh what a 'Feeling.'" *Chicago Sun-Times* 30 March 1997, 87.

8. Change Within Continuity

1. Bruce Cassidy, *Dinah! A Biography* (New York: Franklin Watts, 1979) remains a good beginning for her life as do the two entries in *Current Biography* (1966 and 1994).

2. Albert Morehead, "For Fifteen Years Nobody Finer," *Cosmopolitan,* August 1955, 44.

3. Ibid., 49.

4. Ibid.

5. Dinah Shore, interview, *TV Guide,* 15 December 1956, 13.

6. Ibid.

7. Besides her autobiography, Jonathan Van Meter's article "Mary, Mary Quite Contrary," *New York Times Magazine,* 26 November 1995, 38-41, is very helpful.

Epilogue

1. Betty Friedan, "Television and the Feminine Mystique," *TV Guide,* 1 February 1964, 6.

2. Martha Bayles, "It's Not Sexist. It's Only Rock And Roll," *New York Times,* 28 September 1996, 19. Cher is another rocker who became a successful movie star.

3. *Newsweek,* 24 February 1969, 84.

4. F.R. Crawley, *Janis* (Hollywood: Crawley Films/Universal Pictures, 1974).

5. Tina Turner, quoted in Cathleen McGuigan, "The Second Coming of Tina," *Newsweek,* 10 September 1984, 76.

6. "Tina Turner Tells How She Made It to the Top Alone," *Jet,* 1 April 1985, 62.

7. "Whitney Houston: For Talented Young Star, Singing Is a Family Tradition," *Ebony,* December 1985, 155, ff.

8. Denise Worrell, "Now: Madonna on Madonna," *Time,* 27 May 1985, 81.

9. Karen S. Peterson, "Trash and Frills for Material Girls," *USA Today,* 7 May 1985, 2D.

10. John Skow, "Madonna Rocks the Land," *Time,* 27 May 1985, 74.

11. Camille Paglia, "Madonna-Finally, a Real Feminist," *New York Times,* 14 December 1990.

12. "Now: Madonna on Madonna," 79.

13. Ibid.

14. Meryl Streep, quoted in Monica Eng, "Hollywood's Fallen Women Rise to Stardom," *Chicago Tribune,* 12 January 1997, 1.

15. Jeanine Basinger, quoted in Eng, "Hollywood's Fallen Women."

16. After I wrote this chapter, I read Molly Haskell's latest collection of

essays that includes a final chapter called "Bearded Ladies: Women in Comedy"; she shares part of my view that tv sitcoms have been very good for women. See *Holding My Own In No Man's Land,* (New York: Oxford Univ. Press, 1997).

17. Barbara Ehrenreich, "The Wretched of the Hearth: The Undainty Feminism of Roseanne Barr," *New Republic,* 2 April 1990, 28.

18. Leah Rozen, "Roseanne Barr: Funny, Foul and Fascinating," *Redbook,* January 1991, 26.

19. Roseanne Barr, *Roseanne: My Life as a Woman,* (New York: Harper Publishers, 1989).

20. John Lahr, "Dealing with Roseanne," *New Yorker,* 17 July 1995, 44.

21. Lon Grahnke, "Roseanne Era Ends," *Chicago Sun-Times,* 20 April 1997.

22. Lahr, "Dealing with Roseanne," 51.

23. Ibid., 58.

24. Elaine Dutka, "Candace Bergen: One Cool, Classy Cookie," *Cosmopolitan,* October 1993, 182.

25. Ibid., 187.

26. Susan Douglas, "Put the Blame on Mae, Boys," *Progressive,* November 1992, 18.

27. Ibid.

28. Richard Corliss, "Having It All," *Time,* 21 September 1992, 49.

29. Madelyn Martin, quoted in Betty Friedan, "Television and the Feminine Mystique," Part 2 *TV Guide,* 8 February 1964, 21.

Bibliography

Bargainnier, Earl F., "Melodrama as Formula," *Journal of Popular Culture*, 9 (Winter, 1975).

Baxter, John, *Hollywood in the Thirties* (New York, A.S. Barnes and Company, 1968).

Bergman, Andrew, *We're in the Money: Depression America and Its Films* (New York, Harper Colophon Books, 1971).

Berle, Milton, "Remembering vaudeville: where a fancy dressing room was a new nail," *TV Guide* (January 24, 1987) p.32.

Black, Shirley Temple, *Child Star: an autobiography* (Boston, G.K. Hall, 1989).

Blythe, Cheryl and Susan Sachett, *Say Good Night, Gracie!* (New York, E.P. Dutton, 1986).

Bonderoff, Jason, *Mary Tyler Moore* (New York, St. Martin's Press, 1986).

Butsch, Richard, *editor, For Fun and Profit: the transformation of leisure into consumption* (Philadelphia, Temple University Press, 1990).

Byars, Jackie, *All That Hollywood Allows: Re-Reading Gender in 1950s Melodrama* (Chapel Hill, University of North Carolina Press, 1991).

Cantor, Muriel, *Prime-Time Television: Content and Control* (Beverly Hills, Sage Publications, 1980).

Carson, Tom, "The crystal ball: More than 30 years ago, "I Love Lucy" foretold the future of the sitcom," *American Heritage* 14 #9 (July-August, 1989) p.14.

Curry, Ramona, *Too Much of a Good Thing: Mae West as Cultural Icon* (Minneapolis, University of Minnesota Press, 1996.)

Dalton, David, *Piece of My Heart: The Life, Times, and Legend of Janis Joplin* (New York, St. Martin's Press, 1985).

Deming, Barbara, *Running Away From Myself: A Dream Portrait of America*

Drawn from the Films of the Forties (New York, Grossman Publishers, 1969).

Di Meglio, John E., *Vaudeville, U.S.A.* (Bowling Green, Bowling Green University Popular Press, 1973).

Douglas, Susan J., *Where the Girls Are: Growing Up Female with the Mass Media* (New York, New York Times Books, 1994).

Edwards, Anne, *Shirley Temple: American Princess,* (New York, William Morrow, 1988).

Erens, Patricia, editor, *Issues in Feminist Film Criticism* (Bloomington, Indiana University Press, 1990).

Fedler, F., J. Hall, and L. Tanzi, "Popular Songs Emphasize Sex, Deemphasize Romance," *Mass Communication Review* 9 (Spring-Fall, 1982) pp.10-15.

Fernley, Allison and Paula Maloof, "Yentl" *Film Quarterly* 38 (Spring, 1985) pp.38-46.

Feuer, Jane, et al editors, *MTM 'Quality Television'* (London, BFI Publication, 1984).

Fissinger, Laura, *Tina Turner* (New York, Ballantine Books, 1985).

Griffith, Richard, *The Movie Stars* (New York, Doubleday and Company, 1970).

Harrison, Daphne Duval, *Black Pearls: Blues Queens of the 1920s* (New Brunswick, New Jersey, Rutgers University Press, 1988).

Haskell, Molly, *Holding My Own in No Man's Land* (New York, Oxford University Press, 1997).

Intintoli, Michael James, *Taking Soaps Seriously* (New York, Praeger Publishers, 1984).

Jewell, K. Sue, *From Mammy to Miss America and Beyond: Cultural Images and the shaping of US social policy* (New York, Routledge Publishers, 1993).

Kael, Pauline, *Kiss, Kiss, Bang Bang* (Boston, Little Brown and Company, 1968).

Kaminsky, Stuart, *American Film Genres* (New York, Dell Publishing Company, 1974).

Kibler, Alison, "Female Varieties: Gender and Cultural Hierarchy on the Keith Vaudeville Circuit, 1890-1925," PhD dissertation, University of Iowa, 1994.

Lieb, Sandra R. *Mother of the Blues* (Boston, University of Massachusetts Press, 1981).

MacDonald, J. Fred, *Don't Touch That Dial! Radio Programming in American Life, 1920-1960* (Chicago, Nelson-Hall Publishers, 1979).

Marling, Karal Ann, *As Seen on TV: The Visual Culture of Everyday Life in the 1950s* (Cambridge, Harvard University Press, 1994).

May, Elaine Tyler, *Homeward Bound: American Families During the Cold War Era* (New York, Basic Books, 1988 paperback ed.).

Maychick, Diana, *Meryl Streep: The Reluctant Superstar* (New York, St. Martin's Press, 1984).

Mayne, Judith, *Directed by Dorothy Arzner* (Bloomington, Indiana University Press, 1994).

McClay, Michael, *I Love Lucy* (New York, Warner Books, 1995).

McLean, Albert F., Jr., *American Vaudeville as Ritual* (Lexington, University Press of Kentucky, 1965).

Meehan, Diana M., *Ladies of the Evening: Women Characters of Prime Time Television* (Metuchen, New Jersey, Scarecrow Press, 1983).

Meyerowitz, Joanne, editor, *Not June Cleaver: Women and Gender in Postwar America, 1945-60* (Philadelphia, Temple University Press, 1994).

Miller, Randall M., editor, *The Kaleidoscopic Lens: How Hollywood Views Ethnic Groups* (Englewood, New Jersey, Jerome S. Ozer Publisher, 1980).

Modleski, Tania, editor, *Studies in Entertainment: Critical appraoches to Mass Culture* (Bloomington, Indiana University Press, 1986).

Nasaw, David, *Going Out: The Rise and Fall of Public Amusements* (New York, Basic Books, 1993).

Ringgold, Gene, *The Films of Bette Davis* (New York, The Citadel Press, 1966).

Robinson, Beverly Jean, "Beyond Folktype and Stereotype: American Cultural History Through the Eyes of Edith Wilson," PhD dissertation, University of Pennsylvania, 1983.

Sabino, Laura, "Bad Girl at the Mike: Roseanne, Gender and Stand-Up Comedy," M.A. Thesis, The Ohio State University, 1994.

Spangler, Lynn C., "A Historical Overview of Female Friendships on Prime-Time Television," *Journal of Popular Culture* 22 #4, pp.13-23.

Spigel, Lynn, *Make Room for TV: Television and the Family Ideal in Postwar America* (Chicago, University of Chicago Press, 1992).

Stoddard, Karen M., *Saints and Shrews: Women and Aging in American Popular Film* (Westport, Connecticut, Greenwood Press, 1983).

Turner, Tina with Kurt Loder, *I, Tina* (New York, Morrow and Company, 1986).

Walsh, Andrea S., *Women's Films and Female Experience, 1940 to 1950* (New York, Praeger Publishers, 1984).

Walters, Suzanna Danuta, *Material Girls* (Berkeley, University of California Press, 1995).

Weibel, Kathryn, *Mirror, Mirror: Images of Women Reflected in Popular Culture* (New York, Anchor Books, 1977).

Welsch, Janice R., *Film Archetypes: Sisters, Mistresses, Mothers and Daughters* (New York, Arno Press, 1978).

Special Issues

The Winter 1971-72 issue of *Film Library Quarterly* (v.5,#1) focuses upon women in film.

The Winter 1975-6 issue of *Film Heritage* (v. II, #2) also deals exclusively with women in film.

Index